CHAPTER 1

Ukraine

Post Perebudova

(Perestroika in the Soviet Union), 1991

n 1991, my significant other Doreen and I were recuperating from a grievous monetary slump in Alberta, Canada that guaranteed the majority of our resources in the mid 1980s. We were into our seventh year with another business (Tanks-A-Lot Ltd.) that I had established to make substantial wastewater treatment plants like septic tanks, consumable water storages, and precast pipe.

After going to an enormous Edmonton gathering for Ukraine's President Kuchma in 1993, my musings were overwhelmed by Ukraine, the nation of my parentage. Fervor undulated up my spine when finding out with regards to a time of Perebudova (restoration) in Ukraine that was in the front line of the separation of the Soviet Union's defective framework. Ukraine pronounced Independence in August 1991. Not a shot was discharged; the coldblooded counter-useful framework essentially fell. Promptly, Canada and Poland turned into the main nations to perceive Ukraine as a free country.

eing of Ukrainian lineage I pondered could it presently be investigated? Would I be fruitful in tracking down far off roots? Would having independent company experience take into consideration an undertaking or two? My psyche and heart were available to permit senses to lead the way. The feeling of experience was high. My better half Doreen shared the energy. The kick the bucket was projected. Ukraine, here we come. Yet, first some examination was essential prior to going, as I probably was aware very little of my family. We had no contacts in Ukraine as Canadian Moiseys never spoken with their country. I started to explore Ukraine's set of experiences, and I immediately found it to be old and convoluted as it was a significant intersection of civilization.

Ukraine's Long History

Scholars believe that people have involved the region that is currently Ukraine since around 700,000 BCE. By around 40,000 BCE, agrarian tribes possessed a large portion of the district. Agribusiness, trained creatures, and advances like earthenware and weaving started to show up by around 5000 BCE, before long followed by copper working. Between c. 4000 and c. 2500 BCE, the Trypillian culture thrived, based on the Dniester River valley, however coming to the Dnipro also. The Dniester River bowl was at that point, logical the most developed culture in Europe. Eleven different spaces of Ukraine had less progressed societies. Close to Galicia and Bukovina (home to the Moisey family) the Stanove culture existed from the fourteenth to the twelfth hundreds of years BCE.

Because of its long and muddled history, the geographic space of the present Ukraine has passed by many names: Trypillia, Cimmeria, Scythia, Sarmatia, Rus (articulated as in duce) and Ruthenia (a term at times used to portray the terrains possessed by individuals of Kievan Rus, and in some cases used to depict Eastern Slavic individuals like Ukrainians and Belarusians, yet not Russians.) Iranian Cimmerians showed up nearby around 1500 BCE. The Scythians dislodged them in around 750 BCE. The principal thousand years BCE likewise saw the Iron Age in Ukraine, as horticulture, metallurgy, and business kept on progressing. As ahead of schedule as 700 BCE, Greek city-states had exchanging provinces the area. Attacking itinerant horsemen intermixed with the Scythians and made a domain that was sufficiently amazing to repulse an intrusion by Persian King Darius in 513 BCE.

The antiquated Greek Herodotus (c.484 - c.425 BCE) is acclaimed to be the "Father of History" since he created the principal book that can be viewed as a methodical history. In Chapter IV in his "Accounts," he incorporated the historical backdrop of Scythia, antiquated Ukraine. Afterward, the Greek Thucydides (c. 460 – c. 400 BCE) composed what is recognized as the first basic history in quite a while "History of Peloponnesian War," positioning him as the best antiquarian in ancient times. Thucydides said of Scythian Ukraine:

The Empire of the Odrysians was an extremely incredible realm, in income and general success outperforming all in Europe in populace and military assets coming unequivocally close to the Scythians, with whom for sure no individuals in Europe can bear examination. No gathering in Asia was comparable to

them. They were not on a level with different people groups overall insight and artistic expressions of enlightened life.

round 250 BCE Sarmatians attacked and involved the district. Like the Scythians, who they had likely acclimatized, they exchanged with the Greek city-state provinces. A few of the more prosperous of these provinces on the Black Sea's north coast framed the Bosporan Kingdom in the fifth century BCE, which went on until Rome crushed its last ruler in 63 BCE. Meanwhile, Sarmatian branches like the Alans and Roxolani occupied with teeter-totter battles among themselves and Goths from the north.

In the main thousand years of the Common Era (CE), what is presently Ukraine saw a progression of intruders and occupiers more than a few centuries. Germanic clans from the Baltics vanquished the Sarmatians in 200 CE. Eastern Germanic Goths battled Rome and held onto settlements in the locale in the third century. The roaming Huns surpassed the region in the fourth century as most Goths escaped west of the Danube, with a couple of staying in Crimea. In the fifth century, the Volga Bulgars involved Ukraine. The Avars did likewise in the 6th century, as did the Khazars in the seventh, trailed by the Magyars in the ninth.

From this all around complex storyline of societies in the locale, a city-state fixated on Kyiv started from dinky beginnings in the ninth century, and began to turn into a provincial power. Kyiv's Slavic and Persian roots gradually spread to Europe and grounds toward the north. The Kievan Rus ruler Volodymyr was submersed in 988 and Christianity thrived in the district. The city of Kyiv turned into the social and political focus of Kievan Rus, a free league of realms extending north to the Baltic Sea and overseeing the greater part of Eastern Europe from the late 10th to the mid-thirteenth hundreds of years. At that point, Kievan Rus was the biggest European state, and one of the richest and most socially progressed, in spite of its moderately scanty population.

Through marriage and youngsters, the sovereignty of Kievan Rus started to interlace with the imperial lineages of Western Europe. For example, in 1051, the little girl of Kyiv's amazing King Yaroslav the Wise, the Kyiv-conceived Princess Anna Yaroslavana, wedded King Henry the first of France. Upon Henry's passing, Anna's seven-year-old child Philip became King of France. For the following fourteen years, King Philip the first controlled France overseen

by Queen Anne, his Ukrainian mother. Anne's three sisters–Elisaveta, Anastasia, and Agatha–likewise wedded European sovereignty, turning into the Queens of Norway, Hungary, and England, separately. Yaroslav's child Vseveolod the first likewise fathered Eupraxia, who through marriage turned out to be Holy Roman Empress of the German Kingdom in 1089. During the following around 200 years, there were 38 Ukrainian regal relationships with European rulers. Anna Yaroslavana and her sisters transformed Europe, in any event, stretching out their qualities to Britain's present Queen Elizabeth, which she has acknowledged.

Meanwhile, Kievan Rus kept on confronting attacks from Pechenegs,

Turks and Cumans in the 10th, 11th, and twelfth hundreds of years, individually. Kievan Rus became divided, and started to decay, somewhat in light of the fact that its primary exchanging accomplice Constantinople was additionally in decrease. At long last, in the thirteenth century, the Mongol Empire attacked somewhere in the range of 1237 and 1240 assaulting and annihilating a few Ukrainian urban areas including Kyiv, which it went for all intents and purposes to rubble in late 1240.

Mongol standard went on until 1362, when the Grand Duchy of Lithuania ingested the greater part of present-day Ukraine. In 1569, Poland and Lithuania joined under a Polish-Lithuanian Commonwealth. A few pieces of Ukraine were as yet constrained by the Crimean Khanate as of now. During the 1650s, portions of Ukraine fell heavily influenced by an expansionist Russia, and in the late eighteenth century Poland was divided, the Crimean Khanate was crushed, and Ukraine became parted between the Russian Tsardom and Habsburg Austria.

After the 1917 Russian Revolution, and keeping in mind that WWI actually seethed, Ukraine slipped into a tumultuous battle for its autonomy. Present Soviet Ukrainians allude on this conflict as the Ukrainian-Soviet War: a conflict between the Russian Bolsheviks and the Ukrainian People's Republic (a free state announced following the Russian Revolution). The UPR was fleeting, ousted in 1918, yet is considered today to be a forerunner to present day, autonomous Ukraine. In 1922, the successful Russian Bolsheviks involving Ukraine made it a republic inside the Soviet Union. Other than a couple of long periods of Nazi occupation during WWII, Ukraine stayed under Soviet control until the mid 1990s.

Ukraine Map.

Throughout its long history, Ukraine has sat at the junction of significant shipping lanes: a north-South one connecting Scandinavia to the Middle East along the Baltic Sea, Dnieper River, and Black Sea; and an east-west course from the Caspian Sea to Central and Western Europe. Ukrainian individuals have consistently assumed a significant part, strategically and monetarily, in Eastern Europe. The numerous unfamiliar political powers that have involved Ukraine have given it a rich and various heritage, one that can be found in a portion of the pressures in the nation today, and one that makes it harder to recount a straightforward story of Ukraine's set of experiences. Western, focal, and eastern districts of the nation have had various encounters after some time. Incalculable intrusions have delivered a muddled composition of Ukrainians. The shared factor bringing together Ukrainian grounds and state arrangements has been, and is today, the Ukrainian public, who are joined with a typical language, and some novel social, social, and strict specificities. Intruders came, yet individuals won under cruel mastery. These trespassers, thus, were supplanted by even more impressive intruders. The latest (2014) trespasser is the despot Vladimir Putin of Russia. His essence is a minor injury contrasted with what Ukrainians have encountered in the course of the last 1000 years.

Contrasting Ukraine With Russia

Through quite a bit of its set of experiences, however particularly in the Golden Age of Kievan Rus, the district of present-day Ukraine has piled up well in contrast with Europe, and conversely, with Russia. Measurements recommend that around the year 1,000 CE, Kyiv's populace was higher than that of Paris or London. Its brick work and gold-plated engineering of that time additionally show more abundance and power than presumably all European urban communities outside of the Mediterranean. For something like 200 years in the late Middle Ages Kyiv was one of the main financial and political focuses in Europe.

ompared to Russia and Moscow, the high level phase of Kyiv and Ukraine in the late Medieval period is much really striking. European mapmakers in the Middle Ages considered Kievan Rus a piece of Europe, and depicted Muscovy as a component of Asia related with the Mongol's Golden Horde. A few early narratives notice Ukraine by name. The Hypatian Chronicle does in 1185, for instance, portraying occasions in Kyiv, Galicia, and other Ukrainian areas from as far back as 860 CE. Some early narratives, call the area Krajina (nation), or Galich Ukraina. Moscow was first referenced in a narrative in 1147, at which time it was just a little town. Interestingly, the city of Kyiv, established in 482, is perhaps the most seasoned city in Europe. Kyiv's Metropolia area additionally traces all the way back to a few centuries before Moscow's comparable Patriarchate.

truth be told, Moscow just developed to turn into a significant focus under Mongol occupation somewhere in the range of 1238 and 1480, long after Kievan Rus had for a really long time been a noteworthy political, social, and monetary focus. In any event, with regards to the Mongols, Ukraine was in front of Russia, having shaken off the burden in 1362. Ukraine quit being constrained by the Mongols 117 years before Muscovy did. Indeed, even after 1480, the Tsar of Russia kept on giving recognition for the Crimean Khan (the Golden Horde's replacement) until 1700, in the primary long stretches of Peter the Great's reign.

kraine likewise embraced significant patterns in Western Europe prior than

Russia did, building up its first higher learning foundations at the Ostrozka Collegium in 1576, and first colleges at the Kyiv-Mohyla Academy in 1632 (its archetype began in 1615), and Lviv University in 1661. Russia's first advanced education organizations, on the other hand, were the Saint Petersburg Academy of Sciences, established in 1724, and Moscow University set up in 1755. Foundations of higher learning showed up in Ukraine almost a century and a half before Russia. Printed books showed up in Ukraine in the late sixteenth century, quite a few years before they did in Russia. On April 5, 1710, the recently chosen Ukrainian hetman (a high-positioning military title) Pylyp Orlyk reported a 'Settlements and Constitutions of Rights and Freedoms of the Zaporizhian Host'. This was one of the primary state constitutions, setting a norm for the partition of abilities in a cutting edge edified country, and coming well before comparable constitutions were taken on in the United States in 1787, or France in 1791. Apparently, Russia's first (brief) endeavor at a comparable constitution was the restricted State Duma presented by the dictatorial Tsar Nicholas II in 1906.

The 20th century, which saw the development and fall of the Soviet Union, has fairly joined Ukraine and Russia in the famous creative mind. Acknowledge however, that Ukraine has had a long and complex history autonomous of Russia. Certain individuals today are in any event, looking profound into hereditary contrasts among Russians and different Slavs to attempt to isolate indeed these unmistakable gatherings of individuals. In 2013, Russian news stories asserted that geneticists at the Russian Academy of Medical Sciences still up in the air that Russian individuals are not even Slavs, however more firmly identified with Finnish individuals. To comprehend the unmistakable contrasts of Ukraine-Rus and Moscow-Russia, read the 1904 antiquarian Michael Rusedski's Traditional Scheme of Russian History and Andrew Gregorovich's Anna Yaroslavana, Queen of France. It just so happens, my Mother Nellie (née Palichuk) Moisey went to class with Gregorovich.

What's in a Ukrainian's Genes?

DNA testing has developed as an estimating instrument to interface individuals of today to their far off predecessors of millennia prior. My DNA test results from "Starting points" (www.familytreedna.com) are 95%

European (focused in Ukraine), four percent Turkish and one percent sprinkled between

Norwegian, Finnish and Spanish. My qualities, in the same way as other Ukrainians', have no hint of Russian.

Only a minority of Russians has hints of the Ukrainian and European qualities. This is intelligent as there was not any justification for Ukrainians from the breadbasket of Europe to move to the freezing scope equivalent to that of Canada's southern Northwest Territories. Ukraine is the advanced province of Medieval Rus, and as I have noticed, the name Ukraine made a difference well before the name Moscow did. Ukraine's normal language, social, social, and strict attributes today resemble those of 1000 years prior. The mixture of Russians on Eastern Ukraine soil happened generally during the seventy-year time of Soviet control, and fundamentally during Stalin's standard. Soviet Russia's predominance, generally during the 1930s to 1940s, constrained huge number of Ukrainians into the Siberian Gulag and to a great extent supplanted them by bringing in Russians to Eastern Ukraine.

any blended relationships happened are as yet happening. In 2017, there is a slight noticeable contrast among East and West Ukraine occupants due to intermarriages, which happened with a portion of my Ukrainian family. Unavoidably, they ingested each other's traditions. A portion of my Ukrainian family members living in both Ukraine and Russia have blended relationships. These Russian life partners are among the most pleasant people I know and have awesome, caring families. I presently can't seem to meet a Russian I loathe. They are extraordinary individuals. Their tyrants are another story. Tyrants, Tsars, Lenin, Stalin and Putin carelessly set people in opposition to one another, using weighty portions of publicity. Their type of overseeing couldn't care less with regards to the devastation they made and the misery and loss of guiltless life. They are the most reduced of mankind, the filth of the Earth.

Recently, self-declared history specialist Putin has hailed the profound significance of Chersonesus–an old Greek province established around 2,500 years prior outside of present-day Sevastopol in Crimea–for Russia, saying in a 2014 condition of-the-country address that the Ukrainian region has a "gigantic civilizational and sacrosanct signifying" for the Russian Orthodox Church (ROC), similarly as the Temple Mount in Jerusalem has for Jews and Muslims. In 2015, Putin fixed his command over the ROC Church. As a definitive top of the ROC, Putin isn't tested from inside Russia, as the State forces difficulties for those that do. Numerous political adversaries have paid and continue

to die when scrutinizing the Russian State, which is inseparable from despot Putin. It isn't insightful assuming one wishes to live. In 2015 Putin started supplanting history books in Russian schools to mirror his perspective on history. It ought not be a shock in case he changes the name of the ROC to the Putin Orthodox Church. He fantasizes about turning into a divine resembling the forerunner in North Korea does today. Blending legislative issues in with religion overall resembles blending oil and water. The two don't promptly blend; be that as it may, demi-divine beings accept this doesn't matter to them. Still up in the air to make Moscow the third Rome for the Orthodox Global Churches. This drive was sought after by Stalin in the last part of the 1940s, and it failed.

Seeds of Nationalism

Over the beyond 400 years, when Ukrainian regions were involved by four unfamiliar powers, a few people became instructed to the methods of their oppressors. Resistance began gradually and became dug in the Ukrainian brain, basically to get away from serfdom. The desire toward disobedience is as yet solid in many Ukrainians, as they adapt to the 2014 intrusion by Russia's tyrant Putin.

For four centuries, enormous canine trespassers, particularly the severe Tsars and despots, adjusted Western Ukraine's outlook into defiant activity. By the nineteenth century, a patriot development was coming to fruition, initiating around the time my extraordinary granddad Stefan Moisey was brought into the world in 1846. The precursors of numerous Ukrainian Canadians, including my family from Western Ukraine, have been refered to in the chronicled record as making nationalistic moves. In 1910, Chernivtsi University fumed with understudies and a couple of educators cultivating nationalistic thoughts and making defiant moves. One of these understudies was Olena (Yarema) Kuz, brought into the world in Banyliv, fifty kilometers due west of Chernivtsi University. Olena is my third cousin eliminated, the niece of my distant grandma Wasylena Moisey (née Kuz). Called Yarema by her companions, she has been perceived for her heroics in aiding impede the last Tsar's intrusion of Ukraine in 1915. She is a genuine courageous woman of Ukraine.

My thirteen visits, north of 24 years to Ukraine have responded to certain inquiries, however more were raised. From nearby towns, how should kin, fathers and family members be contradicting dynamic members on rival sides of WWII? For what reason did family members decide to be Nationalists, Communists or Fascists? For what reason were there family clashes in picking distinctive Christian Churches?

To disentangle these inquiries, it was obvious I needed to more deeply study Ukraine, particularly its set of experiences during WWII. New to me, and most in the Western Hemisphere, was Ukraine's set of experiences after WWII and during Perebudova (the social and political movements happening in the decade prior to the breakdown of the Soviet Union in August 1991).

Similarly significant were changes noted in Ukraine during my visits from 1994 to 2016. These progressions are as yet happening now in 2017 and characterizing present day Ukraine, which is producing more grounded attaches with Europe. Without a doubt, Ukraine has swung away from Russian strength to incline nearer to Europe. From its harsh history, solidified Ukrainians are advancing to be driving individuals in the European theater. It is the biggest country in Europe with fantastic assets that will at this point don't be taken advantage of by unfamiliar powers. Ukrainians pledge to never again be serfs or live like dogs.

Finally, on the grounds that Ukraine is presently free, we are accepting their point of view on WWII history as it happened on Ukrainian soil. Ukraine currently presents to the world its actual job and forfeits in WWII, according to its perspective, no longer another person's adaptation of its set of experiences. It isn't the German, Russian, Hungarian, Romanian, American or British and its partners' viewpoint, all of which have their own flavor.

One show of Ukraine's WWII history happened in 2015 at Kyiv's Ukrainian Institute of National Remembrance by the Institute's Director, Volodymyr Viatrovych. The show explained some the intricacies of WWII in Ukraine, especially in clarifying a portion of my predecessors' conduct. It clarified, large numbers of the family stories and tributes I heard throughout the last 24 years. It is pitiful how Ukrainians were moved to kill each other for different countries. Ukraine made unimaginable forfeits in WWII. The show talked about raw numbers and people, showing a mind boggling example of world showdown on Ukraine's dirt and of Ukrainians on all conflict fronts of the worldwide struggle. I will return later to Ukraine's rendition of WWII (see Appendix 2, p. 227), which explained the sights and sentiments Doreen and I experienced. For the time being, I will share my recollections of our first visit to Ukraine and our endeavors to track down my predecessors and living family members. On our first about six visits, we were genuinely guileless. We didn't avoid any circumstance and attempted to relish the experience. Doreen, a genuinely incredible supporting spouse, permitted me this freedom.

Chapter 2

Finding the first Moisey

Our First Visit to Ukraine

Our first visit happened in 1994, not long after the time of Perebudova finished with the fall of the Soviet Union. Doreen and I were welcomed by Yaroslav at the Odesa air terminal. I had met Yaroslav a year sooner at a get-together of Canadian financial specialists, where he created introductions on business open doors in Ukraine. Yaroslav was familiar with both English and Ukrainian and had Ukrainian political associations. He was booked to go to Ukraine on business, so courses of action were made for us to meet him in Odesa, to check out some business openings and to investigate Bukovina to find my relatives.

had data that my Moisey Ukraine family members lived in a town along the Cheremosh River. I had no names or other contact data. Yaroslav had family members living in a town at the Cheremosh River who were able to help us in looking for my hereditary family. A portion of my Canadian family members had recently ventured out to Ukraine. My dad and cousin Mary Ann Tymchuk (née Moisey) uncovered what they was aware of these past visits.

In the 1970s, my Canadian-Ukrainian relative Anna Navalkowsky (whose mother was a Moisey) and her significant other Ludwig visited Moscow and afterward traveled to Chernivtsi, Ukraine, to track down the Moisey family. Anna is a cousin to my dad. Socialist limitations at the time kept them from passing on Chernivtsi to visit the Cheremosh River region; nonetheless, Chernivtsi authorities permitted them to host a get-together for Ukrainian family members. A couple of family members from the Cheremosh River region were reached by government authorities who welcomed them to go to the Chernivtsi party. Anna said she met a Kateryna Mandruk from Banyliv at the party. Kateryna is a niece to Canadian Mary Ann Tymchuk's grandma. At an ensuing Moisey hundred-year festivity in Banyliv in 1998, Mary Ann addressed Mrs. Mandruk, who affirmed she went to the Navalkowsky party in Chernivtsi. Mrs. Mandruk had several

photographs of the Moiseys in Canada.

Also during the 1970s, Anne and Mike Chorney went from Chernivtsi to the Cheremosh River to track down family members. Anne is likewise a Moisey. Their recruited driver drove them to Banyliv where they were captured by the military and accompanied to Vyzhnytsia for cross examination. They were addressed independently, Anne for two hours and Mike for four. In 2014 I met a Mykola Grygorovych Moisei, who saw the Chorneys in Vyzhnytsia, however was not permitted to speak with them.

Doreen and I were investigated along these lines as the Chorney's in a similar police expanding on our 6th visit to Ukraine in late 1996. One evening Valentyn our attorney referenced he was told to illuminate us to answer to the police headquarters. The following morning, we strolled with Valentyn down the central avenue to the structure where a formally dressed cop stood watch. We climbed the couple of steps and entered the structure and were met by two formally dressed officials. Valentyn shook their hand and presented us. After amiable talk Valentyn continued to clarify our quality in Vyzhnytsia. I articulated a couple of inadequately expressed Ukraine words I thought suitable, which plainly showed I didn't have the foggiest idea about the language. We were getting ready to leave when one official highlighted a flight of stairs prompting the second level of the structure and let us know his boss needed to see us.

At the highest point of the flight of stairs stood a man wearing folded pants and a very much worn green suit coat. He drove us past his work area to a seat situated along the divider. He got back to the work area where he nonchalantly hit his cigarette into a half-filled ashtray of butts. He then, at that point, harshly saw us, causing us to feel uncomfortable to be in his office. Out of nowhere he grinned and strolled towards us, stretching out his hand to welcome Doreen. She wouldn't shake his hand, which promptly eliminated the grin and he suddenly went to sit at his work area. He then, at that point, addressed Valentyn to clarify our quality in Vyzhnytsia. I accepted he heard all our conversation down the stairs from his ideal vantage at the highest point of the steps as he addressed just Valentyn. Occasionally Valentyn would persistently request that I explain some detail the prevalent mentioned. After an extensive season of cross examining us, I took one of the explaining issue events to strongly fight that in Kyiv, Lviv and different towns we were not needed to report our appearance. I stressed decently well with Valentyn's assistance to clarify Ukraine was presently an autonomous country free from the tight

control of the Soviet framework. I attempted to incapacitate the prevalent's harsh position and it worked. Exploiting the adjustment of disposition of the meeting, I squeezed Valentyn to see the composed law the police headquarters had specifying where guests should report. The prevalent then lead us first floor, addressed one of the officials and returned up the steps without further recognizing us. An official told Valentyn there could have been no further business and wished us a wonderful visit. After a day Valentyn got a two-page copy of the old Soviet law. It most likely was the specific law used to catch and grill Canadians Mary and Mike Chorney. We later scholarly the unrivaled was the KGB accountable for the Vyzhnytsia region.

Another individual from the Canadian Moisey family went before us to Ukraine when the Chernobyl atomic fiasco happened in April 1986. It was my second cousin Dr. Clarence Moisey, a new alumni in pediatrics from the University of Alberta, who Greenpeace had employed. He planned the war zone for radiation tainting and was effectively perceived on many broadcast news reports, as he wore an Indiana Jones cap and conveyed a Geiger counter. After this venture, he remained in Ukraine for a considerable length of time, zeroing in on his calling and working essentially at Kyiv's Hospital

Number One. With a portion of his Alberta college educators, he spearheaded a few of the main Alberta specialist trades that saw Kyiv Hospital Number One redesigned. He turned out to be notable in Ukraine and Canada for his endeavors, and frank assessments. Many individuals from the Cheremosh region think about him as a hero.

The Navalkowsky and Chorney guests have passed on. I have never met or addressed Clarence Moisey to acquire data he might have uncovered with regards to any Moisey family in Ukraine. Nastasia, girl of old Nikolaij Moisey from Banyliv, referenced she kept in touch with Clarence at the Kyiv Hospital a few times without getting a reaction. The Canadian Moisey family has connected with our Ukrainian family members at whatever point a chance emerged and there have been stories and magnificent reunions that should proceed for somewhere around a couple generations.

Odesa and Yaroslav

On our first visit, we fixed our safety belts as we moved toward the Odesa air terminal. Cigarettes were splashed, while an attendant eliminated void glasses of devoured vodka. As we handled, an awakening applauding reverberated all through the airplane. We strolled down the compact flight of stairs to a pausing, grinning Yaroslav, who whisked us into the rearward sitting arrangement of a huge dark Mercedes. We never left the vehicle at the air terminal. Close to the leave, a non-formally dressed authority stepped our identifications that we stretched out through the vehicle window. No inquiries were posed and off we went. We avoided the arrangement at movement and customs. On this visit, we went with just hand baggage and immediately showed up at a shabby apartment complex. We strolled up one stairway, were allowed in and told to be prepared for dinner in 60 minutes. The dark fit escort controlled our developments, including conveying Doreen's hand baggage and giving us the loft keys.

The one-room condo was sumptuously beautified in radiant red tones and conspicuous Chinese red-lacquered furniture. A red and white spotted tea kettle with coordinating with cups and dishes sat on the kitchen counter. We immediately showered. Yaroslav showed up and took us to a midtown inn restaurant.

he roads were frightfully abandoned, and business structures were dark; most were blocked. The inn outside and inside were sufficiently bright. Two tables had men drinking, smoking and snacking on snacks. Most recognized Yaroslav. I expected they were security.

The back eatery divider and enormous road windows were designed with weighty, pretentious, wine-hued shades from roof to floor. The windows likewise had fine semi-sheer draperies. The café put forth a valiant effort to give us common Odesa food, which was heavenly. Looking out the window uncovered the roads were as yet abandoned. I saw in the furthest corner in excess of 100 electrical discharges sheer draperies, similar to those hanging the windows. Yaroslav referenced this was his stock. He had practical experience in semi-sheer shades. We immediately ate and got back to the loft for much required sleep.

toward the beginning of the day, a house cleaner showed up to plan breakfast. We washed down the caviar, salmon roe and lox with fresh dainty bread with squeezed orange and champagne. We got done with back bacon, eggs and home grown tea. There was

something else to Yaroslav than we anticipated. Our interest was intense.

We visited the most delightful pieces of Odesa (Ukraine's third biggest city), a structurally perfect city worked by Catherine the Great exactly two huundred years prior. Tragically, it was dismissed by the Soviets for a long time and required fix. Downtown was to some degree occupied with youthful office individuals. All were thin, and the ladies for the most part blondish and excellent, decked out in short skirts and the most recent high-heel styles, requested a subsequent look. We experienced no vacationers. At the wonderful Opera House, additionally needing care, we met an artist Oksana from Canada, who was practicing. In the early evening, driving with Yaroslav, we visited the ocean side regions. Yaroslav constantly highlighted properties he as of late procured with his Odesa companions. There were not many cars.

Odesa Opera House.

The next day after breakfast, we visited the Black Sea coast toward the north. Most huge production lines were skeletal demolishes and were deprived of all that could be moved. Not a light or window remained. One huge prestressed-precast substantial processing plant had a huge overhead, unused crane with a chronic number tag with the date 1990, exactly four years prior. What was going on? For what reason would this new piece of hardware, too weighty to even consider moving, except if large equipment was utilized, be in an unfilled structure that was destroyed of windows, entryways, electrical, plumbing and furniture? Everything moveable by physical work was no more. Who delivered these huge production lines to skeletons? Was it the different mafia or simply the nearby people? No one appeared to know and tried not to give an opinion.

We halted at a gathering of painstakingly kept little homes, whose nurseries were tended by Tartar ladies. They were modest, amicable and not very informative. I was captivated by their multicolored shaded eyes. Somewhere far off, we could see where Hammer, of Occidental Oil distinction, had left colossal synthetic plants that had discarded side-effects straightforwardly into the streams, causing ecological ruin. Smoke stacks were presently idle.

ion's Den

One evening back in Odesa, Yaroslav and I went to a conference in a subterranean wine bodega. The entry was off a dark, abandoned sidewalk.

Inside, the bodega's block lined dividers tenderly bended to the low multi-curved roof. Ongoing sand impacting uncovered a delicate red-orange brick.

The jam-packed room had a couple of artworks and a huge vinyl-shrouded table. We were coordinated to seats toward the finish of the table, joining eight men in a faintly lit room loaded up with tobacco smoke. A moderately aged lady in a dim blue fleece cap went into from a side room and sat in the single seat inverse to us. Part of the way burned-through containers of vodka and ashtrays were on the table. After presentations by Yaroslav, and a few shots of vodka, tongues started to loosen.

Author Zen 1994; extravagance in a feeble Odesa condo building.

Although I was unable to communicate in Ukrainian or Russian, I comprehended a couple of words. Yaroslav deciphered, and I immediately perceived that I was being set up to become associated with an undertaking or two. In view of the faint light, it was hard to concentrate on looks. Just two individuals talked during the meeting, Yaroslav and the lady. Yaroslav expounded on my organizations. The lady addressed assuming I approached funds and premium in putting resources into the Odesa region. Yaroslav reacted that cash was not an issue for myself and that I previously had some global transactions. I felt somewhat awkward within the sight of these individuals, detecting they were sneaky go getters. I was restless to leave and tracked down a reason to end the gathering. Yaroslav guaranteed he would keep in touch with them

Early next morning, Yaroslav showed up with a driver. Doreen and I went through a tiring day visiting an enormous chicken activity, a substantial cluster plant and an inactive precast substantial processing plant. These were evidently possessed by a portion of the participants finally late evening's gathering in the bodega. Yaroslav urged us to put resources into these elements. I knew the substantial activities (as I possessed one in Canada) would be a calamity as the innovation and broken down gear required a total makeover. The chicken activity was all around focused on and expertly managed.

Yaroslav answered to the fleece cap lady about our visit. I tried not to meet them once more, as we were drained and restless to plan for our visit to track down the Moisey families in Western Ukraine.

Moldovan Border

In the early morning, with Yaroslav, we stood by to board our five star seats on the train to Chernivtsi, Bukovina, to track down the Moisey family. Vagabonds with their youngsters were working the group on the multitrack stage. Numerous travelers were boarding trains in the two ways. Our train would go through crook a controlled area in Moldova. The top of the line semi-compartment seats were isolated by a tight table that collapsed vertically from the train divider. The windows were fixed with screws. The climate control system had not worked in numerous a year, despite the fact that we paid extra for this extravagance. We were invigorated and popped a jug of delightful champagne as the train jolted into movement. Most men and the odd little youngster boarding were smoking. Train travel was the normal method of crosscountry transportation. We were off to track down a Moisey in Bukovina (presently Chernivtsi Oblast).

Our discussion held us back from survey the open country. Quite expeditiously, we showed up at the Moldovan-line, where we introduced our records to enter. Doreen and I cleared the furnished boundary however Yaroslav didn't, as he failed to remember an archive. A speedy choice was made not to happen without Yaroslav, so we crossed a few tracks toward the south to board a cargo train to get back to Odesa.

A little group was gathering for the ride to Odesa. We followed local people and boarded the antiquated diesel cargo train with its couple of traveler vehicles fixed with wooden seats. There were no cargo vehicles connected. Most travelers had sacks of nursery produce, calm fowl with safely corded feet, just as one fastened pig, probably for the Odesa market. A couple of bikes remained in the middle path close to their owners.

We were the interest of the train. Yaroslav was awkward and regretful for the environmental factors. For our purposes, we were in a natural component, as we had gone regularly to different landmasses with hand bags, wearing pants and T-shirts. We were more quiet here than on the top notch train. We handily traded well disposed grins with passengers.

The train arrived at its greatest speed of 30 km/h, and it was not difficult to notice the open country. Both Doreen and I were stunned to see worn out people and numerous youngsters with widened stomachs and rosy streaked hair, a trademark indication of hunger, strolling the equal back road. Absence of adequate food was very apparent, and pictures of malnourished youngsters were engraved to us. We detected a couple of single pony drawn carts and bikes. The Moldovan line seemed, by all accounts, to be a troublesome spot to exist.

On the train to Moldova, 1994.

A formally dressed train conductor at the furthest finish of the vehicle started gathering tickets. We showed him our paid five star, unused tickets, and he went to the following travelers. At the point when he finished his assortment, he got back to us and demanded cash for the admission. He turned out to be very bold. Abruptly, straightforwardly behind Doreen, an ample, fair, moderately aged woman leaped to her feet and strolled into the essence of the conductor. With a boisterous voice, for all to hear, she admonished him for being discourteous to unfamiliar guests and attempting to blackmail them. The helpless person felt fortunate to escape with his life. He vanished, and we never saw him again.

One doesn't know Doreen until her Irish is stimulated. It very well may be to guard a position or to give a demonstration of grace. As the woman sat down, Doreen promptly went to the back, put her knees on the seat, and accepted the woman for her courage. In a similar movement, she eliminated from her handbag a couple of Canadian banner hoops and introduced them. The woman rejected. Doreen continued and helped until the hoops hung from her ears. Doreen continued to have Yaroslav illuminate the woman that with her valiance and consideration, Ukraine would be an extraordinary country. There were tears.

Yaroslav would habitually ask which business I thought was ideal to put resources into. He additionally squeezed for how much cash I and others could bring to Ukraine. I tried not to give an opinion.

Back in Odesa, we demanded Yaroslav track down a vehicle with driver to take us to Bukovina. While sitting tight for his hunt, we met Yaroslav's sweetheart, the little girl of the police boss. He frequently suggested his political contacts and individuals like the police boss would keep a speculation from wandering off. He boasted about a $10,000 gift he made to a gathering running the undertakings in Odesa and region.

We were content with the inquiry after a concise meeting with the driver and review the state of the vehicle. We were gotten the accompanying sunrise. The driver's English was superior to my restricted Ukrainian, so we had adequate communication.

If we drove the entire day we would be fortunate to arrive at Milijev, Bukovina, on the Cheremosh River an estimated 450 kilometers distance on streets evading the northern Moldovan line. Yaroslav had family members that would put us up for the evening. We realized the Moisey family was from some town along the Cheremosh River at the lower regions of the Carpathian Mountains.

e discovered that Victor our driver had been the individual protector for Kim Philby, the popular British MI6 and Soviet twofold specialist who had surrendered to Russia and experienced a portion of his last a very long time in Odesa. Victor was thin and strong. He had amazing driving abilities and was sharp for the drive, as it was forever his fantasy to visit the Carpathian Mountains. We persuaded him to bring his significant other, who had never been outside the city. She would likewise be great organization on his re-visitation of Odesa. We would leave Ukraine from Lvov, presently spelled Lviv.

Bukovina by Car

We voyaged twelve hours, experiencing little traffic, for the most part green armed force trucks. Vehicles were in every case full and were for the most part Russian Ladas and Skodas, of old vintage. We saw the odd Mercedes and no American vehicles. Unusually, we saw no traveler buses!

Every hour or thereabouts, the generally cleared street would unite with up to four different streets. Here was a significant protected designated spot, monitored with numerous tactical work force. Every street had a draw bar. We halted and were cross examined. A couple of equipped, formally dressed gatekeepers looked into the vehicle as Victor hand-turned down his window. An enormous compound of put away vehicles was close by, which I accepted that were seized. Victor smoothly pulled out his wallet and blazed a couple of records. He was approached to delay until an unrivaled drew closer, who, in the wake of review the reports, grinned, saluted and allowed section. Up exceeded all expectations stabilizer obstruction. This happened at all designated spots, with next to no issue. It felt consoling to be with Victor.

We made our first stop before early afternoon at an unassuming lush side of the road region. It was great to escape the vehicle and stretch. As there were no washrooms, we utilized the shrubbery. The young ladies utilized the opposite roadside. We had not experienced a gas administration station or eatery almost 33% of the way into our excursion. The wide open appeared to be abandoned. Ranch fields were congested with weeds and overwhelmed by a cover of dark red poppies, which are viewed as a weed in Ukraine. Victor opened the storage compartment. It was stuffed more tight than the vehicle. The greater part the storage compartment was fixed with jerry jars of gas and the offset with apparel and food. We refueled from one enormous jerry can.

Out came a red and white-checkered decorative liner, which Doreen helped spread it on the long grass. A material pack was unfastened, and we sat on a cover and devoured chilled seared chicken, fantastic bread, pickles and sweet tarts. We exhausted a huge container of red pop, and we were off once more. At a resulting stop, Doreen was stunned when a square of smoked pork fat was cut into pieces, and one was given to her on a thick cut of hand crafted bread. I recollect well my granddad relishing this bite. Two comparative stops were made before we showed up in obscurity at Milijev on the Cheremosh River.

It is astonishing that the long excursion we took from day break to nightfall was bereft of side of the road administration stations, washrooms or cafés, with the exception of the odd rear, where outside a hibachi typically consumed, powered by wood or charcoal. Close to the rear were a table or two and a colossal compartment of hot herbata (tea).

It was presently dull and a few requests tracked down Yaroslav's relative in the town of Milijev, where we went through the evening. Most neighbors were snoozing. We were very much welcomed and had a couple of vodkas and a nibble of bread and garlic hotdog. Following an hour of energetic talk we were headed toward bed. Getting up to a crowing chicken, we had a huge breakfast and went to find an interpreter who lived close by. The sky was dark with voronas, crows with white head fixes that attack the region. Crowds darkened the sky as they plunged on each corn fix, disregarding ornamental scarecrows.

everal enquiries in Milijev uncovered a Moisey may live in Banyliv, a town toward the north on the Cheremosh River. At Banyliv after more enquiries, we were told to check a house found four houses toward the north of the enormous Ukrainian Orthodox Church of the Dormition, where an elderly person lived.

Meeting the First Moisey in Ukraine

Bingo! Older Nikolaij was the principal Moisey we found. He was eighty years of age and strolled with a stick in a stooped stance. As we went through the veranda, entering the kitchen, he eliminated his cap, uncovering pure black, wavy hair with the odd strand of white.

Nikolaij, Doreen, the interpreter and I accumulated by the kitchen pich (an enormous artistic, wood-consuming oven). Nikolaij and I sat on the edge of his bed situated close to the pich. We were charmed in talk among his thronw records and photographs. He clarified how he was identified with the Moisey family that moved to America in 1898. His charcoal eyes would enter mine every now and then. He rehashed a few times "a supernatural occurrence" had recently happened. He proceeded to say that every year, with a more seasoned cousin Ivan Moisey, they petitioned God for the left Moisey spirits, whose transport they thought had been sunk on the excursion to America. It was so great to be close him.

Our gathering was hindered by an eruption of energy from Olena

Paraniuk, Nikolaij's more youthful little girl, a kindergarten educator from down the road. Word spread rapidly and soon we were joined by the oldest girl, Nastasia, additionally a teacher. Tears were shed, herbata made, photographs taken, and plans were made to rest at the places of Nastasia in Vyzhnytsia and Olena in Banyliv. Olena's home is close to the left bank of the Korytnytsya Creek, which enters the close by Cheremosh River. The town is around 580 years of age, existing before Columbus came to America.

We found and visited more family members and visited Banyliv, a huge three-section town with no business region, aside from two government stores. Entering a store was similar to entering a huge distribution center with counters. A 1920 sales register, a huge record recording buys and dividers fixed with void racks couldn't be missed. One rack held three containers of jelly and the one beneath had six portions of appealing bread. There were no clients and four representatives. The public authority store was on the primary graveled road entering the town from the north and straightforwardly across the road from old Nikolaij Moisey's house.

enquiries on Banyliv's

Several enquiries on Banyliv's populace drew shrugs. Some got it was 4,000. Most houses were on roughly 33% section of land parts, each with a water well, outside latrine, and a little animal dwellingplace with a pig, a cow, or both. Chickens were all over, hectically scratching in the fenced yards. All yards had apple, cherry or pear trees. Olena's region had columns of houses framing a square shape around a roughly ten-section of land package, where each house had a plain nursery plot. On the southeast edge of Banyliv, across the rail tracks towards and against the old Cheremosh River bank were numerous around one-to-ten-section of land plots, each with zero to four houses spread out in an erratic request. These inadequately fenced bundles were associated by pathways and winding, rutted grass streets. Some house groupings were involved by related relatives. Three of the huge plots were claimed by the Moisey families. Michaelo, Ivan and Frozena (née Moisey) Andryuk were isolated by around two kilometers.

Awaking right on time at Nikolaij's girl Olena Paraniuk's home, Doreen arranged breakfast. I was in the outbuilding hand-turning a silage chopper into which her significant other took care of corn stocks to make them more acceptable for the cow. After breakfast, and with headings from Olena, we set out to Frozena's home, strolling the couple of kilometers. It was a wonderful, somewhat bright, fresh morning.

Here we were on a similar soil, grass-lined street trample on many occasions by Moisey blood. Doreen permitted my meandering aimlessly hypothesis on the things that may have occurred here. We clasped hands and saw smoke from family smokestacks, chickens scratching in yards and ladies occupied with tasks. It was not difficult to recognize a water well as they either had a hand siphon jack or pulley with pail and rope. A cow with milk-loaded articulates was occasionaly driven by a man to a slow down connected to the back of the house.

bout a kilometer from our objective, we recognized a bike. As it moved closer, a tall, babushka-clad, blue-looked at woman in high rain boots, with a major grin, gotten off. She laid her bike out and about edge and hurried to us. She had as of now heard we were in the village.

Arms outstretched, we embraced ruddy confronted Frozena. She was gasping vigorously from accelerating her inflatable tired, vintage bicycle and the energy of our gathering. Investigating each other's eyes and communicating our mutual

satisfaction, we strolled to her home. Frozena left the bike on the side of the road. Before long we were tasting hot herbata, intermittently clasping hands and crying tears of happiness.

Frozena clarified her better half Elai was blamed by the Banyliv Kolhosp (an aggregate ranch initiated by the Soviets), a brief distance toward the east, of taking some pork. He was imprisoned close by, turned out to be exceptionally sick and was gotten back. Elai, unfit to walk or stand, was unloaded over the picket fence. Frozena hauled him into the house, where he kicked the bucket presently on February 16, 1984. He was 58 years old.

Frozena's home with a disconnected summer house, shed and stable with enormous nursery was bound with blossoms and organic product trees. Quickly toward the southeast and toward the west, Frozena let us know this land was essential for the first Moisey home site. This is the place where her (and my) progenitors resided. Further toward the east and simply over the old Cheremosh stream slant (100 meters east of Frozena's home) the Moisey progenitors additionally possessed what she assessed to be in excess of fifteen sections of land. Presently in 2017, the properties toward the southeast are partitioned into little private parcels with recently built homes.

Frozena or other Moiseys got no monetary advantage from these early Moisey properties. In 2017, her leftover one-section of land plot is flawlessly fenced, and abutting toward the southeast is an excellent, recently developed house of prayer with space for around four individuals. It is stacked with symbols and other strict gear. It is all around utilized and generally has one to twenty candles burning.

Later in the day, we strolled the couple of kilometers from Frozena's to a kindergarten, not a long way from the secondary school to again visit Olena, who was one of the kindergarten educators. Her more established sister Nastasia was the headmistress. The school was perfect, splendid and efficient. Nastasia procured twenty dollars each month and Olena three dollars.

After chatting with the youngsters, we strolled to Olena's home, crossing on the Korytnytsya Creek's little scaffold. The street had seepage ditches on the two sides, and its middle was grassed. We strolled on the potholed street as there were no walkways. Going across a crossing street, we ventured over a rusted, ten-inch flammable gas pipeline. Vehicles and steel-rimmed carts rode over this uncovered, compressed line. Houses were warmed by wood in a pich as gas was

for different purposes. Wooden electric power shafts were lashed with weighty wire to short, distending substantial posts. Power was normally utilitarian for half-day time frames. The town framework was cruder than the foundation in Alberta unassuming communities and towns had been in the 1930s.

Late in the early evening, we strolled a few squares through a neighborhood with Olena's sister. Ladies were occupied with yard work. We met a man in his fifties strolling towards us wearing a snow capped cap, conveying a shoulder sack. As the conversation advanced, he ventured into his travel bag and talented Doreen with three champagne bottles. One jug was popped, and we tasted effervescent produced using aged grain. My quick idea was that one should have been intoxicated to continue to taste. I proposed to pay, however he was incredibly offended. An older woman watching her fastened cow grinned at this experience. It was clarified that dealing was average in the town, particularly among individuals who knew each other.

After seriously visiting we arranged to get back to Canada. Victor our aide from Odesa drove us to Lviv, a seven-hour drive over a profoundly rutted parkway. Victor and his significant other from Odesa were extraordinary organization for the significant distances we voyaged. We were never to speak with them again.

After visiting Lviv for a day, we loaded onto a plane for Canada, by means of Frankfurt. On the get back we investigated our discussions with Frozena and her two Moisey sisters, Maria Shandro and Paraska Vatrich and how they all experienced the severe Soviet system.

Paraska's better half, Michaelo Vatrich, was dynamic in one of numerous nationalistic obstruction gatherings. I partook in Michaelo's depictions of conflicts and hanging out in the intensely forested Carpathian slopes. He gloated about stores of weapons he and companions (some of them hired soldiers) had, some actually covered close by. Michaelo was a man of activity with digestive courage. He let me know the area of a cache.

Maria experienced in the mid 1930s; on a few events, Soviet fighters came and eliminated every one of Maria's chickens and livestock. They then, at that point, continued into the house and took her food. Furthermore, they bayoneted her huge designed pads and eliminated portions of bread she had stowed away. Just a little to be left for the youngsters, yet without any result. Maria, Paraska and Frozena, alongside neighbors, experienced comparative cruel treatment.

Of the three sisters, just Frozena and Paraska are alive in 2017 and live in their homes in Banyliv and Ispas, separately. Maria, a cheerful lady with an interminably friendly character, passed on April 27, 1997. An absence of penicillin and legitimate clinical consideration killed Maria. My holy messenger spouse Doreen, an enlisted nurture from the Edmonton General

Hospital, consistently loaded our baggage with drugs. I recall Doreen regarding Maria's hemorrhoids as they clustered close to Maria's pich. Maria frequently warmed her hemorrhoids adapting to the pich as close as she dared.

In Ukraine, my lengthy Moisey family had numerous divisions due to their political methods of reasoning. Decisions were made by wild conditions compelling them to settle on quick choices to get by. Some became enthusiastic Soviet Communists, Fascists aligned with Germany, or stalwart Ukraine Nationalists. Many dads repudiated their youngsters as a result of decisions their kids made, particularly assuming the kids favored the Soviets. Frozena, a tall, appealing lady, was recognized as a productive agribusiness field laborer during the 1950s, when the region was under Soviet control. She and a few neighbors invested wholeheartedly in this honor and today are amazing grounds-keepers. Frozena inclined toward the Soviet decision power for monetary endurance, despite the fact that she lost her significant other subject to their authority. Her sister Paraska, an extremely impressive disapproved of individual, was a Nationalist, fundamentally affected by her dynamic Nationalist spouse, Michaelo. He was detained for a long time in the Siberian gulag. His cell was without hotness, and he turned out to be sick following five years and was delivered. He paid for his nationalism with time spent in the Soviet jail and ensuing medical problems. Maria Shandro (née Moisey) additionally helped Michaelo and numerous Nationalist contenders. She was dynamic, helping with stowing away the pursued Nationalists.

Tanasi Moisey (Мойсей), 1882 - 19??, born on oldest known homesite where Frozena lives. He had three wives, all predeceasing him.

From Frozena's home, a couple of kilometers north, downstream of the Cheremosh River and along the railroad track, is Nikolaij Moisey's parcel, by the congregation, confronting the principle Banyliv road. I discovered that the road is alluded to as the old Turkish Way. The house is enormous with a couple of sheds loaded up with his very much worn smithy instruments, manufacture, stock of dry oak, metal sheets and steel level bars. In a joined shelter stood a somewhat finished pony drawn cart under development. The back shed was for livestock. Nikolaij hand-cut oak into spokes, centers and areas of the border wheels. He likewise manufactured and molded a band of steel to tie the wheel pieces safely and fill in as the part that turned over rough streets. He handily produced every part of the cart, selling it for what might be compared to around 200 Canadian dollars. I couldn't want anything more than to have a finished, painted cart on our Canadian farm.

Banyliv 2017.

Nikolaij, seriously twisted from age and for the most part from beatings by Bolsheviks, was his own man. There was nothing very sensitive in his assertions. He detested the Bolsheviks, a few times calling attention to their ineptitude. It is astonishing he endure mishandles experienced on his property from Bolsheviks, Germans and Romanians (who were the manikins left in charge after the German quick assault). His little girl Olena gave me twelve pages of manually written data about her dad's past (see Appendix 13, page 298).

On August 7, 1932, Stalin announced capital punishment for anybody taking a couple of bits of grain from a field. Prior to the appearance of the Bolsheviks and their defective Communist framework, Ukraine was the breadbasket of Europe and its own locale. In 1931 and 1932, Stalin was occupied with sending a large number of trainloads of wheat to hold Moscow back from starving. More trainloads of grain were shipped off China to show the accomplishments of Russian socialism. Mao killed 75,000,000 in his walk to socialism, and Stalin killed 10,000,000. Stalin's declaration was rarely revoked. Numerous distant Kolhosps proceeded to brutally rebuff individuals for minor offensives during and after Perebudova until the mid 1990s.

Lurking Family Shadows

Back in Edmonton after our first visit, we immediately fell into the day by day schedule of earning enough to pay the rent, while recollections of Ukraine streaked through both our psyches. Doreen and I chose to work on something for the Ukrainian families we had met. One day there was a message on the telephone that Yaroslav (from the Odesa place of extreme peril meeting) called! I detected he was searching for cash and disregarded his telephone call.

Visions of the principal visit continued. Pictures of malnourished youngsters entered my fantasies. Deserted, void distribution centers and manufacturing plants lacking windows, entryways, encircled with whole grass and greenery, helped me to remember phantom towns found in films. Great many square kilometers of farmland growing weeds and poppies lay inactive. Individuals briskly strolled streets, and one never saw a solitary traveler transport. Either the people couldn't stand to pay, or oddly enough, the socialist framework didn't make transports available.

A trace of relatives, politically partitioned from the severity of war and numerous accounts of difficulty would once in a while hose our eyes with tears. We before long started to ask ourselves how could we deal with give my far off Ukrainian family some assistance up?

Canadian-Ukrainian social gatherings are among the most grounded all around the world, however we had negligible association with them. After a couple of requests we tracked down the Edmonton office of Meest, a business transporting office conveying administrations from Canada to Eastern Europe. We furnished Meest with a rundown of mass food things we thought would give alleviation to the family members we had met, things like huge sacks of sugar and flour, flavors, cooking oil, hams and canned products. These things were bought in Ukraine and conveyed to explicit families for dispersion to their nearby families.

Our Canadian business was attempting to extend from a past downturn. I paid myself low wages, while Doreen filled in as an enrolled nurture. We stayed away from bank obligation as the previous downturn nearly guaranteed every one of our resources, including the house. Doreen said we should accomplish something so we acquired
$10,000 to buy food to be disseminated to my far off family.

We got thanks from astounded relatives for the merchandise. Bundles were shipped off the oldest in a family bunch. We contemplated they would

realize best on the most proficient method to split the food between their kin and other relatives. We had given transitory help for the coming winter, facilitating our concerns.

Subsequent visits to Ukraine uncovered a ton regarding how the food was circulated among the family gatherings. We realized who was mindful, who cheated with the conveyance among their own family. This information helped us in picking relatives for adventures we later started in Ukraine. Purchasing the food kept us from stepping on the numerous business landmines experienced by most unfamiliar undertakings in Ukraine as it battled to continue on from its socialist past.

On the 1996 visit to Ukraine with Dad, Doreen and I rested a couple of days at Olena Paraniuk's (old Nikolaij's little girl) home, where we noticed her child Roman moving toward his adolescent years. He had a mind blowing ability for workmanship and chiseling; winning a couple of public honors. Artistic expressions are his complete concentration. He gave us a portion of his work, and I bought the rest of, we keep in our Canadian Ukraine room.

On the visit in 2014, I saw Roman's forte of metal forming. He strolled me through his welding and smithy shop with three-year-old child Daniel labeling behind. I saw a couple of very much worn apparatuses, which I accepted came from his granddad's shop. Roman's significant other, Oksana, who was brought into the world in far off upper east Russia and concentrated on craftsmanship in

t. Petersburg, sat on a swing with seven-year-old girl Bohdana.

3 meter metallic Angelic face on Mount Makivka commemorating heroine Olena (Yarema) Kuz from Banyliv, by artist Roman Paraniuk.

With interpreter Oksana Chorney and business-disapproved of Tatyana Krasniuk, I immediately comprehended the troubles Roman was experiencing in his endeavors to advance his models. Roman was exceptionally troubled and in tears as he had recently gotten news that he had lost a companion in Putin's intrusion in Eastern Ukraine. After much conversation, he consented to make a figure to address harmony between Western Ukraine and Ukrainians caught in the Donbas fight zone, where war was instigated by Putin's infiltrators. Roman would plan the figure. He requested a couple of days to give us a sketch in the wake of counseling his creative companions. We acknowledged his plan without changes.

n an early visit, Frozena welcomed me to her congregation in Banyliv, and I promptly acknowledged. Her child Tanasi drove us to the congregation, a red-block shell under development actually deficient with regards to glass in the window pits. We went in while child Tanasi sunk into his vehicle for a rest. The churchyard had painstakingly stacked blocks, holding back to be mortared into a future position. There were not many parishioners in participation as we stooped on plastic sheeting, on a yet-to-be-developed floor. The congregation, a Russian Orthodox Church (ROC) controlled from Moscow, is vital to Frozena, an exceptionally strict person.

Two meter metallic fine art by Roman Paraniuk from Banyliv.

Not excessively far away, on Banyliv's central avenue is the old Ukrainian Orthodox Church of the Dormition (Assumption), went to by a portion of her kin. To numerous relatives, particularly the more youthful age, there was little significance regarding which church they joined in or were hitched in. As of late, Frozena took in the Russian Orthodox Church is a branch of the Russian government. She was stunned to know a portion of the ministers were Russian supporters, giving political data and sending her congregation gifts to help Putin. It took a few of her kids and grandkids to persuade her with regards to the exercises of the ROC. There are instances of how the Russians throughout the years fled with reserves or despoiled a great many Ukrainian places of worship. The majority of these taken Ukrainian church resources are as yet heavily influenced by Russia, through the ROC. Most towns basically acknowledged this burglary, avoiding the chance cause trouble. After Perebudova, locals started to develop new houses of worship as per their religion. One model is the new church in Ispas, twenty minutes south of Banyliv, which Doreen and I upheld with a gift. The congregation elderly folks set our commitment in their affirmation book on page 100.

Ispas Ukrainian Orthodox Church, Kyiv Patriarch.

Our 1996 Visit with Dad and a Family Reunion

My dad John Roman Moisey, Doreen, and I went to Ukraine to find more Moisey family stories, to solidify subtleties for our Lingcomp school that we were creating, and to hold an enormous family reunion.

Dad's order of the Ukrainian language was amazing as per old folks. He was loved, and the more established people held nothing back from him. The older were glad to hear Ukrainian words like Tak, Tak (yes), rather than Russian Da, Da. They were glad Russia didn't totally obliterate the Ukrainian language. The Soviets were fierce with their abuse of Ukrainian culture. Father brought a stockpile of Ukrainian banners (the shade of a blue sky with gold wheat field), which were quickly raised to housetops and up long poles.

Each day, father went through hours with old Nikolaij. They fortified right away and appreciated each other's conversation. Nikolaij was brought into the world in 1914, and my father a year after the fact in Canada. Watching them put in half a month together was a fantastic association to notice. Father likewise reinforced with Michelo Vatrich (wedded to Paraska Moisey, Frozena's sister) and Ivan Moisey, who was quite a long while more established than old Nikolaij.

Zen and father 1996, sign at the south access to our tribal town of Banyliv.

These three old folks scorned the Bolsheviks and Nazis. They irritated these systems sooner rather than later, and were rebuffed when captured. Nikolaij recounted to numerous anecdotes about himself and his family. He was an impassioned Nationalist, opposing the Bolsheviks, the Germans and their possessing Romanian manikins. Later he was recruited by the Soviets and was on the bleeding edges of awful fights to stop the Germans at the edges of Moscow. A significant number of his companions were killed, expelled to Siberia, or detained. Numerous others endured, including Nikolaij.

Dad and Nikolaij's gathering, 1996.

His sly activities were depicted to me by his cousin Maria (née Moisey) Shandro, who like clockwork assisted him with getting by. She was his main contact who knew his whereabouts. Maria clarified she would carry water and food to his different underground refuges. One kind of safe-house comprised of a shallow opening in an open field, with a couple of branches covered by

earth, and disguised with encompassing vegetation. She portrayed an event when his smell was perceptible from a few meters away. When caught, the Bolsheviks beat him with weapon butts, crushing his fingers, breaking his shoulder and harming his back.

Maria Shandro (nee Moisey { Мойсей}) 19?? – 1997, most established little girl of Tanasi's third spouse, conversing with my dad John Roman.

At one at once, to local Romania, expecting the name Moisiuk. I saw his Romanian recognizable proof archive. In Romania, he proceeded with his metal forger exchange. Back in Banyliv, he was shipped off the Russian front, where he fixed tanks and gunnery during fights. He would hold his ears as he portrayed stunning blasts of huge firearms that shook the earth. Long a while later, he had dreams of these occasions. Nikolaij frequently referenced his disdain of the Bolsheviks. He called them inept little men. Maria couldn't accept the cruel treatment Nikolaij got, and the ruthlessness she suffered from the Soviets, Germans and Romanians.

My dad was amped up for an enormous family get-together he and Nikolaij were arranging. They sorted out for it to be held at old Nikolaij Moisey's Banyliv house, north of the congregation on Main Street (Turkish Way). Families regularly met at weddings and burial services, so a gathering was a peculiarity, yet invited. A day was chosen seven days before we were to withdraw for Canada. Father prevailed with regards to welcoming a few dads and their youngsters who recently would not meet one another. Some were isolated logically in light of WWII and the Soviet framework. These individuals had not addressed each other for quite a while. Father figured out how to conquer this separation by persuading them that blood was thicker than water and their political perspectives. Many shed tears of since quite a while ago held responsibility. Father had a particular method of bringing individuals together.

Ukrainian ladies are local area coordinators and practitioners, and they taught Dad to supervise the acquisition of a pig. They would deal with different subtleties. The Kosiv week by week market across the Cheremosh River had domesticated animals for sale.

he Kosiv marketplace is the biggest nearby, where every item under the sun is accessible. Trucks with carpets from Turkey, exceptional meats from Poland, wine from Romania, utilized attire from America and snuck vehicles from Hungary extended as should have been obvious. The mass of moving humankind mixed gradually, raising dust storms. Galicians and Bukovinians with sacks of items, including tobacco, domesticated animals, home jam, woodcarvings, customary embroidery and attire satisfied the faculties. Stock was conveyed by foot, cart, bikes and machinas (vehicles and trucks).

Enroute to the Kosiv Bazaar to acquire a pig for a large family reunion 1996. Lady is transporting two sacks of potatoes uphill by bicycle.

Dad and Ivan, our escort, wrangled for a live pig, which the seller drove a significant distance to Ivan's vehicle. A significant conversation between Dad, Ivan and the seller focused on the best way to move the pig in the little vehicle, a Citroën. They attached the pig to keep it from kicking and getting away. The seller immediately delivered some twine from his back pocket and he and Ivan tied the hoard. Four of us battled to lift the pig into the back compartment of the Citroën hatchback.

Dad and I stacking the pig into a vintage Citroën to the entertainment of the crowd.

We all jumped in, and Ivan put the vehicle into high gear. Doreen shouted that the pig was free and was pushing the cover behind her seat. We leaped out, opened the hatchback to by and by get the pig. It leaped out and limped not too far off with Dad and I in pursue. With a strong jump, I handled the monster, covering its body. The screeching pig contorted and cut a vast opening in my pants, however I hung on. Father then, at that point, assumed responsibility and hoard tied the monster so it was practically unmoving. The Citroën drove up and in exceeded all expectations, crap what not. Five of us heaped in with our buys, and off again we went, gradually moving with the weighty, screeching load down the dusty road.

The day preceding the family gathering, father butchered the pig and left it with the ladies at Nikolaij's home, where a whirlwind of movement was occurring. Nikolaij's home and yard got the best cleaning it had found in many years. In Nikolaij's studio, pyrohies and holobtsi were made, while fitting tunes were sung, which made for its own party. One tune, which appeared to continue for an hour was tied in with making pyrohies. Ladies alternated depicting a short amusing scene and afterward totally participated with the pyrohy chorus

All was prepared the following early evening, and sixty or more visitors showed up, each man with a container or two of custom made spirits. There was a great blend of youngsters and older people. Father was right at home with the old, recounting to a large number of stories and responding to inquiries concerning Canada. Many approached ten kilometers to join in. At last, as scattered homegrown tasks entered individuals' psyches, the party finished. Father persuaded those with vehicles to make a few excursions to commute home those residing the farthest away. An enormous Moisey love-in across the huge sea had occurred.

Dad and Nikolai the 3rd

Old Nikolaij was the attendant of the Moisey graves across the railroad tracks from his home. His folks, grandparents and other old relatives involve the super upper east corner of the burial ground. These graves are all around set apart with steel-pipe crosses, welded by Nikolaij. His significant other Wasylena's (née Maksymiuk) grave is set apart with a snow-white, substantial gravestone, containing an encased photograph of her and the date of her passing in 1980. Nikolaij never remarried.

Yabluniv Internat resident school for homeless students. Andre had a severe cold,   1996.

Nikolaij's child Nikolai the second has one kid, Nikolai the third. We discovered that Nikolai the second hitched Luba, who had two young men from a past marriage. Liquor before long annihilated the association. Nikolai the second was inebriated on the entirety of our visits. Luba with the three young men lived across the Cheremosh River in Stari Kuty. Nikolai the third, around twelve years of age, was in an Ivano-Frankivsk State foundation called an Internat. This Oblast (region) has around eleven Internat schools for parentless kids. Nikolai the third's Internat School, which has both male and female youngsters, is in Yabluniv, across the Cheremosh River, west of Banyliv. Yabluniv is the town from where the main Ukrainians relocated to get comfortable Canada in 1891. In the wake of talking about the kid with old Nikolaij, my dad's eyes met mine. We right away realized we needed to venture out to Yabluniv to find the twelve-year-old.

We showed up sooner than expected morning at the Yabluniv Internat School. The air was sodden with a chilling breeze. Three pre-youngster young men were going across the road to enter the school grounds. Two little youngsters leaving the schoolyard connected at the hip welcomed the young men, trading a couple of snickers. We saw the young ladies' objective was a vacant part fixed with open air latrines against an unpainted picket fence. A couple of understudies stood around close to the latrines. Frozena's child Tanasi, our loyal, affable driver, drawn in the young men in some giggling. Every one of the three were

crouched in grown-up winter apparel, and one had a runny nose, which he cleaned with his jacket sleeve. We learned they inhabited the school and had no guardians. They cherished their instructors. Tanasi extricated the area of the school chief's office. We partook in the experience with the young men, as they crunched on treats we offered.

Dad, Tanasi and I strolled to the open office entryway and acquainted ourselves with the chief, who was interested and genial. She called high temp water and poured enormous cups of herbata (tea from nearby spices, berries and orange strip). Halfway during our time cup of herbata, in came a couple of educators, and we learned of Nikolai the third's conditions. The instructors, and particularly the chief, were loaded up with compassion for the kid and said they would really focus on him at the school for up to one more year. They didn't need him to return to Stari Kuty as they knew about awful impacts there that were hindering to the youthful boy.

he chief set up for the kid to join we all accumulated in her office. He was treated as a grown-up and was told what our identity was. Father and I needed to put in almost no time with him in private, and this wish was allowed. The kid, father, and I tracked down a seat under a tree, where we accepted this wonderful kid. He shed tears every once in a while, and father and I broke down as we found out with regards to his troublesome youth. Nikolai shuddered in the cool air, and I eliminated my multi-hued coat, covering his boney shoulders. He sat among father and me. We discovered that he beyond a doubt adored his mom, Luba, and that he realized the Internat was beneficial for him. The kid would have rather not discuss his father.

Yabluniv Internat School instructors with occupant understudy Nickolai third Moŭceŭ with my skilled Guatemala
coat of many shadings remaining before me and the school chief, 1996.

We got back to the chief's office, where the educators were gathered, and with youthful Nikolai third , we tasted steaming herbata. Tanasi was napping in the vehicle. As we bid farewell, this lovely kid began to take off the coat, which I immediately got back to his shoulders. It looked so great on him, and he bashfully said thanks to me for the gift.

We were presently alone with the chief and told her that we needed to attempt to add to her great work. Father gave her two US hundred-dollar notes, one for herself and the other for what she thought fitting for the kid (instructors in 1996 acquired \$40 to \$80 each month). I told her I was a Rotarian and what we Rotarians do. I knew a couple of Rotarians at the Ivano-Frankivsk Club and said I would investigate further if they could be keen on banding together with a Canadian Rotary Club to help the school.

At a gathering with the Rotary Club of Ivano-Frankivsk, the club consented to deal with a Rotary World Community Service Project for the Internat school. The venture, whenever acknowledged by the school, would see them getting a forty-foot long, by eight-foot wide, by nine foot-four inch high sea holder of materials they desired.

The school chief faxed the Ivano-Frankivsk Rotary Club a list of things to get of

what things would make the school a superior spot. The Ivano-Frankivsk Club and I moved toward Caritas (a Catholic Charity) in Ivano-Frankivsk and got confirmation from the priest that he would set up for import papers to get the holder in Ukraine. The club would then empty the holder and transport the list of things to get things from Ivano-Frankivsk to the Yabluniv Internat school. I would track down a banding together Rotary Club in Canada to fill the holder and pay the delivery expenses for Ukraine.

From the Yabluniv Internat school, we drove south to Stari Kuty to track down the kid's mom, Luba. The house was in a scattered group of little houses, open by a grass-lined trail. We stopped in a great deal close to an enormous house with signage clarifying that this was the place where Ivano Franko spent a decent piece of his initial life. The house was well kept.

We found Luba's home, where we met one of her children, who set out to track down Luba. We were in a rush and following a half hour chose to leave without meeting her. As we drove from the stopping region, we saw Luba and her child running toward us. Father and I left the vehicle and strolled a piece for security with Luba, clarifying what occurred with our gathering with her child in Yabluniv.

Apple time, south of Yabluniv.

Luba educated us regarding her trouble bringing in cash. Her best cash source was gathering boxes of apples and other produce from neighbors and taking the train to Moscow to sell them in the city. She knew Valentyn and Maria Krasniuk, as Maria likewise ventured via train to sell woodcarvings in the city of Moscow. Father gave Luba $100. He prompted her that Maria (Frozena's

little girl) and Valentyn would be the most ideal method for staying in touch and that we loved her kid. Luba, a unimposing, battling mother, was energetic about the minutes we went through with her, and she shed tears. I started crying a few times as we hugged.

Luba said he was a decent kid and needed to eliminate him from exceptionally terrible impacts around. She said he dozed in her bed, where he had a sense of safety. He didn't procure the road smarts of his more seasoned relatives and their companions and was diminished the Internat school acknowledged him.

Edmonton Rotarians immediately filled the Internat school list of things to get of materials and put away them at their Rotary Humanitarian Aid Warehouse, where in this way the products were stacked in a compartment. Tanasi, Frozena's child from Ukraine, was in Canada and at the distribution center to assist with stacking the compartment. After a year in 1997, the holder was dumped by Ivano-Frankivsk Rotarians, and their report was empowering; a couple hundred kids would have some material security before they were turned out on troublesome streets.

Later on another visit, Rotarian Laetitia de Witt from the Vegreville, Alberta Rotary Club, her Ukrainian-talking companion and I visited the Ivano-Frankivsk Club and the Yabluniv Internat school. The visit to the school was unannounced. Climbing the steps to the principle corridor carried tears to my eyes. Everything was newly painted with incredible consideration. Banner estimated understudy drawings covered every one of the dividers. Passages had working lights. Word spread rapidly. We disturbed classes by playing ping-pong on one of a few tables sent from Canada. The passages were warm and dry. Kids dressed impeccably in T-shirts and pants amassed us when they understood what our identity was. I heartily accepted many kids and the school chief. We both shed tears as we embraced.

Classes were suspended. Herbata, Coca-Cola and orange soft drink were poured. Laetitia and her companion were an incredible hit with the instructors, and they occupied with vivified conversation after the energized youngsters got to their ping-pong games and a sudden opportunity to play outside.

We were taken to the residences. The dividers were brilliantly shaded, showing kids' drawings. There were genuine draperies on windows, and each bed was flawlessly made. Gone was the weighty, moist sheet material that probably been 50 years of age. Each bed had a little carpet on the all around worn tile floor.

After much fervor, I pondered where youthful Nikolai third was. No one knew his whereabouts. I later gained from Maria and Valentyn that

the kid and his Mom had been in touch with them. They helped Luba a piece and had last heard the kid was chipping away at a huge pig ranch and his manager was content with him. I anticipate ideally meeting him once more, the grandson of old Nikolaij, the principal Moisey we met in Ukraine.

he Trust Factor

Yaroslav had been hassling me for an impressive time frame to put resources into his numerous chances. Ordinarily, I declined. At some point, Yaroslav called, reporting he was in Edmonton with his better half and child. He welcomed me to be the youngster's back up parent at an Edmonton Orthodox Church administration. Doreen and I met them at the congregation. His better half was a wonderful individual and appeared to be a lot more youthful than Yaroslav. I became adoptive parent, and Yaroslav's sister became godmother.

I next heard from Yaroslav when he called from Odesa. He sounded frantic and argued for cash for a definite arrangement. I denied, and he discourteously hung up. Half a month after the fact, I got a compromising transcribed letter requesting cash. By and by, I felt the dismal foreboding shadow of the Odesa bodega place of extreme peril. I disregarded the letter and never heard from him again. In Ukraine, a few months after the fact, I heard he got a shot to his head.

I was all the while searching for certain organizations in the Ukraine to put resources into. I squeezed father to name somebody I could trust, as I had turned into somewhat suspicious after the Odesa experience with Yaroslav and the way that a portion of the food bundles had neglected to be genuinely conveyed earlier.

I kept on asking father whom to trust, as I needed to turn out to be more engaged with the Lingcomp tuition based school. Without a second thought or capability, he chose Valentyn Krasniuk, who was exceptionally peaceful at all our past get-togethers. In the first part of the day, I gave cash to Valentyn to purchase Mila's condo and set it up for a school. Gradually pieces were becoming all-good with great people.

We bought extra work areas, tables, PCs, and so forth, for the school and had them introduced. Inside the following two years, we maximized at north of 200 selected understudies, everyone prepaying for their examples. Numerous understudies were instructors from in excess of thirty close by high schools.

It became clear the Vyzhnytsia region required an Internet framework. A fifty-kilometer line from Chernivtsi was introduced. We gave a PC to be the server. Inside a year the local area had eight clients on the web. This was refined with help from Ivan Paliy from Chernivtsi, a specialized wiz for the public phone organization. Ivan is hitched to Olga, the amiable little girl of

Lucian Moisey from Ispas, a stepbrother to Frozena.

Our first visit to Banyliv had carried us to find our first Moisey, to open a bigger local area of family members and to start some magnanimous chances to work on individuals' lives. Be that as it may, we were not yet done investigating, or being molded by, Ukraine and its kin. Resulting visits saw us grow our quest for my familial roots and en route my comprehension of, and association with, Ukraine.

Chapter 3

Ancestral Roots

Origins of the Moisey (Мойсей) Family

Tracing Ukrainian family roots is troublesome. It is muddled on the grounds that intruders have frequently involved Ukraine. There have been numerous intrusions and time and again, they have even happened all the while. Numerous documented records, particularly those from temples, were destroyed.

There is an amazing Egyptian association between the Moisey name and the scriptural Moses. Moses in Egypt is known as Moshe. Numerous Ukrainians think about Moisey to mean the scriptural Moses. The root "Moi" is additionally said to come from Moldavia in the sixteenth century. There are different names known to be connected or that might be associated with these roots. These include: Moisey, Moysey, Mojsej, Majsej, Mojsaj, Moisie, Moiseiek, Moisei, Moys, Moyse, Moss, Moyes, Moyses, Moisa, Moisan, Mosha and Moisii. All through this book, I will generally utilize my own spelling of the name for the good of effortlessness, despite the fact that occasionally I might be alluding to somebody whose name might be spelled differently.

There were Moiseys in middle age England in the thirteenth century. The

1199 Yorkshire Pipe Roll records have an Elyas Moyses showing up in 1210 and a Moyses showed up in the Norfolk Roll in 1230. A 1414 "Lease roll" posting land gifts to the Battle Abbey in East Sussex, England, records Jeffrey Fitz Moyse and William Fitz Moyse delivering rent for their territories. In somewhere else and time, the Sept. 1 1678 records of St. Michael's Parish in Barbados, in the Caribbean, records a Susanna Moysey.

In Ukraine the family name is Мойсей in the Cyrillic letter set. Мойсей was changed automatically to Moysey, Moisie and Mojsej during Austrian and Polish occupations. There were likewise other chipped in changes during Romanian and different occupations. These spellings exist today, and some can

be followed in files, school enrolments and different archives, a confounding circumstance to say the least.

My distant grandparents Wasylena and Stefan Moisey, pioneer ranchers in Western Canada, 1898.

Records of the Moisey name in Ukraine and area date back to the mid 1700s. The Moisey name isn't normal, however it is found in numerous nations. A couple of my Canadian and Ukrainian family members have explored the Moisey ancestry. Most Moiseys are found in Western Ukraine. The Cheremosh waterway valley, which incorporates Banyliv, has a convergence of Moiseys. Of those I met living in Bukovina, and different pieces of Ukraine with the name Moisey and forms thereof, most follow their heritage to this area.

In nineteenth century Ukraine, the Chernivtsi 1840 Marriage Archive records Wasyl Moysey's introduction to the world in 1794 in Banyliv. Wasyl is the granddad of my extraordinary granddad, Stefan. Wasyl's marriage enrollment is likewise in the Chernivtsi files. He was hitched in a town a couple of kilometers south of Chernivtsi, close to the Romanian line. The document contains his age, dates for three pre-marriage warnings; his significant other's name; his town; and notes that he was a trooper positioned close to the Romanian line. Relationships were recorded in the spouse's town. They had a child Tanasi Moysey (1821-April 19, 1881), who wedded Irene (Gregory) Andryuk.

My father John Roman Moisey, 1996 at the corner of Banyliv's second school on the west side of the Turkish Way, where his father attended when he was ten years old in 1897. The oak tree is estimated to be 100 years old. Banyliv's first school opened in 1856 with Moisey enrolment. It no longer exists and was located nearby, about a block east of the Turkish Way.

School registers are one more great method for tracking down tribal records. At the point when Banyliv school opened in 1856, one of the initial five schools to open in Bukovina (presently Chernivtsi Oblast), the main day of school enrolled the accompanying Moyseys: my incredible granddad Stefan (at the time matured nine), Ivan (matured twelve) and Tanasi (matured eleven). The involving Austrians opened these five Bukovina schools, after more than 100 years of insubordination, and requests for social change from the Ukrainian local people. A significant resistance had happened only a couple of years prior, in 1848, when Stefan was just two years of age. In the principal year at the Banyliv school 32 young men and one young lady (all between the ages of six and twelve) enlisted from a sum of 558 kids in the town. After 50 years, the scholarly year of 1906-07 had a greatly improved 412 out of 629 young kids enrolled.

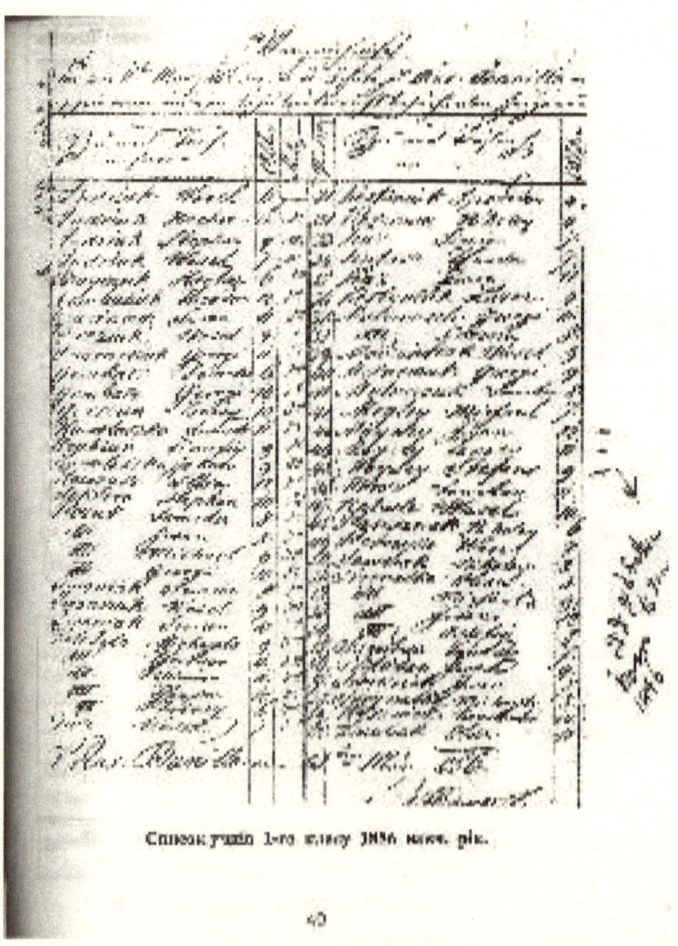

First Banyliv School Registry. Only four other Bukovina Schools were allowed to open for the first time ever by occupying Austrians. My greatgrandfather Stefan and his two brothers are near the middle of the right column.

There are additionally a couple spellings of Moisey in Canadian records, regularly because of Canadian authorities compelling name changes to fit English spelling shows. Since there were no guidelines on the most proficient method to roll out those improvements, one individual frequently even wound up with more than one method for spelling their name. For instance, Stefan Moisey's child Oleksa came to Halifax, Canada, on the

S.S. Bulgaria in April 1898 and is recorded as both Moysey and Majsej. At the point when Stefan and his leftover family showed up in New York, on the S.S. Pretoria in August 1898, they were recorded as Moysey and Mojsej. Once more, this is confounding no doubt, yet don't get too hung up on the spelling of names.

Homestead-related records of the "Canadian Dominion Land Office" list a few of Stefan Moisey's children with various spellings of the keep going name, on occasion on a similar report. Generally fascinating to me is one archive containing the names Stefan, Oleksa, and my granddad Gregory. The dad and children have various spellings of their last name.

Other of Oleksa's property reports likewise have various spellings. Oleksa's residence report from the "Domain Land Office" in Edmonton, stepped with the got date Dec. 23, 1902, and stepped got in Ottawa on Jan. 2, 1903, shows his name as Alexander Moisey. This archive (No. 59915 748020) likewise noticed that he was single, that he entered the property site on Jan. 25, 1899, and that he started residency there in February 1899. When missing from the residence, he expressed, he was a worker at a Blairmore, Alberta, coal mineshaft. Another residence record (No. 1367602) on Form No. 46 for this equivalent land bundle situated on SW1/4-32-57-15W4 shows his name as Alex Morse, matured twenty-five.

While discussing Ukrainian names in Canada, it is actually quite significant that in excess of a couple of Western Canadian towns and towns take their names from Ukrainian spot names. Here are only some of them: Bukowina, Chernowci, Sniatyn, Kysylew, Skowiatyn, Sachava, Wostok, Luzan, Ispas, Zawale, Czahar, Lwiw, Molodia, Krakow, Huwen, Zhoda, Kaluz, and Paraskevia. I went to grade one at South Bukowina School, starting in 1946.

In Canada, the family battled to observe an anglicized spelling utilizing the English letters in order. To acknowledge Moysey, the spelling demanded by their Austrian oppressor, was not adequate; the family in Canada picked Moisey. Ukrainian Canadians like my Moisey precursors spelled their names in manners that opposed the unfamiliar powers that involved their country. Throughout the long stretches of occupation in Ukraine's violent past, various occupiers had forced their frameworks of how they figured Ukraine ought to be and how family names ought to be recorded. This inconvenience fizzled. Unimaginably, Ukraine

has on various events switched these changes, holding just the qualities its kin wanted. Their way of life, music, craftsmanship, close family ties, values, customs, agrarian abilities, hard working attitude, religion and language remained solid.

his flexibility reminds me how when I originally visited Ukraine, following Perebudova, the vast majority of homes had effectively eliminated photographs and memorabilia of Lenin. Out came strict symbols hung with the best weaved wraps (rushnyky). A couple of stalwart socialists wanted to hold their white mortar busts of Lenin, which they showed all through their homes. Starting around 1991, Ukraine twice changed its cash from the Russian ruble, at long last choosing the hryvna, which was utilized in the district in the 11th century. Soviet profaning of Ukrainian customary expressions, customs, writing, history and language started to end. The markets and shops are presently loaded up with complex customary show-stoppers. The forced Russian language is gradually vanishing, and pride in the Ukrainian language is escalating.

oday, the nation is flooded with the blue and yellow shades of the Ukrainian banner. This is reasonable in light of the fact that since Ukraine's commencement severe abuse by unfamiliar trespassers gradually made pockets of opposition all through the country. Russian Tsars and despots, Poles, Germans, Romanians, Austrians Hungarians, and Putin today have pushed Ukrainian patriotism to a breaking point. Ukraine's blue and yellow banner is gladly shown all over the place. Any place one looks there is an ocean of blue and yellow. Transport stops, homes, fences, temples and even extensions are painted in these shadings. On one of our first visits, we gave Nikolaij Moisey an enormous banner, which he promptly raised and flew at his home. No other Ukraine banners were apparent in Banyliv at that time.

New distributions of Ukrainian verse and history are richly accessible. In my tribal town of Banyliv, Степан Кузъ (Stefan Kuz) has distributed a book of verse named Не Діліть Україну (Ukraine Do Not Believe). His subsequent book will before long be printed. He and his better half both work to self-finance these distributions. The current city hall leader, Nicolai Andryuk, in 2013 distributed Банилову, 580, a book on 580 years of Banyliv history. He self-financed and printed it locally. Another variant is destined to be distributed. Another model comes from the home of my Baba Moisey's folks Kalyna and Semon Worobetz (Оробець) whose town of Zaluce (Залуччя) on the north-east

edges of Chernivitsi distributed a quality hardcover town history book in 2004. Quickly, a nearby distributing industry has developed in humble communities all through Ukraine. Today, many towns have recorded their set of experiences. It is simpler now for Ukraine's Diaspora to find their country families and town narratives. Distributing actually part of a relentless influx of public pride, which enormously disturbs the dictator Putin.

Living the Life of a Dog

In the 2014 Maidan Winter Rebellion, Wasyl Moisey, 21 years of age, was the fifth dissident to be killed by a rooftop rifleman, upheld and prepared by Putin's Russia. Assuming that you view the narrative "Maidan Winter Fire," you will observer Wasyl kicking the bucket, as his companions, on two events call out to out him for help. This present book's title is gotten from an ideology Wasyl purportedly announced: "Preferred to Die a Wolf over to Live the Life of a Dog." I feel the same way, as do a couple of Moiseys I met in Ukraine. As I hear additional report from Ukraine, I infrequently wind up with clammy eyes. On these events, I sense a torpid attribute kicking in to take on Wasyl's maxim. I trust more Diaspora Ukrainians, on learning of Putin's awful activities, will speak out to help Ukraine. My significant other Doreen doesn't have Ukrainian blood, however is a savage fighter for Ukraine. She is current with every day losses of life and happenings in Ukraine and is dynamic on the Internet supporting Ukraine.

Throughout the year 1838, another Wasyl Moisey (my extraordinary incredible granddad with his better half Anna and their child Tanasi, matured seventeen, alongside many confided in family members, dozed precariously. They had burnt their property manager's stables, homes and carts. Individuals struck food canisters. They took some coin. The uprising is known as the Bukovina Great Revolt. Twenty years sooner, Wasyl, at the age of 24, had been engaged with a minor Bukovina Revolt. On the Cheremosh River lining Galicia, Banyliv was a simple getaway course for them, as they probably were aware how and where to cross the waterway, particularly at higher water levels.

Living as serfs and serving in the property managers' armed forces, ultimately drove numerous Ukrainians to defiance. Mass insubordination initiated in Galicia and Bukovina in the mid 1800s, with some killing and disrupting of property managers' resources. This prompted, and included, a significant uprising in 1848 in Western Ukraine, where large number of property managers were killed. The basically Polish property managers were now

supplanted by Austrians, with guarantees of change to serfdom. The year 1848 was a key year, when most serfs in Western Ukraine began to accept there was desire to circumvent carrying on with the existence of a canine. A wolf was allowed to wander and do as it wished, while canines were tied and taken care of supper scraps. After 50 years, numerous from Banyliv accepted it was "Smarter to Die a Wolf than to Live the Life of a Dog," as the normal serf change had not shown up, to the majority of the population.

In 1849, the Austrian Empire gradually allowed concessions to mollify Ukrainians, a large portion of who were living in serfdom. Suppression resembled subjugation in America. Most serfs and slaves were attached to the property manager and as a rule stayed a resource when land was sold. Slaves comprised for the most part of vagabonds and Tartars. Not very many were freemen. My predecessors from Western Ukraine's Bukovina were predominately Ruthenian, otherwise called Rusyans (nothing at all to do with the name Russia). My mom's predecessors (Palichuk), who came from across the Cheremosh close to Kosiv, Galicia were Hutzels. Palichuks are found there today.

Bukovinian defiant activities brought about the Austrians allowing minor social concessions, for example, opening the initial five schools ever in 1856; one was in Banyliv, where the three Moysey young men were selected. On my twelfth visit to Banyliv, I looked as a huge new house was developed on exactly the same recognize that the school once stood, and I pictured the three young men joining in. For quite a while, a sizable level of Moiseys have picked training as their occupation. This is valid in Ukraine and Canada.

In the late nineteenth century, the Moiseys took an interest as constrained work assembling a rail line that went through Banyliv while heading to Vyzhnytsia. These were plentiful occasions for the landowners, as they wrongfully fussed over the brutal Austrian laws beginning from far off Vienna. Insubordination was as of now not a choice in Western Ukraine as troops could quickly show up by rail in generous numbers to put down any defiant act.

A touch of disobedience runs in many Moiseys, on the Canadian side of the family as well. I clearly recall my dad John Roman portraying how he opposed a schoolmaster who had given brutal actual discipline for a minor demonstration of defiance. One day after school, Dad held up under the little Whitford Lake river span with a sharp stick. As the instructor's buggy

crossed, Dad jabbed the lance through a break between the boards straightforwardly into the pony's paunch. The surprised pony shot out the instructor from the buggy and hustled off into the distance. This defiant quality appears to be pervasive in the Moisey hereditary code, as Moiseys in Ukraine and Canada are known to participate in comparative insubordinate acts.

In my childhood, I knew about a Moisey in Ukraine during the 1890s who was pursued by the Austrian armed force. As of late, I referenced this to my second cousin Mary Ann Tymchuk (née Moisey). She reacted that it was her granddad Nikolai Moisey from Shandro, Alberta. Nicolai is the most seasoned child of Stefan, our incredible granddad. Mary Ann depicted what her grandma, Nikolai's significant other, told Mary Ann on more than one occasion.

Mary Ann's simply hitched grandma was leaving Ukraine for America with the Wasylena and Stefan Moisey family. Arriving at Hamburg, Germany, they wanted to board the S.S. Bulgaria in the spring of 1898 for Halifax, Canada. They realized the Austrian armed force was chasing after Nikolai and consistently looked for police and military. In the setup for boarding, child Olexsa drove and went too far to the protected stacking region. The leftover family saw the presence of the Austrian armed force police, so they left the arrangement. Assuming they bet and followed Olexsa to the protected boarding zone, the German specialists would have kept the Austrians from catching Nikolai.

After the nearby experience, the family most likely held up in Hamburg, as the get back was 1,500 kilometers, and there was the consistently present Austrian armed force keeping watch for Nikolai. Going underground in Hamburg would set aside cash and take into account contacts to track down one more entry to Canada. What a brilliant encounter for the kids to observe many societies and get familiar with a tad bit of the German and English dialects, which consequently ended up being of worth, particularly for Gregory (my granddad matured eleven) and his sister Mary. They returned a couple of months after the fact in July and boarded the S.S. Pretoria, leaving for New York, then, at that point, on to Edmonton via train.

y incredible grandma Wasylena Moisey's (née Kuz) grandsons, John Roman (my dad), his more seasoned sibling Steve, and their mom (my caring Baba) have talked about Wasylena frequently. Wasylena was dainty however requesting. She disdained my dad and Baba. She inclined toward Steve, who looked more like her child Gregory. They resided in a similar little, crude Canadian house, where many tense minutes happened. My Baba let me know her significant other Gregory was Wasylena's top choice. Wasylena was consistently present and administered like a tactical official. She requested Baba Paraska to do the entirety of the house and yard errands. Harsh Wasylena never dirtied her fingers. Baba frequently let me know she loathed Wasylena, in light of the fact that she dealt with Baba like a worker, not in any event, allowing her to eat until every other person had completed their meals.

Nobody smoked in Wasylena's home. After Wasylena's burial service in 1923, Baba said the family was quiet. Baba, mother of ten, didn't back off on the standard against smoking in the house, with the exception of when the climate was sharply cold, and afterward she permitted the young men to blow their smoke into an open oven damper while they laid on the tile covered floor, eliminating the smoke from inside the house better compared to cutting edge building exhaust systems.

Thirteen visits to Ukraine make them accept Ukraine is a more matriarchal society than Canada. My translator Ohla said most ladies realize the man is the head and the lady is the neck. The head should follow where the neck turns. Possibly many long periods of men being away from homes while enrolled in militaries helped made this matriarchal society. Men were frequently away in nearby Carpathian woods for stretched out timeframes to chase wild creatures to enhance the small food acquired in serfdom. Subsequently, Western Ukraine had to have ladies as head of families. Today, following 25 years of visiting Ukraine, Doreen and I concur Ukraine ladies appear to surpass North American ladies as top of the household.

tatistics in the Internet Encyclopedia of Ukraine show that, in 1897, there were 1,008 ladies for each 1,000 men at twenty years old. The awkwardness expanded to 1,090 ladies in 1926 and 1,040 ladies in the mid 1990s. Conversely, Diaspora Ukrainian men in the West surpassed the quantity of ladies. Battles in Europe and migration from Europe added to these numbers.

My Great-grand relatives

Doreen and I went to a few weddings on our visits to Banyliv during the 1990s. We have long periods of recordings of these broad services. A wedding kept going three to four days. More established people let us know marriage procedures presently were as old as they were youngsters. Numerous visitors we noticed approached sixteen kilometers to the merriments. An unexpected agnostic dance is regularly fused, as a rule after visitors have burned-through bountiful amounts of home-blended vodka. Visitors wore customary ensembles; men hit the dance floor with men to a live band. We moved on a rose, wood-planked floor. All were wearing winter dressing, numerous with hide caps to fight off the virus. The drunkest I have

been in many years (and without a headache) was at one of these agreeable weddings. There was a steady stockpile of homemade libation and food over the four days.

t was a severe cold evening, after a wild Ispas wedding, when Doreen and I previously rested at the Moisey familial site. We had shown up later than expected with confided in driver Tanasi, Frozena's child. Everyone realized we were from Canada. Doreen swears she moved twice with each man, and a few ladies. Her dainty feet were stepped on a few times during the wild moving, and before the finish of the evening her feet were wounded. I recollect that evening I had the most odd contemplations and rested close to nothing. The agnostic moving and incredible homemade libation added to a night we both will always remember, which finished with us tucked under the thick blanket. We didn't know it at that point, yet later recorded examination uncovered that my soonest precursor Wasyl Moisey, brought into the world in 1794, additionally dozed here.

e arose late morning, and after a strong breakfast, Frozena applied a natural solution for Doreen's swollen foot. Gradually we limped a couple of kilometers in unpleasant cold towards focal Banyliv to visit different family members. Doreen looked charming enclosed by Frozena's babushka. Most wooden-fenced yards were occupied with ladies going to day by day tasks. All bustling yard occupants were well disposed and many had recently met us. A chicken declaring to the world that it had laid an egg, and the clank of a metal bucket as it reached the stone lined water all around was exceptionally articulated in the still severe virus air. These sounds made a symphony to the crunching of our boots on the fresh snow.

It was a maybe correspondingly cold morning on October 13, 1868, when quarter century old Ignati Tanasi Moisey, brought into the world in Banyliv, apprehensively held up at a little town church for his lady Anna Wirtsty (a widow), matured 34. The wedding was occurring in a little town close to the Gerza armed force base, only south of Chernivtsi (and today a postion of south Chernivtsi, the legislative center of Bukovina). The Gerza dormitory watched the antagonistic Romanian-Austrian line. Ignati was positioned as an infantry trooper at Gerza, while Anna (brought into the world in Korytne, a town near Banyliv) lived close to the base. Chronicles register that Ignati and Anna showed up at the congregation on three events, to record their goal to wed. To go to the wedding, Ignati's folks, Irene and Tanasi Moisey, and Anna's folks strolled from Banyliv, fifty kilometers away. The single direction venture from Banyliv to Graza was a

two-day walk. Ignati's more youthful sibling Stefan (my extraordinary granddad) was serving in the Austrian armed force, positioned at another area, and couldn't attend.

For an obscure explanation, Ignati's union with Anna finished a few years after the fact, and he remarried. On January 21, 1879, Ignati wedded 33 year-old Wasylena Ilchuk. They resided with Ignati's folks on the home site, where Frozena (née Moisey) Andryuk resides today. Frozena is the extraordinary granddaughter of Irene and Tanasi. This data depends on marriage records from a 1860-1899, Banyliv chronicle in Chernivtsi. Those chronicles record Banyliv as the birth and passing spot for Ignati and Wasylena. His folks (Irene and Tanasi) and grandparents Anna and Wasyl are likewise covered in Banyliv. Anna and Wasyl are the soonest Moisey predecessors found in files to date.

Ignati's sibling, Stefan (my incredible granddad) was additionally recruited into the Austrian Army. He served something like twice in the military. The initial time, he was enlisted on Verlust-liste Nr. 871 and was displayed as Stefan Mojsej. He wedded Wasylena Kuz October 25, 1870, when he was roughly 24 years of age. Stefan is additionally enlisted in now digitalized records at the National Library of the Czech Republic as "Mojsej Stefan, Infantry, k.
k. LIR. Nr. 30, 6. Camp, Galizien, Zubrze, 1874; kriegsgef, Moskau, Rubland." By that year, Stefan had one-year-old Nickolaj Moisey, who in 1898 moved to Canada with the family. The Czech National Library likewise enlists Stefan in the infantry, IR Nr. 24, at camp Ispas in 1875.

any more Mojsej, Moysey, Moise, Moisse, and Moisze guys are recorded in armed force records. Absence of fathers and more seasoned children at home clearly added to food deficiencies and the ensuing beginning of illnesses, prompting high baby passing rates. Wasylena and Ignati had nine youngsters, five of whom passed on before the age of five. Extraordinary granddad Stefan's three-year-old little girl Irena kicked the bucket of red fever in 1879 in Banyliv. Times were cruel and troublesome, as liberation from serfdom guaranteed by the Austrians never entirely happened in a manner that gave genuine opportunity. Two ages of high demise rates, notwithstanding the help of affectionate Banyliv families, happened. So pitiful. See Appendix 6A and 6B, pages 253-255 Family Tree.

Zen's Ancestral Village Банилову (Banyliv)

Still, individuals of Ukraine, and of Banyliv, have endured, made due, and endeavored to improve their lives. Nikola Andryuk's 2013 book Banyliv 580 Years Old is an important record of the Moisey's hereditary village.

Nikola Andryuk's book incorporates a photograph of Doreen and Zen.

It shows a portion of the advancement that has been made there. The stressed segment over the course of the following a few pages is carefully interpreted from his book.

Banyliv is first referenced in 1433 in writing by O. Dobroho, a Moldavian lead representative. There are a few forms of this name. To begin with, the name of the town comes from the Moldovan cash "showers," which were gathered by the Turks' station. Second, it might come from the Turkish word "boycott," which signifies "lead representative" in the Ukrainian language. The authentic records notice that the town existed during the Shypynskoyi land control of the fourteenth century. This is exactly 100 years before Columbus came to America.

On the boundary of two states, Banyliv has for quite some time been a focal point of struggle

between the Polish lords and Moldovan lead representatives. In 1538,

Bukovina was under the control of the Sultan of Turkey. Banyliv right up 'til the present time has a "Turkish" Way (Main Street) on account of it being a "Turkish" watch post. In 1775, Banyliv fell under the Habsburg Empire. In 1886, Banyliv Ruska opened a mail center. During the 1890s, it had a railroad station adjoining the first Moisey homesite, with rails reaching out from Vienna to Vyzhnytsia along the right bank of the Cheremosh River.

During WWI, Banyliv was the location of battling between the Austrian and Russian armies.

During WWII, on April 8, 1944, Soviet soldiers entered Ruthenian Banyliv. 300 occupants battled the Nazis. 53 were killed and missing. For Military Merit, five locals were granted the Order of the Red Banner, the third Order of Glory III; fourteen residents were granted the decoration "For Valor." Many others were granted different other medals.

n 1950, the Banyliv state ranch (Kolhosp) was set up. A clinical center likewise opened. In 1952, the Melnivka Creek hydro plant started to function.

Banylivskoyi, the design of the Village Council, represented two settlements, Banyliv and Berezhnytsya, with 4,555 hectares and 999.9 hectares, respectively.

Educational institutions:

Two optional schools: Banylivska auxiliary school degrees and optional school Bereznytska UC-II levels. In south Banyliv the preschool instructive organization works, which is intended for 63 kids. Open Music School.

Health care and social help: In the town, the committee works a clinical center and family medication practice (south Banyliv), which has a rescue vehicle and wellbeing posts in south Berezhnytsya that is completely outfitted with clinical staff and assuming important offers help to all sections of the populace. The town has two stable dental workplaces. There are

three pharmacies.

Culture, game and the travel industry: There is a library in every town. The People's House has the public society bunch "Banylivska toloka," drove by Mazuryaka VM, taking an interest in all occasions held in the town, region, and area and beyond.

In the Banyliv People's House, there is an exhibition hall of history.

The primary room of the exhibition hall covers the historical backdrop of the town of stone "yanoho age" to the furthest limit of the nineteenth century. The second room of the gallery covers the time of the mid twentieth century to 1940. The fourth little room is an inside room from the late nineteenth and mid twentieth centuries.

In the town situated close to the school exercise center, there is a wonderful arena with a bituminous running track, football field, volleyball court and b-ball court.

There are four enrolled strict networks. They are 1. Supposition of the Blessed Virgin Mary, Ukrainian Patriarchate. 2. St. Nicholas Church Moscow Patriarchate. 3. Supplication House ASD. 4. Michael Church of the Moscow Patriarchate. The town has an Orthodox, Jewish and Polish cemetery.

Another intriguing record of Banyliv comes from Irina Belova. Her expounding on Banyliv particularly shows the advancement made there since the fall of the Soviet Union. She likewise clarifies how Nikola Andryuk is significantly more than simply a creator and antiquarian, and assumes a significant part in Banyliv. Coming up next is from Irina Belova:

On October 14, 2014, in the town Banyliv raised a landmark to Olena Kuz, an individual from Sich, a Ukrainian military gathering, who exhibited exceptional mental fortitude during the threats of 1914-1918. The thought for a bust came from Kuz's niece Helena, who, alongside George Menzak and different contributors, brought it alive and diverted her from somebody consigned to blankness into a perceived champion. The landmark is situated on school property, and hence is an eminent illustration of invulnerable soul and gallantry to the more youthful generation.

The uncovering occasion was gone to by Deputy Head of District Administration Claudia Nazarenko, Manager of the District Council George Ivonyak, Head of Education District Administration Mikhail Andrych, Chairman of the District Committee of Union of Education Yaroslav Badger, Chairman of the area part of the All-Ukrainian Association "Edification" Dmitry Nykyforyak, Head of Banyliv Village gathering Nikola Andryuk, instructors, guardians, understudies and villagers.

Father Elijah favored the bust and read a sacred petition for harmony and peacefulness in the country. Tending to the crowd, Claudia Nazarenko noticed Banyliv's part in history and that the local area respects huge figures who made that set of experiences. "Without a doubt, Olena Kuz is an illustration of female bravery. Also that is the case of such recorded figures we should teach the more youthful age about, so they grow up genuine loyalists, broadly cognizant residents of Ukraine," she said. The Banyliv school understudies' fables outfit "Banylivska Toloka" performed and invited the members to the authentic occasion regarding the town hero. At last, Nikola Andryuk expressed gratitude toward the backers and every one of the members and said that slowly all the saints whose names were eradicated from history in Soviet occasions would be gotten back from obscurity and honored.

In the Chernivtsi area, trout took care of the whole town of Banyliv. Banyliv has one the greatest fisheries in Ukraine. Numerous Bukovinians know Banyliv town on account of the popular trout ranch. The proprietor, Levon Terteryan, for a long time has controlled the rearing of fish. He is currently developing trout and sturgeon, and anybody can buy straightforwardly from the homestead. For instance, a kilo of trout goes for $60 US, sturgeon $100 US. Also 90% of the fish taken from the town are sent alive. This is an exceptionally amazing economy. The greater part of the trout in the Ukrainian market are taken from here. The proprietor develops trout in the most flawless water, utilizing the most recent innovation, as per town head Nikola Andryuk. Individuals from numerous nations visit the site. Close to the pools with trout and sturgeon is a unique seating region where guests can attempt to get fish. To see so many trout together is amazing.

Learning such a great amount about my soonest Ukrainian progenitors, just roused me more to attempt to effectively assist with working on the existences of individuals in Ukraine. Doing as such kept on reinforcing our association with, and enthusiasm for, Ukraine, and to extend the organization of individuals we know there. We even got to meet Nikola Andryuk, and (at his asking) to help pay for the landmark to Olena Kuz that Irina Belova depicts above. The following part portrays a portion of the humanitarian exercises Doreen and I have done as we turned out to be progressively "contributed" in Ukraine.

Chapter 4

Investing in Ukraine

Scholarships

In September 2014, the Krasniuk family and I were welcome to a Banyliv school service respecting my incredible grandparents Wasylena and Stefan Moisey. The school likewise offered thanks to the Krasniuk family and me for making and giving an honor of $300 to a graduating young lady and kid yearly at the Banyliv secondary school starting around 2005. Subtleties of grant victors are at www.moiseyscholarship.org/wswinners2005.html. Ivano-Frankivsk and Chernivtsi Oblasts have likewise gotten this honor, with the absolute number of grant champs presently moving toward 100 understudies. This most amicable gathering was gone to by teachers, chiefs, oblast instructive agents, and neighborhood and provincial government delegates. An uncommon treat were exhibitions by early-grade understudies with their dance and tune. They welcomed me to move. What fun it was.

Dancers, 2014, Banyliv School gathering for the Krasniuks and Zen for financing the Wasylena and Stefan Moisey Annual Scholarships.

Dancers and visitors, 2014, Banyliv School gathering for the Krasniuks and Zen for subsidizing the Wasylena and Stefan Moisey Annual Scholarships.

Dedicated educators with Zen at the Banyliv School, 2014.

Immediately after the merriments, Mayor Andryuk welcomed Tatyana, interpreter Oksana and me to his office in a nearby school building. The city hall leader showed us heaps of old photographs and records, and provided us with a speedy visit through the historical center. Oksana was an understudy at our Lingcomp English School and later moved on from the University of Chernivtsi with five years of English as her major. She was a diamond in keeping me informed in regards to the gathering and meeting with the Mayor. During this visit, Mayor Andryuk, additionally the town's informal history specialist, tapped me for $300 to purchase concrete and materials to raise a bronze bust of champion Olena (Yarema) Kuz. It was at this meeting that I initially educated she was a Ukraine heroine.

An instructor holding the secondary school understudy prize. 47 $300 understudy grants were introduced in 2007 by the Doreen and Zenith Moisey Canada Scholarship in the Ivano-Frankivsk, Lviv and Chernivtsi areas. Each likewise gotten a prize and diploma.

as well as getting sorted out another Lingcomp School (portrayed in the following area), we furnished existing government funded schools with new understudy grants. One gathering of grants stays at the Banyliv School, to pay tribute to my Canadian incredible grandparents, Wasylena and Stefan Moisey. Doreen and I had financed the grant to respect Wasylena and Stefan, brought into the world in Banyliv, Bukovina, who had moved to western Canada in 1898 with their six youngsters. Banyliv School grant victors have their names engraved on a wood prize, which incorporates a cut image of Wasylena and Stefan. Grants worth $300 have been conceded every year starting around 2005. Every year a Banyliv young lady and kid are chosen, in view of the best test scores. Assuming there are a few competitors with a similar score, then, at that point, the champ will be dictated by a jury of five instructors, including the school head. Victors should enter a higher instructive foundation. The committed administration of the Banyliv

Scholarship grants is directed by Valentyn, Maria and their little girl Tatyana Krusniuk from Vyzhnytsia. They likewise give cash to the honors. The Banyliv showing staff and their chief, Mrs. Nykoforik, select the triumphant students.

Scholarships and prizes are regulated by legal counselor Valentyn Krasniuk. The Lingcomp School project was fruitful as a result of him.

We gave a second gathering of grants through the "Doreen and Zenith Moisey Canada Scholarship Fund" we have at the Edmonton Community Foundation (ECF). Cash from the ECF was then diverted through the "Canada Ukraine Foundation" (CUF) for extra understudy grants. A Scholarship Report by the Lviv Office of the CUF for the 2006-7 school year noticed that 47 alumni from Ivano-Frankivsk, Lviv and Chernevitsi had won awards from our asset. At grants functions all through those locales in May and June 2007, contending schools won regarded covers, and winning understudies got endorsements and grants worth $300 Canadian. The CUF additionally duplicated the quantity of award victors, and gave more grants to understudies in the Physics and Mathematics Lyceum at Lviv University who had won the All Ukrainian Olympiads. The CUF has now shut its Lviv office. In 2015, CUF was intending to open a Kyiv office as Canadian Prime Minister Steven Harper's administration gave $1.5 million to this reason. It is my fantasy for Ukraine to shape its own territorial and city "Ukraine Charitable Foundations." This is not difficult to achieve, whenever dependent on the Canadian model of the "Edmonton Community Foundation," which can be seen at: www.ecfoundation.org/

One of Wasylena and Stefan's youngsters was my granddad Gregory, who until the age of 11 likewise went to the Banyliv School, prior to leaving for Canada. In Canada, Gregory turned into an educator, Canada's first Ukrainian Justice of the Peace, and a Reeve of Alberta's Wostok District, all while raising his family on a ranch. Numerous Canadian Moiseys set up the "Jean and Gregory Moisey Scholarship" at the secondary school in Andrew, Alberta. The Scholarship is overseen by the Edmonton Community Foundation (ECF) and has been granted yearly since the 1990s.

anyliv School grant victors can be seen at www.moiseyscholarship.org/wswinners.html. This site is overseen by Nick Bilak from Chernivtsi. A rundown of CUF grant victors and grants occasions can be found in Appendix 4, on page 247. Assuming that you are of Ukrainian legacy from Alberta or Bukovina (presently Chernivtsi Oblast), you are probably going to observe your family name recorded there.

Lingcomp (Our Private School)

Increasing the proficiency rate in non-industrial nations is one of the best ways of propelling the way of life locally. In Ukraine, we found a particularly high proficiency rate with 70% having post-secondary school training. Ukraine's proficiency rate positions fourth in Europe and surpasses the United States. High proficiency, shockingly, didn't mean a decent way of life. Ukraine's way of life was not exactly many non-industrial nations we had visited. We experienced numerous family members with unfriendly ailments, some who passed on rashly, for absence of normal drugs. Doreen, an enrolled nurture, was particularly perplexed.

Schoolteachers, now and again, were not being paid for a really long time, and when they were paid, in pieces of Bukovina, it was with vodka from the state-possessed refinery. An instructor would get jugs of vodka at retail value worth and afterward go to the road to offer them at underneath discount costs to procure their compensation. Times just after Perebudova in 1991 were hard for most government representatives, particularly educators. We saw numerous ladies passed on Ukraine to work abroad and send cash home. The breakdown of the Soviet Union obliterated whatever alleged useful implies that remained. Ladies worked for lower than negligible wages in nations they headed out to illicitly. In the mean time, Ukraine, the biggest country in Europe, has the fourth most

instructed populace, with an education pace of 99.7 percent. Europe's most impressive programming powers are in Ukraine. Online business is developing at a shocking pace of 20% per year.

Between 1994 and 1996, Doreen and I visited Ukraine another multiple times and hardened all the more family and non-family associations. Ukraine was advancing a few stages forward and one back. Everybody was glad, aside from old stalwart commies, gradually being pushed out of their situation of advantage. During these visits, we gathered enormous bags with utilized eyeglasses and PCs, accepting this would help the Cheremosh River valley stay aware of huge city training. Carpathian country schools were not treated on an equivalent premise to Kyiv schools. Ukraine needed assets, and when assets were free, the large urban communities progressed while rustic regions were neglected.

We chosen to invest our amounts of energy into building up a tuition based school called Lingcomp (Linguistics and Computers) to help understudies in the English language and the most recent in PC innovation. A Canada/Ukraine Joint Venture established by me in 1994, Lingcomp was a pioneer in Ukraine, preparing on occasion multiple hundred understudies to be capable with PCs and English from its tuition based school in Vyzhnytsia, Chernivtsi Oblast. Following 10 years, each encompassing local area had contending non-public schools. Lingcomp has coordinated more than thirty secondary schools in the Vyzhnytsia Region of Bukovina. A couple of Edmonton Rotary Clubs gave the very first PCs, printers and Internet associations with the schools. Taking an interest schools gathered $100 from guardians to start the interaction. One educator offered his pony to help raise the required $100 for his secondary school to take an interest. In the mid 1990s, Kyiv's victories with immense amounts of cash infused into its school for PC preparing could not hope to compare to the accomplishments of the private Lingcomp school.

Some of my Ukraine family members, Ivan Vatrich from Ispas and Valentyn Krasniuk from Vyzhnytsia, immediately tracked down Nick Bilak and Taras Masaruk. Them four solidified an arrangement to make a Computer and English School, and turned out to be important for Lingcomp's spine. Scratch had recently finished five years of college in PC designing. Our Lingcomp tuition based school requested PC parts from China, and Nick Bilak and his gathering collected them. Taras had was a school head who talked faultless English. He recently accomplished public acknowledgment for his progressive instructing. Taras won a rivalry that permitted him to visit Canada and the U.S., and he had concentrated on Saskatchewan's instructive systems.

Author Zen and the inconceivable Taras Mazaruk (Lingcomp English School Director) 1996.

The primary PC classes started in Valentyn's home and Taras' school office. Understudies paid for each class they went to on PCs or English. Understudies' expenses of fifty pennies for each illustration helped pay the educators. The educators got the biggest level of charges gathered. We paid for all important materials like PCs, printers, programming, course readings, earphones, recording devices, and so on Doreen and I gave funding to essential things, including the acquisition of study hall space. This was a method for surrendering some assistance. The more we got involved the more we developed to like the caring people of Ukraine.

We before long tracked down Olena, from Vyzhnytsia, a splendid youthful alumni with five years' PC preparing and fantastic English, to instruct from her home. Olena worked for the public authority for $50 each month, and we paid her $25 for late night educating. Her better half sold alcohol. They just had a child. Olena was working herself ragged.

It became obvious an extremely durable office was required for advantageous advancement to be made. A principle concern was to track down a super durable, all around found structure to fill in as a tuition based school. Ivan, Valentyn and I visited the mayor of Vyzhnytsia, who showed us a few government structures that could be bought after an extended interaction including Chernivtsi government authorities. We finished up we would be going around and around and squandering energy attempting to get an unused government building.

Valentyn knew where there was a loft available to be purchased, claimed by a single parent named Mila who had been given the condo by the Soviets. We were informed that it was all at once a Polish ruler's royal residence, a terrific old structure that was currently separated into five condos. Situated on 78 Ukrainian Street, Vyzhnytsia, close to the town's focal square, it remains on the edge of the business locale and across the road from a couple of skyscraper condo buildings.

Three of five aparments (pink) bought and remodeled for the private English and Computer Lingcomp School in Vyzhzytsia.

At sixty years old, Mila was troubled with medical issues, and she needed to live approach her sister in Chernivtsi. She had a thirty-year-old girl keen on going to New York, where her companions were working in bars. The condo required broad fix, yet was great for the Computer and English School. We consented to buy the condo for $8,500 US. Mila gifted us with a ruby glass, hand-painted decanter and six coordinating with glasses, which when we use them bring affectionate recollections. They are finished with hand-painted white blossoms. She said it was made in Romania and acquired by her mother.

First homeroom bought was Mila's loft. Mila's endowment of ruby dish sets to Doreen, which was acquired from Mila's Moldovian

To make the school, we wanted a proficient legal counselor, and we were fortunate. Frozena's girl Maria Andryuk had hitched Valentyn Krasniuk, a new alumni with a law degree. Maria had been brought into the world on a similar property as my extraordinary granddad Stefan. Valentyn, a cautious scholastic who tried not to twist rules, consented to assist us with framing a legitimate substance, which was urgent for the arrangement of Lingcomp. This was not a simple errand as post-Soviet standard had no strong and demonstrated interaction to frame a lawful substance, similar to we have in the Western world. Valentyn counseled his lawful contacts, and we chose to frame and enroll "Lingcomp Canada/Ukraine Joint Venture". Rapidly, Valentyn arranged records with assistance from universities, which the lawful delegate of Vyzhnytsia district in this manner endorsed. Valentyn paid ahead of time for the administrations and left cash for others in the muddled interaction. Close to the furthest limit of 1994, we got the legitimate element "Lingcomp Ukraine/Canada Joint Venture." Lingcomp was the principal joint endeavor among Ukrainian and Canadian elements to be set up in the district. The Linguistics and Computer school worked at 78 Ukraine Street just a little over 10 years. A sign to remember the school was gladly raised at that location, and one can in any case see it today.

The one-condo school was quickly loaded up with understudies, driving us to buy two nearby condos from Orletsky for $10,500 and Klym for $11,500 separately. (See Appendix 3, page 245 for subtleties). We presently had three adjoining lofts of the five. The condos were held in Valentyn's name for quite a long time and later moved to my name.

Ceiling of Mila's apartment redecorated for the school classroom. Note stenciled wall work unique to this region and common in the 1800s.

Within months, a total reclamation, inside and outside, was finished to what the families accepted the structure resembled about 200 years sooner. Within dividers were a lopsided mortar, which the family fixed and hand painted with an old stencil framework totally unfamiliar to me. For ages, more established homes and some houses of worship along the Cheremosh River among Banyliv and Vyzhnytsia have fused the framework. Relatives chose by Maria Krasniuk, Valentyn's significant other, the girl of Frozena, finished all the work.

On the entirety of our first visits, we brought PCs and extras. Once in Kyiv, customs addressed us for conveying three PCs and printers. In the wake of illuminating traditions about Lingcomp, they hoped everything would work out for us of karma and we continued without covering charges. Whenever authorities were recounted our exercises, they never bothered us, in any event, when we were bringing things and bountiful measures of U.S. dollars into the country.

Tatyana modelling her creative skills in 2014. Sales are as far away as Costa Rica, USA and Canada. Ukraine and Canada signed a free trade agreement in 2017 that should facilitate more sales to Canada.

In May 2000, my splendid companion, David Salues from Miami, headed out to Ukraine with me. He effectively acclimatized into the Moisey family. He regularly investigated all alone, not knowing an expression of Ukrainian however figuring out how to speak with the guide of an interpreter. David was dazzled with the affectability and imaginative pizazz of youthful Tatyana Krasniuk. At the point when he left, he gave Tatyana his camera. David, a five-year move on from PC designing and the proprietor of a couple of Miami Beach stores, consistently had the most recent and best of gear. David and I went with Ivan and Boris Vatrich to the Polish line, where David left to visit adjoining nations. I proceeded with the siblings to Warsaw to meet Doreen and a couple of our Edmonton Rotarian companions who were important for a Polish group arranging a "Turning Projects Fair."

oris' twelve-traveler van moved at greatest speed when it was not moving around potholes. Ivan and Boris knew every pothole, as they crossed the line roughly double seven days with items and travelers. Inside forty kilometers of the Polish line, trucks would in general bundle together in long queues. Ivan was continually in the passing path evading approaching traffic. Only sometimes did we experience a traveler transport, and this was nine years post-Perebudova. The last ten kilometers before the line were packed with trucks, halting and beginning, and moving at an agonizingly slow clip. Our van kept to the passing path with numerous an approaching vehicle dropping its wheel onto the street shoulder. This moving proceeded to the front truck at the boundary door. A speedy crush to one side had us situated to meet the boundary guard.

The watchman grinned and welcomed Ivan as though he was a closest companion. He took a few reports to the stand, where they were immediately handled and returned. Once more, I saw Ivan slip a roll of cash to the watchman. On an earlier year's intersection, when Boris got me the Warsaw air terminal, the truck traffic didn't confront an arrangement as the Poles had a productive line crossing framework. I likewise noted Boris lubing the watchman's palm. Inside the following two kilometers, Boris was waved somewhere near Ukrainian alleged 'town police', whom he paid more cash while trading cordial talk. These three stops were taking into account each other.

Ivan said a few cops claimed the greatest of houses. I let the siblings know that pay-offs didn't exist in Canada. They feigned exacerbation at my gullibility about carrying on with work. I never offered an incentive, even at the Thai-Malaysian train-crossing line, where Doreen and I were once confined. Numerous a pay off was

mentioned, however we won't ever surrender. My Miami Beach companion David, brought up in Bolivia, was interested at my addressing, as he comprehended this type of private tax collection. A couple of years after the fact, after a few thwarted Ukrainian government endeavors to control pay off at borders, one of the siblings was gotten and couldn't get away, even with multiplying down on his pay off offer. He was fined a few additional occasions the yearly compensation of a generously compensated Ukraine employee.

At a Warsaw inn, we were met by Doreen and two great Rotarian companions, Eunice Maris and Betty Screpnek. They showed up the other day, as we were to take part in a Rotary International Projects Fair in Kielce. These three vigorous ladies had no difficulty in visiting Warsaw, purchasing their cherished Glenfiddich scotch and loosening up after their overseas flight. Quickly in one of the rooms, after drinks streamed and much chuckling, we examined a potential business drive the Vatrich young men and I had recently investigated. Betty talked superb Ukrainian, and with her demonstrated business record, she immediately interpreted the issues. She winked at the young men without me seeing the wink and let them know I was a great fellow and would gift them the compartment of paintbrush hair. I quickly hindered and exhaustingly protested with a "no" "no". The young men broke out in wild chuckling. Eunice, an effective business visionary, added explanation where required. Fundamentally, I would head out to China with the siblings and asset the acquisition of a holder of paintbrush pig hair for the siblings' paintbrush processing plant. They had huge deals, inside and outside Ukraine. An understanding was made, dependent upon the siblings' affirming subtleties of the China visit. Beverages and giggling proceeded, and the young men left to take care of business.

Entrepreneurs 54-year-old Ivan Vatrich and 76-year-old author Zen Moisey; obviously   related.

half a month after the fact, Ivan Vatrich informed us that he didn't require subsidizing for the compartment of pig hair. Obviously, bypassing their agreeable Polish provider might actually risk a portion of the siblings' global deals. The siblings' deals were somewhat worked with by the Polish provider. Ivan is a sharp financial specialist, in the same way as other I met in Ukraine. His old mother, Paraska, (née Moisey, sister to Frozena), in my essence advised the siblings to be cautious about the Russian bear. She said the bear never quits any pretense of attempting to control Ukraine. The siblings, with their Mercedes vehicles, inn, bars and different organizations, impolitely ignored the danger. In 2017, we presently see Russia's severe animosity in Ukraine. The siblings keep on succeeding, yet they keep a much lower profile. They should notice their mom's warning.

The following day after the siblings left, Eunice, Betty, Doreen and I spent comfortable hours in focal Warsaw. The region was a promenade, recently developed after the bombarding obliteration of WWII. It was re-developed from photographs and rescued records. It was an uncomfortable inclination, imagining the occupants as they were bombarded. Snapping back to the warm radiant day under an umbrella, tasting from an iced brew mug and watching the walker march made a fantastic differentiation of feelings. That we were so fortunate to be Canadian. We split up to go window shopping. Doreen liked a blossomed customary Polish tea set, and some golden studded, precious stone alcohol glasses. Afterward, I investigated a second hand store searching for high quality glass beads.

On our movements, we generally keep an eye open for the sort of dots my extraordinary grandparents Wasylena and Stefan Moisey brought to Canada from Ukraine. The dots were given over from past ages from either Wasylena or Stefan's family. A legend, frequently rehashed by Wasylena Moisey to her grandkids, recounted a Moisey male youth taken to fill in as a Turkish slave. The Turks additionally took numerous ladies. The kid, tall and solid, served in the Sultan's castle in a distant land. He worked in the pens really focusing on the Sultan's ponies. Numerous years after the fact, in the wake of acquiring favor with the Sultan for his expertise as a horseman, he got away with the best ponies and the dots. For a long time he was pursued yet would get away from catch by intersection the Cheremosh River and living in the mountains.

hese globules were given over through the family, as a rule from female

to female. In 2015, my uncle Arnold Moisey gifted one dot to Doreen. The excess dabs are with a couple of my dad's kin. One dot was gifted back to Ukraine by my auntie Angie Brower. As a kid, laying down with my grandma Paraska, I saw an ashtray of free dots on her bureau. A Warsaw shop had a total jewelry of comparative looking dabs, which we bought, that had a place with a ninety-year-old Ukrainian woman.

One of the dabs brought to Canada from Ukraine by Wasylena and Stefan in 1898. It is the main thing of theirs know to exist.

As I clarified in Chapter One, my DNA has a hint of Turkish family line. My four percent Middle Eastern qualities most likely were acquired in the period of the globule story. On visits to Ukraine, I met Turkish vacationers who said they were agreeable in homes of old Ukrainians. They remarked on the ear-splitting quality in conventional Ukrainian society melodies, fairly like their own, the enormous divider and floor enriching mats of Turkish plan, and the rational invite they got in the homes.

Rotary International

Rotating is a significant piece of my life. I joined the Rotary Club of Edmonton West in 1968. Rotational was established in 1905 and is the most seasoned and biggest NGO, working in multiple hundred nations and locales, with 35,800 Rotary Clubs in excess of 500 characterized geological areas. Community Clubs, Districts and Rotary International choose another president, chief and directorate every year. Turning doesn't engage in political, strict or racial issues.

Each club endeavors to serve in the accompanying five Avenues of Service: 1.

Community Service: gives advantages to its nearby local area. 2. Worldwide Service: works with a Club/s in one more nation or district to give benefits, ordinarily to a less-created region. 3. Professional Service: typically happens inside the club's region. 4. Club Service: includes week by week gatherings to improve cooperation to individuals and family. 5.

Generational Service: by sustaining youth, Rotarians assist with giving the abilities youngsters need to prevail as future local area pioneers. Rotational is additionally founded on a straightforward 4-Way Test: "The 4-Way Test of the things we think, say or do: Is it reality? Is it reasonable for all concerned? Will it construct altruism and better kinships? Will it be advantageous to all concerned?"

My energy was and is International Service, and I so far have insight in more than 100 self-supporting activities; principally in Central America. Revolving had two clubs (in Kyiv and Lviv) when I previously showed up in Ukraine. Lviv's Rotary Club, had recently been disbanded by the Soviets in 1939. 38 Ukraine Rotary Clubs sprang to activity by 2000 after the fall of the Soviet Union in 1991. Today there are more than 1.2 million dynamic Rotarians around the world. Today, there are 46 Clubs in Rotary District 2330, which incorporates Belarus and Poland. Until this point in time, some Edmonton clubs have finished fourteen Ukraine International Projects.

I am particularly glad for three tasks done in associations with the Rotary Club of Ivano-Frankivsk, which was sanctioned in 1995. Rotarians Volodymyr Humennyk, Rostyslav Hul and Ihor Komar, alongside Club secretary Natalia Ifonska, were the key contacts working with the Rotary Club of Edmonton West. The primary venture provided eleven PCs and accomplices to the Ivano-Frankivsk School of Business. In the subsequent venture, we transported a forty-foot holder of dress, sheet material, athletic gear and school supplies to the Ukraine Internat School for destitute youngsters. I visited the school, situated in Yabluniv, prior and then afterward the compartment shipment. The main visit pulled at my feelings, bringing tears. The school worked without heat, and awful outside latrines were situated across the street.

Ivano-Frankivsk Rotary Club members. The indespensible Natalia Ifonska stands between me and the Bishop. Great active Rotarians.

Rotary was fundamental for our Lingcomp, providing current PCs, modems and printers to 35 of the 37 secondary schools in the Vyzhnytsia School District of Chernivtsi Oblast. Eddie Southern, addressing the Government of Alberta, Canada, was available when the 35 school directors, numerous educators and neighborhood city hall leaders went from their towns to get the gear. A festival was held in Vyzhnytsia, where the Rotary Club of Ivano-Frankivsk was all around hailed. Turning and Lingcomp's work in the Vyzhnytsia School Region, moved the locale forward toward PC and English language abilities, more than in the enormous urban areas of Ukraine. Many understudies are currently working abroad due to these skills.

Rotary Project Fairs began in Central America over twenty years prior, with American and Canadian Rotarians meeting yearly in turning Central American nations to accomplice in Central America Community Projects called "Uniendo America." More than 1,000 activities have been collaborated. Doreen and I have been lucky to go to eleven of these useful yearly gatherings.

The main Rotary International "Undertakings Fair" for post-Soviet Union nations was held in Kielce, Poland, from May 5-7, 2000, and united Rotary members from Belarus, Ukraine, Poland, Norway and Western Canada. Four clubs from Russia intending to go to didn't show up. In 2017, tyrant Putin prohibited Rotary Clubs in Russia; nonetheless, numerous Rotarians there stay dynamic and some go to Rotary International's yearly meetings. It is difficult to kill the possibility of Rotary and its great works.

The Kielce Fair showed local area projects from Belarus, Ukraine and Polish Clubs that were looking for monetary or material help, and collaborated them with European and Western Canadian Rotary Clubs. The three-day occasion was reached out to four days, and it was focus in, meet eye-to-eye, from morning to late night to make practical local area projects a reality. Enduring fellowships were manufactured. Following two years, seventeen ventures were collaborated. Western Canadian Rotarians Eunice Maris, Betty Screpnek, Doreen Moisey and a holy messenger from Poland, Rotarian Halina Stepien coordinated the Kielce Fair. Betty said, and I concur, that we "worked like a dog" to work with Rotary-banded together ventures, contacting and working on the existences of thousands.

r. Larysa Bondarenko from the Kherson, Ukraine Rotary Club ventured to every part of the longest distance (via train for two days) to join in. As the head of the city's neglected youngsters' safe house obliging 900 kids, Larysa put her entire being into the expectation of finding outside help. She surrendered any expectation of getting monetary assistance from Kherson City and Oblast. The Soviet framework had made ruin in her reality. Just the overview structures, neglected staff and volunteers with really focusing hearts gave on the kids, for the most part matured three to fifteen. Frantic people dropped off boxes of children close to home. Commonly, she said, "Turning is the main expect Ukraine."

Larysa's undertaking was cooperated with Norwegian and German Rotary Clubs. On the final evening, before Larysa was to board her train, Doreen learned Larysa didn't have cash for a spot to rest. I rested on the love seat while they shared the bed. We kept in touch with Larysa for a couple of years, and unexpectedly it stopped. She was genuinely summary and needing rest. Larisa is a genuine Mother Teresa. I feel honored to have met her.

Philanthropy for Ukraine

Through my movements and magnanimous work, I gradually acquired compassion for the difficulties looked by my far off and current Ukraine families, from attacking Tsars, despots and the present mafia, driven by dictator Putin. Most in Ukraine and large numbers of its Diaspora (twenty million resettled all over the planet) hate despot Putin, while regarding the great Russian individuals. The vast majority of my life I was oblivious to the monstrosities carried out in Ukraine, and presently in 2017, my hatred for Putin's suppression in Crimea and grisly assaults in Eastern Ukraine are

equivalent to that of most Ukrainians I have met around the world. Moment advanced interchanges continually uncover these unfeeling atrocities.

Still, Ukraine and its kin are versatile. Astonishing outcomes are moving Ukraine toward turning into a star on the European stage, in spite of the unpleasant conflict with Putin. The young people of post-Perebudova have tasted vote based system and Western ways of life. Nothing will deny them accomplishing their fantasies, not even old commies, presently restricted to their beds, if not their graves. Dinosaur Putin can't win, and the adolescent know this. The Russian Federation empties cash into spreading bogus data to acquire Russians' help to keep up with and extend Putin's inner circle of outlaws who make progress toward self-improvement. Numerous despondent people in the Russian Federation envision Putin joining individual tyrant Gadhafi in a comparative demise. These two despots are among the most detested in the last part of the 1900s and mid 2000s.

Ukraine has again separated itself as a worldwide food bushel and is currently the world's main exporter of sunflower oil and number two in grain. Fields that were inactive and weed-swarmed under the Soviet framework are presently useful. On our first visit in 1994, on two events, we saw a spouse directing a one-base furrow, while her significant other in front pulled like a pony to work a little plot in a tremendous weed-filled field. We watched in one slanted field where a couple conveyed the furrow back to the highest point of the slope to facilitate their work by furrowing just downhill. Blazes of this sort of extremely difficult work that ages of my progenitors suffered in both the Soviet and prior unfamiliar controlled occasions continue to show up in my dreams.

On the authoritative record, in one year, starting in December 2014, Ukraine embraced and drafted new laws that created change methodologies in excess of forty spaces of public interest. This happened while despot Putin battled against Ukraine soil. The Canadian government is at the front line in helping Ukraine. On some random day, there are in excess of 1,000 volunteer Canadians giving their chance to propel Ukraine. Every one of these Canadians has a story to tell, and ideally, large numbers of them will record their accounts. The worldwide Diaspora of Ukrainian individuals have incredibly assisted Ukraine with being strong and ricochet back from its difficulties. The Ukrainian World Congress (UWC) for quite a long time has supported for Ukraine and keeps Ukraine on the global plan. The UWC has public parts, with the Ukrainian Canadian Congress being among the most grounded of Ukraine's supporters.

Ukraine in 2017 is prepared and ready for generosity. Its social and legitimate frameworks have progressed inconceivably since present Perebudova on permit caring residents to have their own Ukraine Charitable Foundation (UCF). However they don't have one yet, a UCF would help its benefactors past any Ukrainian's most extravagant fantasies. The UCF might actually be founded on a model I have known since its commencement: the Edmonton Community Foundation (ECF), which is the fourth biggest such establishment in Canada. There are a couple of instances of Ukraine previously getting benefits from Charitable Foundations like the ECF. The Rotary Foundation (TRF) and the ECF empowered the Yabluniv Internat School to update, a Kherson halfway house to save lives and in excess of 100 Ukrainian understudies to get $300 grant awards. These are only a couple of models; they and others have presented Ukraine to the chance of having its own Ukraine Charitable Foundations.

UCF is easy to make. It requires Ukrainian contributors and their assets to be gotten, contributed, and that a part of the income should be appropriated to those they consider out of luck. The equilibrium of yearly profit is held to build the worth of the asset. The asset develops everlastingly, and its capital is rarely spent. This is the way TRF and ECF work. This demonstrated information is accessible for Ukraine. The key to dispatching Ukraine's own UCF is to ensure the benefactors' cash. We as a whole know a pot of honey draws in flies. The pot of Ukrainian cash should be shielded from flies. This is conceivable as demonstrated by many existing establishments in different nations. Tragically, in 2017 Ukraine needs adequate laws and other framework to ensure a UCF's assets. Gradually Ukraine is propelling this framework to where it can one day join the universe of worldwide foundations.

here exist different establishments in Ukraine, however none demonstrated on the ECF, which permits a huge number of people and partnerships to give, secure and direct asset income to allowed recipients of the givers' picking. In my city of Edmonton, at the time Perebudova was happening, the Edmonton Poole family gave $15,000,000, making the ECF. In 2015, ECF conceded $21,200,000 from profit. In 2016, ECF was esteemed at
$500,000,000. The Poole family was joined by large number of Edmonton givers, including Doreen and me, to construct this gigantic, fruitful establishment. This is the model Ukraine is prepared to follow, however its lawful and financial laws require significant improvement for individual normal Ukrainians to give and to turn out to be valid philanthropists.

Many common individuals comprehend the significance of generosity. Winston Churchill, once said, "We live to get; we make a day to day existence by what we give." My caring Baba Moisey, before she kicked the bucket, parted with the ranch and a house she claimed. She had no ventures, living just from her huge nursery and an unassuming Canadian annuity. She lived efficiently and figured out how to save

$9,000, which she allowed away a year prior to she passed on to those she considered most out of luck. For her entire life, she was a provider of affection and overabundance material products. Baba Moisey realized how to live and was cherished by everyone.

Unfortunately, right now, time won't hang tight for great Ukrainians with an overflow of resources for give consistently, as its laws will require one more decade or so to secure their cash. I prior expressed that "Ukraine in 2017 is prepared for generosity" however actually, right now, any gift of cash would rapidly be tainted or devoured by flies, similarly as would a pot of honey.

Fortunately, today any Ukrainian without the advantage of time can elapse a portion of their resources in an altruistic way through existing demonstrated establishments, concerning model, "The Rotary Foundation (TRF)" with a more than century long record of fruitful encounters. Kindly let me propose how this should be possible. Charge Gates addressed 40,000 of us Rotarians at the Rotary International Conference in June 2017 in Atlanta. After the Conference, I googled data on Bill and read his rundown of 169 names of well off individuals able to make a vow of one billion dollars to noble cause. Shockingly seemed the name of Viktor Pinchuk.

I met Viktor when he visited Edmonton with Ukraine's President Kuchma to address multiple hundred Canadians. They were looking for help for Ukraine and effectively observed some help from handfuls I knew in the room. Today, a lot more have participated in supporting Ukraine. I need to propose to Viktor to frame "The Pinchuk/Kuchma Rotary Endowment for Economic and Community Development in Ukraine" which would give assets in ceaselessness, passing on a commendable inheritance to help his family, neighbors and Ukrainians. This is a basic method for regarding Viktor's vow to Bill Gates.

Doreen and I battled over how we could continue in the strides of Baba Moisey, however on a practical premise. We were persuaded that an altruistic establishment was principal as we saw the helpful work fueled by them. For fifty years at this point, Doreen and I have been associated with more than 100 involved local area projects in Ukraine, Central America and different nations. We have acquired a lot of joy from this humanitarian effort and have been compensated with worldwide long lasting companions. We even have an embraced Guatemalan godchild (Amelia Coroy Chiz), who resembles a little girl to us, who presently has her own family, and a Malawi Minister of Justice (Samuel Tembenu) calling me Dad. We saw how little, inspiring signals can be of colossal assistance for people to help themselves, and to carry on with a superior life. I'm persuaded establishments are fundamental for this to occur.

In late 2016, not long after getting back from Ukraine, our Rotarian companion Betty Screpnek welcomed Doreen and me to meet Rotarian Carolyn Ferguson. We advised her of our bombed work to build up an asset for the penniless in my genealogical country. We underlined the asset should be secure and powerful. Carolyn clarified that this was conceivable. Prior to requiring a second taste of dim rum and coke, I investigated Doreen's eyes and without a word between us, I saw that she acknowledged Carolyn's proposition. Carolyn clarified that the Rotary Foundation's "Curve Klumpf Society" (AKS) has an exceptional center region, where one can give to a nation of decision. Inconceivably, our gifts' profit would in unendingness be assigned to our preferred nation, Ukraine.

A gift to AKS is gotten by the Rotary Foundation, as such gifts have been throughout the previous 100 years. Rotarians in Ukraine utilize the profit of the blessing yearly to help their local area. Our gift of $250,000 US to AKS shaped "The Doreen and Zen Moisey Rotary Endowment for Economic and Community Development in Ukraine." All benefits from the offer of this book will be added to this asset. This implies that Rotary Clubs in the Rotary District that have Ukraine Clubs will get yearly monetary income in perpetuity.

Rotarians in around 200 nations volunteer to make their local area a superior spot to live. They started doing this in 1905, over a century prior, and know their urban communities' and townspeople's requirements, and how to satisfy these necessities. Like us, you can give securely to help a nation of your decision, by reaching a Rotarian living near you and clarifying how

Doreen and I utilized AKS. The contact data beneath will likewise be of assistance:

Carolyn Ferguson, Senior Major Gifts Officer, Zone 24

email: Carolyn Ferguson Carolyn.Ferguson@rotary.org

You can likewise contact the creator at

Zen@incentre.net

Drilling for Oil in Ukraine

The best man at our wedding, designing colleague Steve Benediktson, acquainted me with Eddie Southern. Eddie and Steve intended to bore for oil in Ukraine. Both claimed fruitful oil organizations in Western Canada and Colombia. I put resources into their Ukrainian organization called Kroes Oil (Kroes is Steve's better half's original last name). Eddie, with Darrel Zakreski, spearheaded bringing Canada's oil industry skill to the Lelyaki, Chernihiv Oblast oil field, through their interest in the Kashstan Petroleum Ukrainian-Joint Venture Company soon after Perebudova. In 1994, Zhoda bought UK-Ran Oil International Inc. On Jan 8, 2002, Kroes Energy Inc. obtained Zhoda 2001 Corporation, which held a 45 percent premium in Kashtan Petroleum. Zhoda's accomplice in Khastan was UkrNafta JSC, the Ukraine State Company. They spudded the principal well on Jan 19, 2001, and hit oil on February 16 that year. Eddie guaranteed this was the primary Canada-Ukraine Joint Venture, which I tested, as Doreen and I had made Lingcomp, a Ukraine-Canada joint endeavor organization in 1994 in Western Ukraine.

oreen and I turned out to be old buddies with Eddie. He was named the Alberta Consular to Ukraine. We invested a great deal of energy with Eddie in Kyiv and Vyzhnytsia, just as during a visit toward the Eastern Ukraine penetrating site. Eddie and Doreen are dynamic, faithful Catholics and turned out to be dear companions. We both preferred Eddie's uplifting outlook, particularly for Rotary ventures in Ukraine, where we fused his abilities and contacts to guarantee Rotary people group projects didn't go awry.

Sketch of Eddie's Ukraine drill site that Doreen and I visited.

During Easter of 1996, Eddie coordinated a train visit to Crimea. A party of sixty, for the most part Canadian oil-business people, gone from Kyiv to Yalta. Kroes Energy Inc. was all around addressed. Steve Benediktson and his significant other Adriana were available. The gathering left from Kyiv on previous President Mikhail Gorbachev's private train, which was all around named and really focused on. They left on a Thursday and returned on Monday. Adriana partook in the visit, yet remarked that the way of life in the open country, especially the lodging, gear, and general consideration of farmland and streets, was crude. Individuals experienced were agreeable and affable. She didn't see any malnourished children.

On June 8, 2004, following a couple of hours' drive from Kyiv, Doreen, Eddie, our driver Victor and I showed up at the Lelyaki oil site, where an apparatus was loudly penetrating inside meters of expected jackpot. We were given new, unpackaged hard caps and wellbeing glasses, the initial time ever such security things had been utilized in the Lelyaki field by guests and workers. Doreen was the very first lady permitted on the drill deck.

The drill apparatus' super primary individuals were made of weighty oak woods, similar to the American and Eastern Canadian oil fields of the mid 1900s. The apparatuses, chains, and administration hardware were all around worn. Five on location lodging trailers molded like portions of bread had little windows and distending wood oven smokestacks. Eddie pointed proudly to the new well victory preventer underneath the work deck. Eddie presented the principal useful victory preventers utilized in the Lelyaki field. Numerous a day to day existence has been saved utilizing victory preventers. The Lelyaki field has been creating oil since the 1960s. Ineffectively made due, the field had recently experienced water flooding, requiring experienced topographical oversight to address, which Eddie brought from Canada.

fter scrambling by the group, the enormous diesel motor with a defective suppressor was closed down. New boots, hard caps and wellbeing glasses were changed. One of the team assisted Doreen with her hard cap. I saw none of the laborers wore steel-toed boots. We mixed up the extended metal steps to arrive at the sloppy drill deck. A driller on each side of Doreen held an arm to direct her so she would not slip on the sloppy region. The amicable team were eager to show us grouped things nearby the deck. The now-quiet diesel motor uncovered that every one of its measures were broken, aside from one.

After a hot espresso with new cream, we headed to the local oil office, where we sat at a splendid, flooring covered worktable, stacked with run of the mill Ukrainian food, huge containers of Coke, soft drink water and a lot of vodka. Twelve men, generally wearing suits, took seats, and numerous a toast was made and tune sung after extended presentations. We were given a hard-covered book on Bukovina, my hereditary Ukraine Oblast. It was given extraordinary display and more toasts. I lurched up to get the book endorsed by generally present, including Chairman of the Board Ivan Kozar of Naftogaz, which is a business entity partnered with Chernivtsigaz. The few hours of devouring reached a conclusion as the sun set.

Kroes Oil had a 49 percent premium with the Ukrainian government-controlled Naftogaz Company. Ultimately, obstruction by the Russian government-possessed Gazprom Oil Company pressed and eliminated Kroes Oil from Ukraine. We as a whole lost cash on this endeavor. Kroes had presented the innovation of multi-well siphon jacks from a solitary stage. The oil was siphoned from the stage to a line, with a meter to record creation. Eddie showed us a covered, valve T-area in the line before the meter. The unmetered oil had a place with the mafia and was moved by rail to treatment facilities. Eddie thought about the redirected oil as a duty and kept drilling.

e remained with Eddie for seven days in his agreeable Kyiv loft, which was a relaxed stroll from the rail travel framework. The condo window investigated an enormous khastan (chestnut) tree, under which older neighbors sat on park seats. Our week's visit through Kyiv, a city of 4,000,000, was pleasant. Kyiv is an exceptionally cosmopolitan city. The previous primary base camp of the Soviet Union in the focal square was currently delegated with a MacDonald's and other normal Western signage.

When the time had come to leave, Eddie drove us to the train station, where we left for Poland. At the boundary close to 12 PM, the rail vehicle wheels were changed to fit the Poles' rail track aspects. This was cultivated by ladies utilizing substantial crowbars, winches and a turntable. It was a loud cycle, however entertaining.

Money Extraction Schemes (Bribes)

Over the years, Doreen and I have experienced pay off plans. When our Ukrainian Lingcomp School participation topped at 205 understudies, I got a message to come rapidly from Canada, as there were issues: government authorities were shutting our school.

No understudies were at the school when I showed up. The fire examiner with a portion of his authorities had visited the school. They guaranteed unknown infractions with the fire code and trained the instructors to promptly send understudies home and close the school. I got a message to contact the fire official, pay a charge and consent before the school could be reopened.

Word spread rapidly of the school shutting. Our understudies were offspring of clerics, teachers, government authorities, entrepreneurs and other persevering people. Valentyn asked me what we ought to do. The choice was to illuminate everyone that the school would stay shut, as requested by the fire official. I would not meet the fire controller. Promptly, people group pioneers brought pressure, reached the fire controller, and the school was returned. No charge (pay off) was paid.

In 1998 we had additionally experienced a pay off conspire at the Lviv air terminal. Seven Canadian Moiseys and four from Romania went to Ukraine to commend the Moisey 100th commemoration of Wasylena, Stefan and their youngsters leaving Ukraine. It was the primary visit for my mom and a couple of others. I was at the rear of the line at the movement booth. Everyone cleared, and it was my move. When requested to pay $15 for wellbeing crisis protection, I declined.

A mediator was found. He evidently was an agent from the insurance agency. Once more, I would not pay, clarifying I had worldwide travel protection and purchasing extra protection was unmistakably excessive. He acquainted me with the central migration official. I declined the main's idea to pay. He was a brilliant advertising individual. At this point, everyone cleared traditions, including my relatives, who paid for the protection. I was the focal point of consideration, and everyone comprehended I was testing a sham scheme.

My mom made some noise, admonishing me to pay, as they were worn out. My relative Valentyn (a youthful legal counselor) was at the air terminal to meet us, and I shouted at him to come and assist with the question. The head of movement consented to our

solicitation to call the Canadian Consulate; sadly, the Lviv air terminal telephones were not working. No different telephones were close by, so the boss consented to release me with his escort and Valentyn to track down a telephone outside the air terminal, passing on our gathering to sit tight for my return. Observing an eatery telephone, Valentyn previously called the insurance agency, and no one replied. We were unable to arrive at anyone at the Kyiv Canadian Consulate, so we got back to the air terminal with regards to a half hour after the fact. Doreen was tensely pausing, and the air terminal control didn't know whether we would be sent back to Warsaw, as threatened.

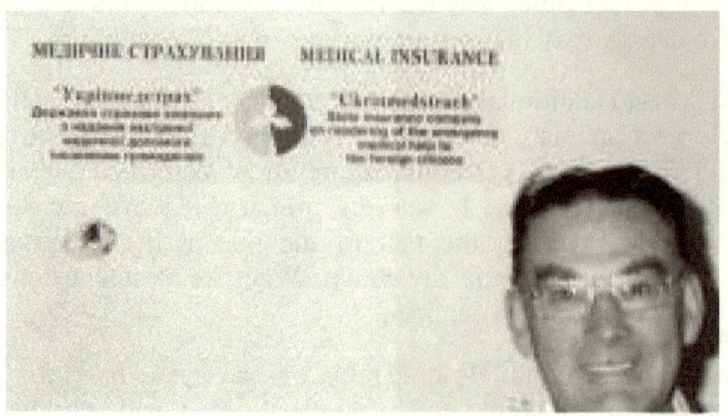

Airport non-existent Medical insurance.

My party was angry when I advised them to happen without me, and that I would get back to Warsaw. We informed the central that nobody replied when you called the supposed "health related crisis" telephone number. The air terminal travelers cleared, and staff needed to return home. Everybody was drained, including the boss. In the end, I was cleared, without a freedom structure. I then, at that point, put $15 in the hand of one of the housekeepers and requested that she share it with different cleaners. On our re-visitation of Canada, Doreen composed a letter to Ukraine Tourism clarifying the issue. She got a decent answer, and on our following visit, we saw the protection sign and structures had gone. Afterward, we heard this was a plan between somebody in Canada and the Ukraine air terminal control officials.

My mother's relative's home north of Yabluniv, where she lived by herself, 1998. A strong minded, self-reliant loveing woman to all.

We encountered one more cash extraction conspire in Kyiv as Doreen and I comfortable walked the space of St. Sophia. We were surprised as two men in their thirties, extremely close to us, ejected in a contention after we saw one of them get a wad of American cash. The man with the cash endeavored to place it in his pocket, however was forestalled by the other. This man then, at that point, addressed us in English, expressing "the cash tumbled from our pocket". In Ukrainian he then, at that point, kept contending with the man to return the cash to us. We said it was not our cash. The man demanded he saw it tumble from my pocket and to check no doubt. As I came to actually look at my pocket, Doreen shouted "trick, don't show them your cash". Doreen was right as she probably was aware the plan from an article she had recently perused. Assuming we had shown our cash they were in a magnificent situation to just snatch it. We likewise saw, what we were subsequently told were wanderer kids causing interruptions at a congregation, and at the jam-packed Kyiv railroad station asking and obviously endeavoring to pick individuals' pockets.

Fewer Ukraine legislators are participating in pay-offs in 2017 contrasted with before Maidan in 2014. The people talked, many giving their lives to tidy up political debasement. The equivalent can not be said for Russia, where debasement spins out of control. I, as most people, can't help thinking about how Putin procured forty to 200 billion (assessed by Forbes Magazine) on his administration pay cheque.

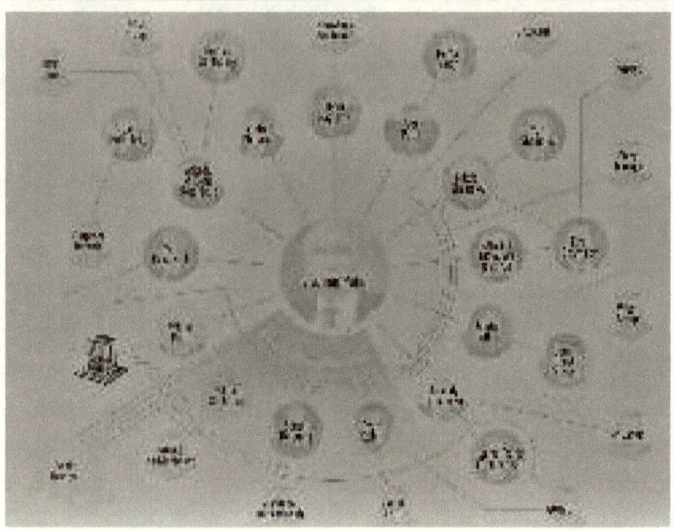

PUTIN AND THE PROXIES The Russian oligarchs have been tamed since Vladimir Putin's arrival to the presidency. The longtime leader has struck a mutually beneficial bargain: Leave the politics to me, chip in when I need you to -- and you can keep, and even grow, your wealth is reported by OCCRP and its long-time partner Novaya Gazeta when they went digging to find out more -- and pieced together   the assets of some of President Putin's friends, family, and inner circle. The Novaya Gazeta and   OCCRP investigation looked into the wealth surrounding Russian President Vladimir Putin; October   24 2017. The Organized Crime and Corruption Reporting Project (OCCRP) is a global network of investigative journalists; who are an investigative reporting platform formed by 40 non-profit investigative centers, scores of journalists and several major regional news organizations around the globe. Their network is spread across Europe, Africa, Asia and Latin America and teamed up in 2006   to do transnational investigative reporting and promote technology-based approaches to exposing organized crime and corruption worldwide. For additional investigative reporting view https://www.occrp.org/en/putinandtheproxies/

Putin Slips Yanukovych $3 Billion

A $3 billion Eurobond gave by Russia to Ukraine entered the pocket of Ukraine's President Viktor Yanukovych in December 2013 and was expected for reimbursement on December 20, 2015. The Atlantic Council Senior Fellow A. Aslund writes:

> "Ukraine has no excuse to pay [Russia]. In February 2014, the
> Kremlin dispatched military animosity against Ukraine, first
> annexing
> Crimea and later seeking after military disruption in southern and eastern

Ukraine. For over a year, Russian-directed soldiers with a combination of volunteers and normal Russian fighters have involved three percent of Ukraine's easternmost domains. Moscow's conflict has made significant harm Ukraine. [...] Ukraine has no justifiable excuse to pay such an attacker; truth be told, Russia should pay compensations to Ukraine. Putin arranged this arrangement actually with previous President Yanukovych to furnish him with a help. It was never intended to help the Ukrainian nation.

The main justification behind Ukraine to pay is that it could risk not getting further subsidizing from the IMF, which is essential for Ukraine's monetary food. The IMF has an old act of not loaning to a nation financially past due to a sovereign, however that training ought not be applied for this situation. [...] The IMF is going to change its act of not loaning into unpaid debts. This is handily finished. The IMF Executive Board can choose to change this strategy with a straightforward board larger part. The IMF has loaned to Afghanistan, Georgia, and Iraq amidst war, and Russia has no denial right, holding just 2.39 percent of the votes in the IMF. At the point when the IMF has loaned to Georgia and Ukraine, different individuals from its Executive Board have overruled Russia. [...] Russia's stubbornness has persuaded a board larger part that the standards should change quick. From that point forward, Russia's contention that the IMF ought not pay Ukraine loses validity.

he full article is accessible at: www.atlanticcouncil.org/online journals/new-atlanticist/ukraine-must-not-pay-russia

Chapter 5

Russian Myth

Great Russia and Russian Myth

Russia has distorted numerous chronicled occasions including the tale of its starting point, and today progresses a bogus history to menace its neighbors. It is a place of cards based on a broken establishment that will implode again from the inside, similarly as occurred during Perestroika during the 1980s and mid 1990s. Ukraine is one adjoining country, among others, that attempts to uncover these recorded falsifications.

The accompanying stressed segment has been taken from the conspicuous Ukrainian antiquarian Yaroslav Dashkevych's article How Moscow Hijacked the History of Kievan Rus previously distributed in 2011 and afterward on the Internet by the Euromaidan Press in 2014.

In making their country, Ukrainians need to look at and examine their own set of experiences, in view of truth, checked realities and verifiable occasions. For a really long time subject to victors, Ukrainians were essentially denied of the chance to impact the arrangement of public mindfulness and the advancement of their set of experiences, with the outcome that Ukraine's set of experiences was created overwhelmingly to the benefit of their vanquishers. Particularly problematic is the subject of the assumptions and requests of Moscow, and later Russia, concerning the recorded tradition of Kievan Rus.

In his authentic work "The Land of Moksel or Moskovia" (Olena Teliha Publishing House, Kyiv 2008, 2009, 3 vol.) Volodymyr Bilinsky presents verifiable sources (overwhelmingly Russian) that vouch for the absolute distortion of the historical backdrop of the Russian Empire, which was equipped to make a chronicled folklore about Moscow and Kievan Rus sharing normal recorded roots, and that

Moscow has "progression freedoms" to Kievan Rus.

Moscow's out and out extortion that appropriated the past of the Great Kyiv realm and its kin managed an extreme hit to the Ukrainian ethos. Our commitment presently is to use hard realities to reveal the untruths and flippancy of Moskovian mythology.

Let's analyze these problems.

The tsars of Moscow and, later, Russia comprehended that without a forcing past it was difficult to make an extraordinary country and realm. Subsequently, it was important to laud their chronicled attaches and even to seize the historical backdrop of different countries. Along these lines, beginning with Ivan the Terrible (1533-1584), the tsars of Moscow applied every one of their endeavors to proper the historical backdrop of Kievan Rus and its sublime past, and to make an authority folklore for the Russian Empire.

This may have been less important assuming their folklore had not impacted the focal worries of Ukraine and on the off chance that it had not focused on the absolute obliteration of Ukraine: its set of experiences, language and culture. After some time, plainly Russian Imperial chauvinists did and keep on doing all that could be within reach to understand this aim.

ver many years, and particularly beginning with the mid sixteenth century, they indoctrinated and keep on programming everybody, saying that the starting points of the Russian country and individuals are the Great Kievan realm. They attest that Kievan Rus was the support of three kin countries — Russians, Ukrainians and Belarusians — and that in light of the fact that the Russians are "more seasoned siblings," they reserve the privilege to the tradition of Kievan Rus. Right up 'til the present time, Russian students of history and authorities utilize this sad falsehood, which is rehashed by the 'fifth section' of socialists and practically all Party of Regions delegates in [the Ukrainian] Parliament.

The ninth century ethno-phonetic guide of Eastern Europe exposes the fantasy of "Three Brotherly Nations" — in the spot of current Moscow, non-Slavic clans lived, while the domain of Ukraine and Belarus were occupied by Slavic (Slavonic) peoples.

Here are the facts:

At the hour of the Kievan Empire, there was no notice of a Moscow country. It is notable that Moscow was made in 1277 as a compliant vassal district or 'ulus' to the Golden Horde, set up by the Khan Mengu-Timur. At that point, Kievan Rus had existed for more than 300 years.

There are no signs of any association of Kievan Rus with the Finnish ethnic gatherings in the place that is known for 'Moksel' or later of the Moscow realm with the Principality of Kievan Rus up until the sixteenth century. When Kievan Rus had authoritatively acknowledged Christianity, the Finn clans in 'Moksel' lived in a semi-crude state.

How would anyone be able to discuss 'a more established sibling' when that 'more seasoned sibling' didn't initially show up until hundreds of years after

Rus-Ukrainians? He has no ethical right to consider himself an 'more established sibling,' nor to direct how individuals are to live, nor to compel his way of life, language, and perspectives. Unmistakably until the finish of the fifteenth century, there was no Russian country, there could have been no more seasoned sibling 'Extraordinary Russian,' nor were there any Russian individuals. All things being equal, there was the place that is known for Suzdal: the place where there is Moksel, later the Moscow princedom, which entered the job of the Golden Horde, the country of Genghis Khan. From the finish of the thirteenth to the start of the eighteenth century, individuals in this land were called Moskovites. Furthermore Moscow students of history are quiet with regards to this inquiry of their public origins.

Moskovites, 'Great Russians' – who are they?

During the 10th to the twelfth hundreds of years, the enormous space of Tula, Ryazan, and the present Moscow locale – this was possessed by individuals called 'Moksel,' including the clans of Muromians, Merya, Vepsians, Mokshas, Chudes, Maris and others. These clans ultimately turned into the establishment of the country who currently call themselves 'Incredible Russians.'

In 1137, the 6th child of the Kievan ruler Volodymyr Monomakh, Yurii Dolgorukii (who had been left without a princedom in the Kievan domain) showed up in this land.

Yurii Dolgorukii started the standard of the 'Riurykovyches' in 'Moksel', becoming sovereign of Suzdal. To him and a neighborhood Finnish lady was conceived a child Andrei, called 'Bogoliubskii.' Born and brought up in the timberland wild among the half-savage Finnish clans, sovereign Andrei cut all binds with his dad's company and with their old Kievan customs.

In 1169, Andrei Bogoliubskii fired and obliterated Kyiv. He annihilated all the holy places and strict antiquities, something incomprehensible in those occasions. Andrei was a savage who didn't feel any familial binds with Kyiv, the blessed city of Slavs.

ithin a short time frame (50-80 years), each Finnish clan was forced with a ruler of the Riurykovyches, whose mother was either a lady of Mer, Murom or Kokshan… Thus, seemed the 'Moksel' princedoms: Vladimir, Ryazan,

Tver, and others. Right now, a few teachers showed up in the place where there is Moksel to spread Christianity. It is difficult to consider a mass 'relocation' of Slavs from the Dnipro stream area, as Russian history specialists demand. For what reason should the Slavs leave behind their rich Dnipro lands and move in excess of 1,000 kilometers through obstructed undergrowth and bogs into an obscure semi-savage land?

Under the impact of Christianity, the place that is known for 'Moksel' began to shape their language, which in time became Russian. Up until the twelfth century, just Finn clans lived in the place where there is 'Moksel.' The

archeological discoveries of O.S. Uvarova (Merya And Their Everyday Life from Kurgan Excavations, 1872 – p. 215) support this. Out of 7,729 uncovered kurgans, not a solitary Slavic internment was discovered.

And the anthropological examinations of human skulls by A.P. Bohdanov and F.K. Vovk support the separated attributes of the Finnish and Slavic ethnoses.

In 1237, the Tatar-Mongols entered the terrains of Suzdal. All who bowed, kissed the boots of the Khan and acknowledged acquiescence stayed alive and safe; all other people who didn't submit were destroyed.

The sovereigns of Vladimir, Yurii and Yaroslav Vsevolodovich acknowledged compliance to Khan Batey. Thusly, the place that is known for 'Moksel' entered the positions of the Golden Horde Empire of Genghis Khan, and its battling powers were joined with the multitude of the Empire. The authority of the Moksel division inside Batey's military was Yurii Vsevolodovich, the ruler of the city of Vladimir. In 1238, Finnish clan divisions were shaped and walked together under Batey in his intrusions of Europe in 1240-1242. This is immediate proof of the foundation of the standard of the Khan in the grounds of Rostov-Suzdal.

While Yurii Vsevolodovich was away partaking in Batey's European attack, his more youthful sibling Yaroslav Vsevolodovich was put at the top of the Vladimir princedom. Yaroslav left his eight-year-old child Alexander Yaroslavich as prisoner with the Khan.

Living with the Horde of Batey from 1238 to 1252, Alexander, just a lot later named "Nevsky," embraced every one of the traditions and authoritative thoughts of the Golden Horde. He turned into a kindred spirit of Sartak, the child of the Khan, hitched the Khan's girl, and in the long run turned into a dedicated vassal of the Golden Horde and ruler of Vladimir from 1252 to 1263. He never partook in any huge fights — every one of the 'triumphs' of Alexander Nevsky are straightforward falsehoods. Sovereign Alexander just would never have partaken in the fights on the Neva in 1240 and on Chud or Peipus Lake in 1242 (fantasized in Eisenstein's film) since he was as yet a youngster.

It is important to mention that the ruling powers of the local princes of Rostov-Suzdal were minimal. Khan Batey installed his own administrators in all the "ulus" princedoms: on top was the Great Baskak, and under him were the regional administrative baskaks. These were full-fledged rulers from the Golden Horde, who followed the laws of the Genghis Khans. Russian historians are lying when they state that the princes of Suzdal, and later Moscow, were independent from the Golden Horde. The Khan's covenant named the primary rulers of the princedoms his baskak, or 'daruha,' while the local princes were relegated to second and even third-place importance.

he big lie was introduced: that Moscow was founded in 1147 by Yuri Dolgoruky. This is a myth with no supportive evidence. Moscow was established as a settlement in 1272. That same year, the Golden Horde conducted their third census of the populations in their domain. Both in the first census (1237-1238) and in the second census (1254- 1259), there is no mention of any Moscow at all.

oscow appeared as a princedom in 1277 at the decree of the Tatar- Mongol Khan Mengu-Timur, and it was an ordinary 'ulus' (subdivision) of the Golden Horde. The first Moscow prince was Danila (1277-1303), younger son of Alexander so-called "Nevsky." The Riurykovych dynasty of Moscow princes starts from him. In 1319 Khan Uzbek (as stated in the aforementioned work by Bilinsky) named his brother Kulkhan the virtual Prince of Moscow, and in 1328 the Great Prince of Moscow. Khan Uzbek (named in Russian history as Kalita), after he converted to Islam, destroyed almost all the Riurykovych princes. In 1319-1328, the Riurykovych dynasty was replaced by the Genghis dynasty in the Moscow 'ulus' of the Golden Horde. Only in 1598 this Genghis dynasty in Moscow, which began with Prince Ivan Kalita (Kulkhan), was finally broken. Thus, for over 270 years, Moscow was ruled solely by khans of the Genghis dynasty.

till, the new dynasty of the Romanovs (Kobyla) promised to follow former traditions and solemnly swore allegiance to the age-old dynasty of Genghis.

In 1613 the Moscow Orthodox Church became the stabilizing force to

safeguard the sustainment of Tatar-Mongol government in Moscow, offering masses for the Khan, and issuing anathemas on anyone who opposed this servitude.

Based on these facts, it becomes clear that Moscow is the direct inheritor of the Golden Horde Empire of Genghis and that actually the Tatar-Mongols were the 'godfathers' of Moscow statehood. The Moscow princedom (and tsardom from 1547) up until the sixteenth century had no ties or relationships with the princedoms of the lands of Kievan Rus.

Great Russians

The tribe of Great Russians, or the Russian people as known today, appeared around the fifteenth to seventeenth centuries from among the Finn tribes: Muroma, Mer, Ves and others. This was when their history started. There is no history of Great Russians on Kievan lands!

The history of Great Russians starts with the 'Beyond the Forests Land' in Moscow, which was never Kievan Rus. The Tatar-Mongols who entered these lands were a big element in the formulation of 'Great Russians.' The Great Russian psychology absorbed many characteristics — the Tatar-Mongol instincts of a conqueror and despot, with the aim: world domination.

Thus, by the sixteenth century was established the type of a conqueror who was horrible in his lack of education, rage and cruelty. These people had no use for European culture and literacy. All such things like morality, honesty, shame, justice, human dignity and historical awareness were absolutely foreign to them. A significant amount of Tatar-Mongols entered the makeup of Great Russians from the thirteenth to sixteenth centuries, and they accounted for the genealogy of over 25% of Russian nobility. Here are some names of Tatar/Turkic origin that brought fame to the Russian Empire: Arakcheev, Bunin, Chaadayev, Derzhavin, Karamzin, Kuprin, Plekhanov, Saltykov- Shchedrin, Tiutchev, Turgenev, Sheremetiev, and many others.

In order to appropriate the history of Kyiv lands and to immortalize

this theft, the Great Russians had to squash the Ukrainian people, drive them into slavery, deprive them of their true name, exterminate them via famine, etc.

krainians had emerged as a nation in the 11th to 12th centuries, and probably, even earlier. Later they were labeled 'Little Russians' when Russians began to brainwash the world with their 'version' of history. For the smallest deviation from this official version, people were tortured, killed, and sent off to the GULAG. The Soviet period was especially brutal and vicious. During that time, Ukraine lost over 25 million of her sons and daughters, who perished in wars for Russian interests, and during collectivization, tortures, and forced relocations.

This is the way the 'older brother' forced the 'younger brother,' the 'Little Russian,' to live in the savage 'embraces of love.'

Creation of the Historical Myth of the Russian State

Back in the times of the princedom of Vasyli III (1505–1533) Moscow gave birth to the idea of its greatness, articulated by the representative of Moscow orthodoxy, the monk Filofey: "Two Romes fell, a third still stands, and there will never be a fourth."

From there, they created the idea of an all-powerful and 'God-chosen' Moscow – the 'third – and final Rome'. These ideas spread and were confirmed throughout Moskovia. And how much blood was spilt by the princes of Moscow, and later the tsars, over this fantasy-myth!

During the reign of Ivan IV (the Terrible), they grasped not only after the inheritance of Kievan Rus, but now also the Byzantine Empire. Thus, according to accounts, the "Monomakh's Cap" was believed to have been given the Kievan prince Volodymyr Monomakh by his granddad, the basileus Constantine IX.

This was considered the symbol of the transfer of power from Byzantium to Kievan Rus. In addition, Yuri Dolgorukii, the sixth son of Volodymyr Monomakh, was the first prince of Suzdal, so the appearance of this cap in Moscow was a 'proof' of the legacy legitimacy of the Moscow rulers not only to the Kyiv Great Throne, but now also to the inheritance of the former

Byzantine Empire. Furthermore, Moscow fabricated a deceptive last will of Volodymyr Monomakh about handing over 'legacy rights' to his son Yuri Dolgorukii, the conqueror of the so-called 'Beyond the Forests Land.' This was all fiction. In reality, "Monomakh's Cap" was a gold 'Bukhara tubeteika,' which Khan Uzbek presented to Ivan Kalyta (1319-1340), who maintained this cap in order to further his fame. (Логвин Ю. Кобила, Калита і тюбетейка «Мономаха» // Час. – Київ, 1997, 27 березня).

Ivan IV (the Terrible) in 1547 was anointed in the cathedral with the title of 'Moscow Tsar' as the 'inheritor' of the Greek and Roman emperors. Of the 39 signatures who affirmed this document sent from Constantinople, 35 were forgeries. Thus, Ivan the Terrible became the 'inheritor of the Byzantine emperors.' Thus, the lie was made official.

Peter I began the massive falsification of his people's history. In 1701 he issued a decree to eliminate from all subjugated peoples all their recorded national historical artifacts: ancient chronicles, chronographs, old archives, church documents, etc. This was especially directed at Ukraine-Rus.

In 1716, Peter I 'changed the copy' of the so-called Königsberg Chronicles to now show the 'joining' of the old chronicles of the Kievan with the Moscow princedoms. The aim was to lay a foundation for the unity of Slavic and Finnish lands. However, both the false 'copy' and the original were sealed.

Peter's falsification became the basis for further falsifications – the composition of the so-called 'General Rus Chronicles Collections' which purported to establish Moscow's rights to the legacy of Kievan Rus. On the basis of these falsifications, on October 22, 1721, Moscow proclaimed itself the Russian Empire, and all Moskovites were now to be – Russians. In this manner, they stole from the legitimate inheritors of Kievan Rus, the Ukrainians, [the] historical name of Rus.

Peter imported from Europe a large number of specialists, including professional historians, who were assigned the rewriting and falsification of the history of the Russian state.

In addition, every foreigner who entered government work, swore an oath not to reveal state secrets and to never betray the Moscow state. The question remains, what government secrets regarding the 'formation of

Russian history' of ancient times could there be? In any civilized European country, after 30-50 years all archives are opened. The Russian Empire is very afraid about the truth in its past. Deathly afraid!

Following Peter I, who transformed Moscow into the Russian state, the Moscow elite began to consider the necessity of creating a comprehensive history of their own country. Empress Catherine II (1762-1796) intensively took on this task.

he could not admit the idea that common Tatar-Mongol elements existed in the dynasty of the Tsars. Catherine was an intelligent and educated European woman and once she had examined the archival sources, she called attention to the fact that all the history of her country was based on oral traditions ('byliny') and had no factual support.

Therefore, on December 4, 1783, Catherine II issued a decree, creating a 'Commission for the Collection and Organization of the Ancient Russian History' under the leadership and oversight of Count
A. P. Shuvalov, with a staff of 10 historians. The principal task before this commission was to 'find' new chronicles, rewrite others, and create new collections of archives and other similar falsifications. The aim was to lay the foundations for the 'legitimacy' of Moscow's hijacking of the historical legacy of Kievan Rus and to create an official historical myth about the origins of the Russian state. This commission labored for ten years. In 1792, 'Catherine's History' saw the light of day. The commission worked in the following manner:

– he gathering of all written documents (archives, chronicles, etc.). This effort had partly begun under Peter I. This collection of materials was conducted not only within the Empire, but also from other countries like Poland, Turkey etc.

– The analysis, falsification, rewritings or destruction of historical materials. Thus, they rewrote the chronicles: 'The Tale of Ihor's Campaign', 'Tale of Bygone Years', 'Lavrentiivsky Chronicles', and many others. Many chronicles were rewritten several times, and the originals were either locked up or destroyed. Thus, were also locked up: the 'History of the Scythians' by A. I. Lyzlov (published in 1776 and 1787), and the 'Russian History from Ancient Times' by V. M. Tatishchev (published in 1747). In his 'Scythian

History' Lyzlov showed that the inhabitants of Moscow were a separate people, who

—

—

had nothing in common with Kievan Rus, Lithuania, Poland, etc.

– The writing of new 'Rus Chronicles Collections' which were now being composed in the eighteenth century, but purported to be from the eleventh to the fourteenth centuries. These collections all propagated the 'General Rus' idea. This was in reference to the times when Kievan lands were inhabited by Slavic tribes (the Polans, the Drevlians, the Severians, and others) who were Christians, while the 'Beyond the Forests Land' was populated by Finn tribes (the Muromians, the Merya, the Vepsians, the Mokshas, and others) who lived a semi-primitive existence, and these tribes had nothing historical in common up to the sixteenth century.

– The new composition of thousands of various collections to establish the 'unity' of Kievan Rus with the Finn tribes. All these chronicles and collections, according to author Bilinsky, exist only in the form of copies, not one original. Not one! All this points to the almost unbelievable in scope and shameless, massive plundering and falsification of the creation of the history of the Russian state. It is impossible to live a lie forever!

It is time for Ukrainian historians to write the actual true history of Ukraine, which would not be based on the lies of the 'Catherine's Chronicles', the falsifications and newly written in the eighteenth century 'General Russian Chronicle Collections', but rather based on historical reality, established in documents, especially those preserved in countries like Poland, Turkey, Greece, Iran and others. People deserve to know the truth.

Ukraine Declares Independence 1917

The website of Ukraine's Ministry of Foreign Affairs contains the following description of Ukraine during World War I.

For the first time in the twentieth century, Ukraine declared independence declared independence during the First World War. In 1917, the Ukrainian Central Rada was formed in Kyiv, who played the role of a transitional government and declared the creation of the

Ukrainian National Republic (UNR).

After the declaration of four fundamental constitutional decrees – Universals – the UNR, as an independent state, instigated diplomatic contacts with England and France along with Germany and their allies.

The Ukrainian revolution began earlier than other countries of this region: in Lithuania, Estonia, Czechoslovakia, Poland, Latvia and the Balkans.

In December 1917, after the Kharkiv puppet government was formed and the Bolsheviks proclaimed a "Soviet Ukraine", the Russian Bolsheviks unleashed war against Ukraine.

The fight against the Bolsheviks continued until 1921. This war and other conflicts exhausted Ukraine and it lost its independence.

The worst of times then began for one of the great European nations. The mass deportations, the Holodomor and the Great Terror claimed millions of lives during this "peaceful" interwar period.

The website can be viewed at: mfa.gov.ua/en/news-feeds/foreign-offices-news/56936-ukrajina-u-drugij-svitovij-vijni (Also, for more information bout Ukraine

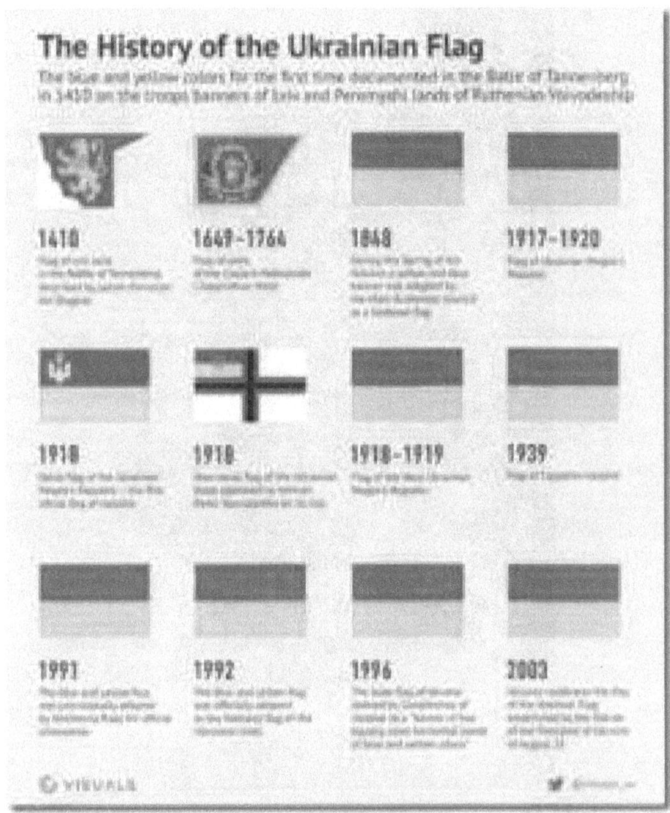

during WWI, see Appendix 9, page 265.)

rigin of Ukraine's flag. National Anthem and National Coat of Arms.

1915 Ukraine Heroine Olena (Yarema) Kuz, my great grandmother's niece from Banyliv, my third cousin.

Mount Makivka and my Heroine Third Cousin

One example of many sparks of independence occurred in my ancestral village of Banyliv in 1913, when my great- grandmother's niece Olena (Yarema) Kuz, aged nineteen, was faced with a tragic dilemma. Her father Tanase was falsely accused of collaborating with the Russians and placed in the notorious internment camp of Taleroff in southeast Austria, where eventually he was tried, found innocent, released, but soon died of typhus. Yarema, one of six siblings, left the University of Chernivtsi as a graduate of teaching. She was active in the sweeping nationalism at universities in

Western Ukraine and was motivated to avenge the death of her loving father. She then volunteered to enroll with the Ukraine Sich Riflemen Sharp Shooters, Calvary division, after taking sharpshooter training in Vienna. She was in many battles against the invading Russian tsar during 1914 to 1916, where she became a heroine at the Carpathian Mountain, Mount Makivka.

efore WWl, 250,000 Ukrainian volunteers and conscripts were recruited into the Austrian army, who were the occupiers in Western Ukraine. The Ukrainians detested the Russians, who were also present, more than they did the Austrians. Under pressure, the Austrians allowed one group of 2,500 Ukrainians to function independently of the Austrian army commanders. This was a first. This independent Ukrainian division immediately attacked the strongholds of the invading Russian tsar. The Austrian army of 250,000 Ukrainians fought under Austrian command.

The Austrians did not trust the large force of Ukrainians to be as independent as the 2,500 Ukraine Sich Riflemen, thirty of whom were women. One of these women was my third cousin, Olena (Yarema) Kuz. She, with eight Sich Riflemen at night removed the last of the tsar's machine gun nests from the top of famous Mount Makivka. The Mount Makivka battle was the first major battle to push the Russian tsar's army east.

I first learned about heroine Olena (Yarema) Kuz in September 2014, when a bronze bust of her was ready for installation at the Banyliv high school. I was being honored, along with the Krasniuks, for our contributions to many community projects.

hen Doreen and I first went to Ukraine, we never saw a Ukraine flag, except for ones we packed from Canada. No sign of nationalism showed its face publicly; however, most Bukovina homes had shed the Lenin busts, photos and other Soviet memorabilia. People were afraid to speak out as the local commie leaders still had some powers.

n September 2014, a few months after the height of Russia's surprise annexation of Ukraine's Crimea and killings in Eastern Ukraine, the country awoke from its slumber. At the Banyliv school reception, I experienced an incredible hyper-wave of nationalism, which was evident throughout Ukraine. My translator's six-year-old son asked his mom to buy him a gun, so he could kill Putin. At the school ceremony, a grade-one student also declared to the audience that he would kill Putin. Clearly, Putin's aggressive acts in Ukraine were felt by the children, creating a new generation of Ukrainian nationalists.

Putin caught Ukraine sleeping in 2014 when he annexed Crimea and committed other criminal bloody acts in Donbas. This was the required fuel to flare Ukrainian nationalism to a fever pitch. The bridges, flagpoles, buildings and many vehicles now match the colour of their beloved flag. Flags are flying everywhere.

After the school reception, my translator Oksana, Tatyana and I were led by Mayor Andryuk to his office, located next to the school, to learn more about the bronze bust of the heroine, which would be erected once funds were acquired. Tatyana and I gave the mayor money to purchase the necessary cement, aggregate and rebar to construct the base for the bust. I could not control my curiosity and began gathering information about Yarema from publications, family members and neighbors.

In 2016, translator Ohla Sokivka, Tatyana and I hiked to the top of Mount Makivka. I carefully studied the mountain and visualized how Yarema would have led a surprise attack on this strategic fortification. Following is my re-creation of events at Mount Makivka:

Six p.m., April 27, 1915: Yarema stamped out her cigarette and with her eight companions carefully inspected their heavy backpacks for the last time. Grenades wrapped in cloth, a loaf of bread, cheese and sausage were packed to prevent shifting of the backpack on the steep slope. Water canisters were full and placed into a side pocket of each backpack.

rom nearby tree branches the holstered revolver belts, fully loaded, were strapped to the youngsters' powerful bodies. All were in their teens or early twenties. As darkness set in, the nine companions draped hemp climbing rope over their shoulders and picked up their sturdy walking stick; waving a slight goodbye to the remaining Sich Riflemen of the Korsaka division, they set off for the base of Mount Makivka, approximately three kilometers distance to directly below the Russian machine gun emplacements. They skirted the forested edge of a few small hayfields. Olena (Yarema) Kuz and her carefully selected group darkened their army attire and faces, as well as shedding the army boots for the comfort and quietness of traditional Banyliv soft, forest-footwear.

The troop, led by Yarema, moved silently while all of Ukraine slept. The climb would take two nights. On the first night, the moon slowly began its ascent at six p.m. and near midnight it partially bleached a section of the Milky Way and prominent stars that could be plucked from the heavens.

Tall, mature pine trees on steep slants gave ideal shadowing to move upslope. Not a word was murmured, and a periodic hand signal was given. On the forested incline, Yarema was right at home, having been raised close to her grandma Kuz's home on the wild at the northwest edge of Banyliv, a short stroll from the Cheremosh River and its overflowed backwaters.

At sundown on the principal leg of the trip, the perspiring, depleted gathering covered their drained bodies protected by a stone outcrop, rapidly nodding off. They were stimulated by hints of evening sunrays, gleaming over their countenances. All stayed in their resting region, moving infrequently to be more agreeable, while chomping food from their rucksacks. They took a taste of water, and most snoozed off to rest once more, as they probably were aware the main short trip was drawing nearer to arrive at the involved key culmination, which Yarema had recently explored somewhat higher up from the stone outcrop.

The second night under moonlight they painstakingly climbed the un-explored region to the space that was very much set apart from past gunfire at the essential pass. The moon would set at four a.m., and all were situated inside meters of the assault rifle emplacements. The principal projectile was thrown into a firearm home, and inside the space of seconds eight different blasts emitted. Under a moment later, many explosives detonated, and a periodic pistol shot rang out reverberating into the backwoods. Commotion broke out on the site with gunfire and shouting.

Yarema and her men hurriedly mixed downslope as dawn was not too far off. They immediately arrived at their tied down ropes to quickly pass steep regions to show up at headquarters in the late morning. They obliterated adequate machine weapon homes, which immediately saw the Russians escaping Mount Makivka with the Ukrainian Independent Sich Riflemen, Korsika division, driving the pursuit. The Austrian-drove armed force possessing Mount Makivka's northwest and focal pinnacles immediately participated. This occured between April 29 and May 4 of every 1915, which started the expulsion of the last Russian Tsar from Ukraine.

Yarema later got an injury while seeking after the escaping Russians to their eastern bleeding edge. Went with an individual officer, riding a horse, they rode to her Banyliv grandma's home, where she recovered for a month and afterward got back to push the Russian line farther east. She then, at that point, gained from a lady that a top Russian general was stowing away in an adjoining house, where with a gun, without any assistance, she caught him. This occasion was therefore distributed in numerous newspapers.

In August 1915, brave Yarema's karma ran out. At the Golden Lipo fight at the Golden Oak River mouth, situated inside Tlumach, Ivano-Frankivsk locale, splinter explosives hit Olena's left side and broke her ribs. She tumbled from her pony and lay oblivious for eight hours, was moved to Budapest for medical procedure, and in pre-winter, she was moved to the Queen Elizabeth Hospital in Vienna for Sich Riflemen of the Makivka fight. She then, at that point, recovered in the popular manor of Mrs. Spat in the wake of being treated by Dr. Kaiser Kervats, the Emperor's doctor, who was keen on the destiny of the fearless Bukovinka.

he columnist for the local news week by week "Association of Liberation of Ukraine" later wrote in 1915 on the destiny of Yarema Kuz, expressing she every day related with her "Kobylyanskaya" sister. The harmed Yarema's fantasy was to get back to battle when possible.

Olena (Yarema) Kuz's sister Wasylena frequently compared with her, and afterward they moved together, and lived respectively in Vienna. Family relatives said they remained in Vienna, and Yarema was utilized giving French lessons.

First two images are of Countess Olena Kuz, whom Austria twice awarded medals for bravery. The brave Bukovinka, from a simple family, to be called Countess; such a great honour. The third image is Zen's great grandmother Wasylena, who is also the aunt of Countess Olena (Yarema) Kuz.

Vladimir Staruk captured Olena (Yarema) Kuz, and presented his photograph to the American Press Association, which then, at that point, showed up in a few papers on January 24, 1916. Vladimir Staruk revealed in 1917, "Olena retired in 1917 and resided with her sister Wasylena in Vienna, where she kicked the bucket; when she passed on isn't known."

and numerous Kuz family members' interests about Yarema's last experiences are as yet aroused and must be fulfilled by survey her headstone, if one exists.

Upon relating this secret to Luba Moisey from the town of Stari Kuty close to the left upper bank of the Cheremosh River, I was told Yarema got back to Ukraine and resided in disguise under the noses of the Bolsheviks close to Ivano-Frankivsk. Luba said this was normal information to numerous in Stari Kuty. Squeezing Luba for additional subtleties, she reacted, "Harmony, we in our delinquent, in reverse town were on the moon offering our products to the space travelers when they landed." Luba is an enterprising, bold mother who accommodated her folks and youngsters by getting and exchanging items in generally capitals of the Soviet Union and then some. She is an extremely road shrewd lady, getting through difficult stretches with alcoholic spouse Nikolai Moisey, while bringing up three kids. What at last befell Yarema, Luba didn't know.

In September 2016, I talked with Maria Tanasiyivna (née Kuz) Luchka, who resides in Banyliv, two or three hundred meters east of where Yarema was raised. Maria depicted how Olena, recovering in Vienna, functioned as an instructor of

French. The family consistently realized her cousin was a champion, however in Soviet occasions, to say this was outlandish. The family realized that the little girl of Tanase Kuz (my extraordinary grandma was his more seasoned sister) was a valiant lady, who went to the Sich Riflemen to respect her dad. Maria's grandma Wasylena Kuz, said that during the conflict, Olena (Yarema) Kuz went to her home. Her grandmother had said that Yarema came riding from across the Cheremosh River, joined by her officers. She was injured in the arm. Maria accepts this was the principal twisted from battling in the Carpathians. She lived with Maria's grandma for a month, until the injury recuperated. Maria's grandma prepared her food. Olena was conveying a guide, which she regularly checked out. This is all Maria knew about her.

The meeting with Maria Luchka occurred in the secondary lounge of Tanasi's vehicle, as Maria's significant other was sick and she didn't need us to become caused. Ohla in the front seat interpreted from a neighborhood paper article Maria expounded on Yarema. There was a slight sprinkle as we sat and talked. It was as of now that I discovered that my extraordinary grandma Wasylena was the more seasoned sister of the champion's dad, Tanase. This was subsequently affirmed from the Chernivtsi archives.

Maria's house is at the north edge of Banyliv, close to the Cheremosh River. She pointed toward the stream to a huge, two-story, uninhabited structure. This structure is on the specific area of an old house where courageous woman Olena (Yarema) Kuz, injured interestingly, was breast fed by her grandma. Yarema lived in interesting nationalistic occasions that saw the reception of the present Ukrainian banner, public song of praise and image. In Appendix 9, page 265, there are more reported records about Yarema.

fter the wonderful gathering, Maria opened an umbrella and got back to her home. Tanasi, interpreter Ohla and I headed to the cleared structure, where we were quickly charged by two German shepherds from a close by fish ranch. We immediately bounced once more into the vehicle, tapping out, and left for Valentyn's home. On my thirteenth visit in September 2016, Valentyn acquainted me with Ohla Sokivka, an astounding interpreter, who lives across the Cheremosh River and was curious about any of my Ukrainian family members and companions. Ohla was fast at getting a handle on and taking care of numerous delicate issues that I needed to all the more likely comprehend to attempt to make this book precise, while not culpable such a large number of acquaintances.

Ohla, a youthful college graduate in English, makes money by giving private English illustrations. She immediately reinforced with Valentyn's little girl, Tatyana. The two young ladies, affable Tanasi and I spent long days as we went to meet my goals. One such day was a visit to Mount Makivka, where Olena (Yarema) Kuz turned into a Ukrainian heroine.

Tanasi and I, as common throughout the long term, were the visitors of Maria (his sister) and Valentyn at Vyzhenka, three kilometers from Vyzhnytsia, adjoining a feeder of the Cheremosh River. We had private higher up rooms in their beautiful Carpathian home. Breakfast was normally imparted to Maria and Valentyn, where we assessed the endeavors of the earlier day and made arrangements for the coming days.

The morning meal table is close to an enormous window, obviously uncovering the rising sun over the vigorously pecan and pine-forested mountain. The nearby yard toward the south is the place where Valentyn's mom resides, and every morning she moved the fastened goat to a crisp touching region and tended the raised bunny pens as chickens hectically cackled close to her home. Dew-covered grass capitulated to the sun's beams creating rising whiffs of steam. Their grass was cut and heaped in three immense, rocket-molded stacks with a tall community stake projecting upward, which sheds downpour and snow while possessing a little impression in the yard.

One day, a piece before dawn, Maria and I were completing a morning meal of potato hotcakes, eggs, cheddar, espresso and cherry compote as Tanasi drove up the precarious grade to the house with Tatyana, who lives at the Lingcomp School, three kilometers away. In practically no time, with my shoulder sack loaded with bites and four void two-liter pop containers, we headed to a close by metal line streaming with cool spring water. In the wake of filling the jugs and taking a taste from measured hands, we were set for get interpreter Ohla for our excursion to Mount Makivka.

Within a couple of kilometers, we got the enormous extension over the powerful Cheremosh River and drove close to Stari Kuty's one-time home of

Ivano Franko towards Kosiv. We passed the enormous field on the right half of the street where the week by week Kosiv market is held, and the memory of my perished father streaked through my brain. That was the place where we handled the pig for a family get-together in 2006. I mumbled to myself, "I love you Dad."

As we entered Kosiv, Tanasi called Ohla. We met her on a central avenue, a couple of squares from her mother's home, which she imparted to her sister. Her mother lives in America. Ohla joined Tatyana in the rearward sitting arrangement. Following a half hour, I napped off into Neverland. This allowed the young ladies their first opportunity to talk continuous. Every once in a while, I was stimulated by an obstruction. The rhythm of their chat expanded, and they oftentimes burst into chuckling. They were holding and today are friends.

We didn't have unequivocal data on the most brief course to Mount Makivka. Enquiring now and again, in any event, when close to the mountain, we were met with shrugged shoulders. The guide and PDA were of negligible worth. After a couple of wrong turns, the projecting mountain was in view. The difficulty was which end of the mountain to approach. Hours could be squandered to track down the right methodology. We needed to be close to the area where Olena (Yarema) Kuz executed her valiant assault on the Russian tsar's fortress. At the southerly finish of Mount Makivka, we were at a crossroads, and noticing Yogi Berra's recommendation ("When you go to a crossroads, take it"), we required one street and inside twenty minutes arrived at a little extension with a sign appearance an eleven-kilometer climb to arrive at the culmination, which was toward the path we had quite recently come from. We turned around and took the other street. A bunch of homes and a couple of more enquiries prompted two more conceivable vehicle trails we could attempt. Inside ten minutes, we showed up at a steel pipe boundary, which was locked. We saw a stone landmark with a sign close to the entryway. Tanasi wound down the engine and promptly shut his eyes for a nap.

e three, with shoulder packs close by, moved toward the stone landmark hung with blue and yellow paint (the shade of the country's banner). A sign appearance a path 4.5-kilometer-long would prompt another landmark, where courageous woman Olena (Yarema) Kuz boldly took out the tsar's assault rifle nests.

We tasted our water, changed shoelaces for the long, tough stroll on the restricted 4x4-wheel-drive trail, flexibility just when liberated from snow and downpour. Best case scenario, we could just see two or three hundred meters in front of the winding barrette street with its thickly covered slant of tall, bolt straight pine trees. We experienced a sign representing twelve distinct mushrooms found on the mountain. We looked, yet didn't track down any. Farther up the path, another sign delineated neighborhood birds. Shrieking falcons and a bird took off high. The path in places with close to vertical cuts was covered with rocks up to football size, and we must be cautious as we kept a lively speed. A portion of the shale contained fossils. The Carpathian Mountains are among the most seasoned of all ranges.

Halfway up the mountain, we halted to lay on a huge sun-warmed rock. The air was cool and new. A light breeze tenderly influenced the pine

tops. Toward the finish of the ascension, the path expanded into a huge, evened out region. Off to one side and ten meters down was an evened out half-hectare region containing a huge landmark and short columns of crosses. Prior to strolling down, the ten-meter drop, we strolled to two shrubbery concealed wooden seats that confronted one another. Not a word was expressed as we drooped depleted into the seats, which confronted one another. It was somewhat past early afternoon hour. We devoured our bananas and peanuts and tasted cool water.

The landmark was encircled on three sides with fifty short peevish. They were snow-white and in lines like those in Flanders Field. I moved toward the closest cross and found writing in Cyrillic followed by two numbers. Ohla interpreted the name Havryliuk, matured nineteen. My idea quickly blazed to Edmonton where a previous long-lasting Mayor Bill Hawrelak's folks came from Banyliv in 1899.

All appeared to be strange and I was constrained to walk and contact each grave marker while Ohla interpreted the Cyrillic names of the young men matured sixteen to twenty, some who were siblings. Most last names were recognizable from my childhood in Andrew, Alberta, and normal in my hereditary town of Banyliv. Incredibly, I saw my mom's original last name (Palichuk) on a cross. Amazing feelings undulated up my spine, as I envisioned the few encounters that butchered the young men at this vital location.

Mount Makivka remembrance with 50 crosses 2016.

It was Olena (Yarema) Kuz who drove eight young men at this strengthened pass that required Mount Makivka in the dead of night and switched things around to eliminate the

last tsar from Ukraine in 1915. Today Putin is attempting to achieve what past tsars and despots neglected to do. Ukraine actually exists, and the world, alongside twenty million in the Ukrainian Diaspora, upholds Ukraine and its drive for freedom.

On the plunge from Makivka, we were good humored and chatty. We gathered brilliant shale pieces engraved with impressions of antiquated life, some of which I have in our Ukraine room in Canada. Back at the vehicle, we arose Tanasi and had a nibble prior to getting back to Vyzhnytsia.

It was dull, and the murmuring vehicle and delicate radio music had us three explorers resting. My psyche floated to what in particular course Yarema and her eight nationalists took up the mountain on their quiet rising under front of obscurity. In 1915, there was restricted admittance to the highest point of vital Mount Makivka's automatic rifle homes. The course we explorers took would have been excessively risky as the simple bends considered covered tsar guard stations. I closed the young, experienced in exploring woodland territory, chosen for make an immediate ascension, stowed away from the view of the as of late imagined automatic rifles (called Chris by the Ukrainians).

Appendix #9, page 265 has a rundown of names on the fifty tombstones, and on the off chance that you are of Ukrainian legacy from the Cheremosh River valley or from Western Canada, you have a fantastic shot at seeing your hereditary name on one of them.

4.5 Kilometer, 1996 trail to East summit of the Sich Riflemen Memorial on Mount Makivka (2.) where the last tsar's forces were removed.

Finally, WWII (Ukraine's Version)

To all the more likely see the present Ukrainians, in their numerous geographic locales, one should know Ukraine's rendition of WWII. The accompanying has been replicated from the Ukrainian Ministry of Foreign Affairs site, which has an archive by the Ukrainian Institute of National Remembrance that portrays the Ukrainian involvement with WWII. The whole archive can be seen at: mfa.gov.ua/en/news sources/unfamiliar workplaces news/56936-ukrajina-u-drugij-svitovij-vijni

The Ukrainian country toward the beginning of the Second World War in September 1939 was split between five nations: the USSR,

Poland, Slovakia, Hungary and Romania.

On March 15, 1939, the Carpatho-Ukrainian Parliament chose Augustine Voloshin as its leader and took on a few state symbols – the blue and yellow banner, "Ukraine has not yet died" as its hymn and St. Volodymyr the Great's Trident as their public layer of arms.

around the same time, Budapest offered Khust a harmony that would annex

Carpatho-Ukraine (Transkarpathia) to Hungary. Voloshin denied and consequently started the overall hostile of the Hungarian troops.

The summit of this was the Battle of Krasne Pole on 16 March 1939. Here, the Ukrainian officers coordinated their protection against the normal Hungarian armed force which included tanks, planes, mounted guns, and substantial weapons. By the evening, the Carpatho-Ukrainian capital fell.

krainians were the first in pre-war Europe to guard their opportunity with arms. […]

ccording to [a] secret convention [the Non-Aggression Pact between the Third Reich and the Soviet Union], Eastern Europe was to be split between two tyrants: Hitler would take Poland and the Baltic States, Finland and Romanian Bukovyna and Bessarabia would fall into Stalin's zone of interest. For a very long time the public authority of the USSR denied the presence of this mystery protocol.

[…] The conflict in Ukraine started on 1 September 1939 and 120 thousand Ukrainians met the Nazis in the positions of the Polish armed force. Lviv and other Western Ukrainian urban communities experienced Nazi bombings on the primary day of the war.

The Soviet Union entered the Second World War on 17 September 1939 as a Nazi partner. Without announcing war, the Red Army crossed the Polish boundary and moved toward the west. The Soviet soldiers helped the Wehrmacht break the Polish obstruction in Przemysl and Brest. On 22 September, Lviv gave up, blockaded by the Wehrmacht from the west and the Red Army from the east. That very day there was a joint German-Soviet triumph march in Brest.

During the Second World War, Ukraine lost a greater number of individuals than the consolidated misfortunes of Great Britain, Canada, Poland, the USA and France. The absolute Ukrainian misfortunes during the conflict is an expected at 8-10 million lives. The quantity of Ukrainian casualties can measure up to the advanced populace of Austria.

coming up next is taken from Ukraine's Version of Who Won WWII by Ukraine's Andrew Hevko.

On the region of Ukraine in WWII, there were three soldiers: The Wehrmacht German Army, the Soviet Red Army and the Ukrainian Insurgent (People's) Army (UPA). What did the German armed force battle for? It battled for the Third Reich. Does the Third Reich exist? No, it was obliterated. What did the Soviet Union battle for? It battled for the U.S.S.R. Does the U.S.S.R exist? No, it vanished. What did the Ukrainian Insurgent Army battle for? It battled for an autonomous Ukraine. Does an autonomous Ukraine exist? Indeed, it exists. I welcome the triumphant Ukraine Insurgent (People's) Army.

WWII in Ukraine saw the attacking Wehrmacht German Army battling for the Third Reich, and the Soviet Red Army battling for the USSR. From the outset, these two intruders subtly consented to an arrangement to isolate Ukraine, however the scoundrels deceived one another. In post-Perebudova Ukraine, the Third Reich had been a distant memory from the substance of the earth. The socialist USSR additionally vanished.

kraine won in view of its initial progressive seeds, developed from hundreds of years of slaughter, delivering enthusiastic survivors. Many Ukrainian sectarian gatherings were shaped. Sectarian Ukrainians battled each other for an assortment of muddled strict, philosophical and fortuitous reasons. A considerable lot of my Ukrainian family members were split between the super hardliner gatherings throughout the previous 125 years. Today, in 2017 not many hardliners are isolated, and patriotism is at a breaking point. Ukraine exists due to its hardliners, while the Third Reich and the USSR have both vanished. (Index 2, page 227 has more information)

Putin Invades Ukraine 2014

Since WWII, Ukraine soil didn't see an equipped intrusion on its dirt until Putin went along and in March 2014 added Ukraine's Crimea and attacked Donbas in the East, using rebel procedures recently executed in Georgia and other areas.

I called Tatyana in Ukraine when the intrusion happened, and she was insanely crying, couldn't rest, and envisioned her room being besieged. She was threatened. Contact with others in Ukraine affirmed that they dreaded an assault was imminent.

Quickly I organized to go to Ukraine in September of 2014. Doreen stayed in Canada. I was on the last leg of a departure from Warsaw to Lviv. The little plane, with two seats on one side of the passageway, made them sit close to a tall, solid, blue jean-clad man in his fifties. I saw he was perusing a manual depicting a WWII fight. Whenever the chance emerged, we recognized one another and didn't quit talking until the flight finished. He was an American, positioned with NATO in northern Italy, and this was his second visit to Ukraine. Clearing customs together and leaving the structure, we waved a farewell, as he met his casually dressed driver, who was driving him quickly to the Donetsk war zone.

half a month after the fact my interpreter Oksana required a three day weekend and was supplanted by Tatyana's beloved companion, who works at a huge Lviv inn, where numerous NATO faculty remained. She worked inviting visitors. She, as most Ukrainians in their twenties, was energetic with regards to Ukraine, promptly taking on the opportunities found in the West. I viewed her as extremely enthusiastic, including her passionate longing to go to the front with a rifle. Among her NATO visitors were two from Canada.

In Vyzhnytsia, we visited the military sleeping shelter and a group of structures, once in the past claimed by a Jewish association. A considerable lot of the youthful volunteer troopers were understudies from our Lingcomp School, and they promptly showed us around. At the point when we were leaving, they gave me one of their outfits, which I put on and modeled for photographs. The majority of this age gathering and some more youthful are valid nationalists. They are encircled by an ocean of blue and yellow banners, images, painted scaffolds, postal boxes, vehicles, light posts and many different constructions. Ordinarily, I thought about how Putin could involve the districts I visited.

Also, 2014 saw Canadian Armed Forces' Captain Mike Dullege convey Operation UNIFIER. Wearing non-military garments, he went without anyone else from Edmonton, Canada, to Lviv and traveled sixty kilometers northwest to Stari, where he worked until March 2017, setting up a preparation base to prepare Ukrainian military.

Captain Dullege made a show on May 4, 2017, at the twenty-fourth yearly pledge drive of Edmonton's "Kyiv Konnection," went to by multiple hundred, generally of Ukrainian legacy. All in attendance,

including Doreen and I, are wild supporters for Ukraine. In Canada, there are in excess of 100 gatherings like the "Kyiv Konnection," and every one of these gatherings' individuals have worked for Ukraine's improvement. Numerous people have given 50 years of administration. Notwithstanding these numerous authority Canadian associations, the Canadian government and large number of people unobtrusively offered material and moral help for Ukraine. They all have a story to tell, and I trust many are being recorded.

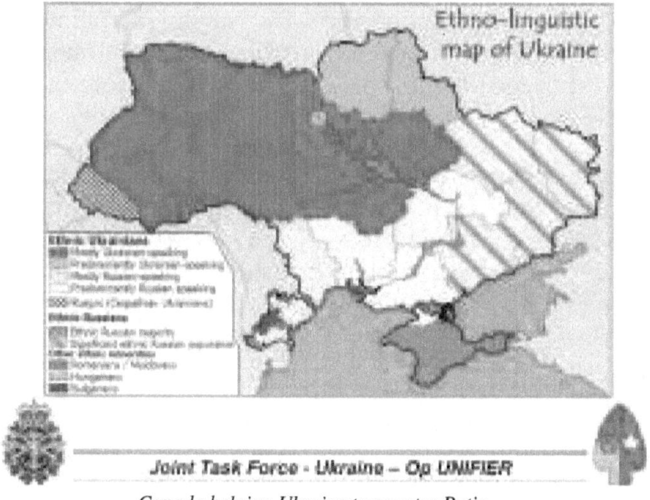

Canada helping Ukraine to counter Putin.

Canada has a heavenly standing and a pile of generosity in Ukraine. All Ukrainians know this. Each filthy deed by Putin slices to our heart, however much it does to a Ukrainian's. Putin, the dinosaur, is a blockhead battling our help for Ukraine, and we in Canada address just five percent of Ukraine's worldwide Diaspora pulling for Ukraine's freedom.

On July 1, 2015 at 10 a.m., menace Putin shut valves conveying gas to Ukraine as the conflict seethed in Donbas, generally close to Donetsk. Ukraine is geologically key for Europe's gas supply, as Europe utilizes Ukraine's organization of pipelines to get Russian gas. Today 33% of Europe's gas supply is from Russia, of which 40% is moved through Ukraine. Russia, with its malignant activities towards Ukraine, charges Ukraine a more exorbitant cost, despite the fact that it is nearer than Europe. Additionally, Ukraine should pay in

advance.

kraine, to the shock of Putin, prevented bringing in gas from Russia and cunningly diminished imports to not exactly half. This was refined by moving forward their own gas creation, executing old strategies for keeping warm (sweaters, covers, resting in one room) and utilizing substitute wellsprings of energy (fundamentally wood and coal).

store and a private home in Vyzhnytsia were currently introducing a Latvian programmed wood-consuming heater to the outside of their homes. It consolidates headways in impenetrable heaters. The heater warmed a liquor and water high temp water framework. The liquor was refined from grapes developed at my property, the site of our Lingcomp non-public school. The expense of wood needed for the year was bought and conveniently stacked, for less expense than one month's past gas bill.

Coal in Ukraine comes from Donetsk and Putin remove the shipments to western Ukrainian warm electric plants and redirected the coal to Russia. Putin might want the Ukrainians to freeze in obscurity. Accordingly, the US inclined up their coal creation and in September 2017 the principal shipment of their coal showed up in Ukraine.

ear of Jesus

Ukrainians by and large have a harder skin than most people as they advanced from hundreds of years of abusive unfamiliar control and serfdom to foster a protection from the dread of death. Cleric Robert Barron of California composed the accompanying with regards to Jesus' Final Teaching, and it addresses me concerning that foster such a protection from the dread of death:

The prior night he kicked the bucket, Jesus gives a bizarre, supernatural discourse to his supporters. This was his last will and confirmation. During this apparently meandering talk, Jesus is baiting them, once and for all, into his vision of things, or, in other words, into a world wherein the dread of death has been overcome.

From the start of his service, Jesus discussed a heavenly love that loves us genuinely, that connects with us in any event, when we wander

far away, and that loves us even through the fear and haziness of death. Similarly as he moved into the disgrace and underestimation of transgression to carry the light to miscreants, presently he will move into the obscurity of death to show us the way through.

Jesus is going to leave this world, and he supplicates that his supporters may realize that they are not of this world. What does this world resemble solidly? Indeed, look around.

The dread of death resembles a cloud, similar to a horrible shadow that falls over human existence and experience. All our general apprehensions are impressions of, and cooperations in, this early stage dread. It cramps us, hands us over on ourselves, and it makes us guarded, contemptuous, vicious, and vengeful.

Further, designs of mistreatment in our reality are predicated upon the dread of death. Since a dictator can undermine his kin with death, he can rule them and execute a wide range of injustice.

Whenever the solid (in any sense) overpower the frail, we are checking out the methods of death.

Jesus came to introduce what he called the Kingdom of God, God's method of being, God's organization. This is a request dependent on the boundless and shocking affection for God. What might the world resemble affected by this adoration? It would be fundamentally changed, altered, supplanted: 'another sky and a new earth.'

What might life resemble assuming we were at this point not apprehensive? We would live as the holy people do – not insusceptible to anguish, but rather, assuming that I can put it thusly, unaffected by it. We would realize that we are adored by a power that rises above death, and this would fill us with an extravagance past measure.

utin basically controls his kin utilizing the dread of death. The Russian state controls the Russian media and those that show resistance are underestimated and surprisingly dispensed with. This is the same than the strategies of the antiquated Romans. Most I met in Ukraine don't have a dread of death from Putin. In 2017, this is particularly obvious among the young, who are eager to get a firearm to kill Putin. Some of them realize it is Better to Die a Wolf than to Live the Life of a Dog.

I get many reports from Ukraine from different sources on Putin's attack, and day by day the number of Ukrainian youth are killed and injured. On March 28, 2015, Banyliv, my tribal town, bid farewell to Alexander Kolotylo (a comparative with my more distant family). In 2014, he was in a counter-psychological oppressor activity in Eastern Ukraine as a sergeant of the third contingent, strategic gatherings of the 80th separate airborne unit and versatile airborne soldiers of the Armed Forces of Ukraine.

A contacting goodbye function for Alexander was held in the Banyliv Church of the Dormition. The greater part of the town joined in. Many battling fighters were in participation. Central avenue was lined on the two sides for the legend, everyone bowing, most with tears and wild eruptions of despondency. Authorities in participation incorporated the top of the area organization, Mikhail Andryuk; representative provincial military commissar of instructive work Valery Movchanyuk; manager of the locale committee George Ivonyak; Banyliv Mayor Nikolai Andryuk, and top of the local state organization Oleksandr Fyschuk.

All knew about Alexander's boldness and gallantry in guarding Ukraine's sway and regional trustworthiness. Official Decree No. 708/2014 was granted post mortem to Alexander. The Order "For mental fortitude" of III degree was introduced to his better half, Valery Movchanyuk. He left two daughters.

Alexander Kolotylo was one of the first to head off to war against Putin's shrewd intrusion of Ukraine, where today in 2017, Crimea is attached, and every day bombardments happen in Eastern Ukraine. Alexander battled and liberated numerous little towns and the towns of Krasny Liman, Slovyansk and Seversk. He kicked the bucket in Luhansk. He was applauded as a mindful dad, a caring child and a decent sibling, incredibly unassuming but then a bold youngster who didn't stop for a second to guard Ukraine's glad future for all.

The congregation service, among an ocean of blue and yellow blossoms, blended in with tears, to the metal band playing the public hymn, finished with yells of "Wonder to Ukraine," "Legends of Glory," "Brilliance to the Nation," "Passing to the Enemy." Some adolescent held Alexander's photograph with the subtitle, "Saints never kick the bucket." The serenade "Demise to Putin" is communicated day by day by grade younger students, who gladly sport blue and yellow on their apparel.

a definitive cost was paid by Alexander Kolotylo, among huge number of contenders and regular citizens ensuring their country. Starting at 2017, almost 10,000 have passed on since Putin's intrusion. Ukrainian contenders are among the fiercest. They battle with mediocre hardware against Putin's military, who are in plain outfits with the most recent of modern armaments.

Crimea

Wikipedia has the accompanying to say about the "Historical backdrop of Crimea"

The written history of the Crimean Peninsula, generally known as the Tauric Chersonese (Χερσόνησος Ταυρική "Tauric Peninsula"), starts around the fifth century BCE, when a few Greek states were set up along its coast. The southern coast stayed Greek in culture for right around 2,000 years as a feature of the Roman Empire (47 BCE - 330 CE), and its replacement expresses, the Byzantine Empire (330 CE - 1204 CE), the Empire of Trebizond (1204 CE - 1461 CE), and the free Principality of Theodoro (finished 1475 CE). In the thirteenth century, ome port urban communities were constrained by the Venetians and by the Genovese. The Crimean inside was substantially less steady, persevering through a long series of victories and attacks; by the early middle age time frame it had been settled by Scythians (Scytho-Cimmerians), Tauri, Greeks, Romans, Goths, Huns, Bulgars, Kipchaks and Khazars. In the

middle age period, it was obtained incompletely by Kievan Rus, however tumbled to the Mongol intrusions as a feature of the Golden Horde. They were trailed by the Crimean Khanate and the Ottoman Empire, which vanquished the waterfront regions too, in the fifteenth to eighteenth centuries.

The advanced history of Crimea starts with the addition by the Russian Empire in 1783. [...] In 1921, the Crimean Autonomous Soviet Socialist Republic was made. This republic was broken up in 1945, and Crimea turned into an oblast, first of the Russian S.S.R. (1945-1954) and afterward the Ukrainian S.S.R. (1954-1991). Starting around a 1991, the area was covered by the Autonomous Republic of Crimea and Sevastopol City inside free Ukraine. During the 2014 Crimean emergency [Putin's invasion].the landmass was taken over by supportive of Russian powers and a mandate on whether to join Russia was held. Soon after the outcome for joining Russia was declared, Crimea was added by the Russian Federation as two government subjects, the Republic of Crimea and the bureaucratic city of Sevastopol.

most of world nations, including Canada, the EU, America and the UN don't perceive Putin's extension and truth be told starting at 2017 instituted extreme limitations on Putin's Russia. Putin responded and in August of 2017 he introduced global long range rockets (IBM) equipped with atomic bombs. Lamentably, atomic weapons are again on Ukraine's dirt. It intentionally surrendered them to decrease the worldwide numbers under an arrangement where the USA ensured an attack from Russia would be forestalled. The USA under the initiative of President Obama should look down in disgrace for not satisfying its understanding. Ukraine has requested that the USA supply protective weapons for the Ukraine armed force without progress. The Nuclear Non-Proliferation Treaty (NPT), endorsed in 1968, came into power 1970: A worldwide deal (as of now with 189-part states) to restrict the spread of atomic weapons. The arrangement has three fundamental columns: restraint, demobilization, and the option to calmly utilize atomic technology.

utin Propaganda

A June 6, 2015 Deutsche Welle paper article noted:

The legal counselor Zhanna Nemtsova, the girl of killed Russian

resistance legislator Boris Nemtsov, says she has left [Russia]. In an open letter, she faulted [Putin's] state promulgation for her dad's death.

"Russian publicity kills," Nemtsova wrote in a segment published … in the business every day Vedomosti, saying that obligation regarding her dad's passing was shared by writers working for state-controlled TV stations who had portrayed him and other resistance figures as "public traitors."

Boris Nemtsov, 55, a frank pundit of President Vladimir Putin, was shot dead in late February 2015 while strolling on an extension close to the Kremlin in Moscow.

"Putin's data machine – like those in Nazi Germany and Rwanda, is utilizing criminal techniques for purposeful publicity, and planting contempt that creates savagery and dread," she said, adding that individuals "tainted with disdain start perpetrating new wrongdoings all alone initiative."

In 2014, Ukraine had no arranged public purposeful publicity set up to counter Putin, an expert at the round of trickery, who had all his administration offices going all out. He controls Russia's media and the Russian Orthodox Church (ROC, a strict division of the Russian government). His publicity, incredibly powerful in Russia, likewise reached out to a couple of neighboring nations. With the fast extension of Crimea in 2014, Ukraine at last got up and made its own purposeful publicity machine to counter Putin.

The world is presently mindful of Putin's act. He leads with an iron mafia clench hand, utilizing KGB strategies of dread of death. His reality is one of falsehoods and duplicity, with purposeful publicity to keep most Russians in the dark.

The accompanying has been duplicated from the article "Putin and the Proxies" on the site of the Organized Crime and Corruption Reporting Project. The full article can be perused here: www.occrp.org/en/putinandtheproxies/

The [Russian] oligarchs have been restrained since Vladimir Putin's appearance to the administration. The long-term pioneer has made a commonly gainful deal: Leave the governmental issues to me, chip in when I really want you

to - - and you can keep, and even develop, your riches. […]

OCCRP and its long-term accomplice Novaya Gazeta went uncovering to track down more - - and sorted out the resources of some of President Putin's companions, family, and inward circle. […] [The] Novaya Gazeta and OCCRP examination investigated the abundance encompassing Russian President Vladimir Putin.

The Organized Crime and Corruption Reporting Project (OCCRP) is a worldwide organization of insightful writers […] an analytical revealing stage framed by 40 non-benefit insightful focuses, scores of columnists and a few significant local news associations all over the planet. [Their] network is spread across Europe, Africa, Asia and Latin America/[They] collaborated in 2006 to do transnational analytical revealing and elevate innovation based ways to deal with uncovering coordinated wrongdoing and debasement worldwide.

Putin has cautioned ordinarily that Russia should shield itself from "shading upsets" like those that overturned presidents in adjoining Ukraine, Georgia and Kyrgyzstan. He utilizes this dread strategy to fix his iron-clench hand hold on the country by specifically picking the 89 provincial lead representatives and the Kremlin elastic stamps the bills they are introduced. A shading unrest is the main expected snag to Putin's control.

According to a November 7, 2017 BBC article, the Russian news organization Tass reports that Rosgvardiya (otherwise called Rosguard) the tip top Russian public gatekeeper now 2017 surpasses 340,000 individuals. They will be positioned to ensure the 89 territorial lead representatives and constrained by the focal Federal Security Service (FSB), the replacement to the KGB constrained by no other than Putin then, at that point, and presently. The BBC reports that "[t]he power has a portion of Russia's most refined military equipment and break troops from unique powers units." This power permits the Kremlin (Putin) to rapidly stop a resistance to him. Political investigator Dmitry Oreshkin has seen that "The lead representatives are presently under more tight [central] control." The full message of the BBC article can be perused here: www.bbc.com/news/world-europe-41900643

Chapter 6

Ukraine strives for freedom despit e Putin

Jews in Ukraine

In Western Ukraine, Jews were referenced without precedent for 1030. Coming up next is reproduced from the Wikipedia page on the "Historical backdrop of the Jews in Ukraine."

Jewish people group have existed in the region of Ukraine from the hour of [Kievan] Rus' (one of [Kyiv] city entryways was called Judaic) and created a considerable lot of the most unmistakable present day Jewish religious and social customs, like Hasidism. As per the World Jewish Congress, the Jewish people group in Ukraine comprise the third greatest Jewish people group in Europe and the fifth greatest on the planet.

While now and again it thrived, at different occasions the Jewish people group confronted times of oppression and against Semitic prejudicial strategies. In the Ukrainian People's Republic, Yiddish was a state language alongside Ukrainian and Russian. Around then [the Jewish National Union was created] ... the local area was allowed an independent status. Yiddish was utilized on Ukrainian money in 1917–1920.

A multitude of Cossacks and Crimean Tatars slaughtered and took into bondage countless Jews, Roman Catholic Christians and Uniate Christians in 1648–1649. Late gauges range from fifteen thousand to 30,000 Jews killed or kidnapped, and 300 Jewish people group completely obliterated. During the 1821 enemy of Jewish mobs in Odesa after the demise of the Greek Orthodox patriarch in Constantinople, 14 Jews were killed. At the point when part of the [Tsar's]

Russian Empire in 1911 to 1913, the counter Semitic perspectives can be found in the quantity of blood slander cases. In 1915, the public authority removed a huge number of Jews from the Empire's line areas.

During the 1917 Russian Revolution and the following Russian Civil War, an expected 31,071 Jews were killed during 1918–1920. During the foundation of the Ukrainian People's Republic (1917–21), massacres kept on being an executed on Ukrainian area. In Ukraine, the quantity of non military personnel Jews killed during the period was somewhere in the range of 35 and 50 thousand. Huge slaughters proceeded until 1921. The activities of the Soviet government by 1927 prompted a developing discrimination against Jews in the area.

Ukraine was attacked by Germany and Russia during WWII.] Total regular citizen misfortunes during WWII and German occupation in Ukraine are assessed at 7,000,000, including more than 1,000,000 Jews shot and killed by the Einsatzgruppen and by their numerous nearby Ukrainian allies in the western piece of Ukraine. [The Jews addressed fifteen percent of Ukrainians killed in this brief period.]

Before World War II, somewhat under 33% of Ukraine's metropolitan populace comprised of Jews who were the biggest public minority in Ukraine. Ukrainian Jews are contained by various sub-gatherings, including Ashkenazi Jews, Mountain Jews, Bukharan Jews, Crimean Karaites, Krymchak Jews and Georgian Jews.

Ukraine had 840,000 Jews in 1959, an abatement of practically 70% from 1941 (inside Ukraine's present lines). Ukraine's Jewish populace declined altogether during the Cold War. In 1989, Ukraine's Jewish populace was just somewhat the greater part of what it was thirty years sooner (in 1959). The mind-boggling larger part of the Jews who stayed in Ukraine in 1989 remaining Ukraine and moved to different nations (generally to Israel) during the 1990s during and after the breakdown of Communism.

Ukraine's President Poroshenko, chose in 2016, and numerous Ukrainian chosen authorities are Jewish. In my thirteen visits post-Perebudova, for the most part to western Ukraine, I didn't see or know about any enemy of Semitic actions.

When I was seven years of age in 1947 living in the little northern Canadian town of Lac La Biche, I initially heard the word Jew. The town made due on fishing, catching and logging. I was great at catching hares and catching wild creatures and at age seven my dad gave me a 22-type rifle. With Dad's assistance, we cleaned and extended the hide pelts. These I would take to offer to old Sam Wolff, the hide purchaser. Sam paid five pennies for a completely ready bunny pelt. He checked out me, continually sharing a couple of peanuts from his container and paying attention to how I put out traps. The town alluded to him as the Jew hide purchaser, and individuals were careful about him, notice that he would "Jew you down" on the cost of your pelts.

When in Grade Eleven in Edmonton, Canada, Steve Rankin, of Jewish drop, selected late in the school year. He sat straightforwardly behind me. Steve had a decent body with wavy dark black hair that diverged from his white T-shirts he generally wore. We promptly turned out to be dear companions, are still companions right up 'til today. We avoided a ton of school classes to chase ducks and birds with our prepared Labrador retrievers. Steve was a decent artist and a hit with young ladies. He was somewhat of a troublemaker, which added to great contentions and us having loads of fun. With insignificant considering, he had good grades in the entirety of his tests. At his home, I was generally welcomed by his Mom and saw a family centered around advanced education. For instance, his six-year-old sister was perusing the 600 page book Ivanhoe. Steve's dad, David, was a material science teacher at the University of Alberta. The family was scholarly contrasted with the wide range of various families I knew. It was in this late phase of tutoring that I previously found out with regards to colleges, because of Steve. I additionally discovered that Judaism is a religion. Steve and his family were not strict. Up to that point, I thought a Jew alluded to an ethnicity and not a religion.

Later, I met Joe Sheckter, another Jew, who was exceptionally committed to his confidence. Joe was more established than my dad, and turned into my coach. He was my subsequent dad. His sibling frequently said he was unable to comprehend the unique relationship we created. My companion Joe joined a Canadian government assignment to Moscow in 1971, where he met First Secretary Leonid Brezhnev. Joe kibitzed with Brezhnev and extricated documentation to venture out to Kyiv. In Kyiv, Joe and Sadie met a family member. They left the following day to the town of his dad's introduction to the world. They loaded an acquired vehicle with gas jars, cooked chicken and bread for the excursion to the distant town. With Soviet documentation, they handily persuaded Kyiv's traffic signal at the exit of the

city to permit them to visit the close by open country. On the edges of Kyiv, there were other outfitted controlled protected stations. Sadie and Joe figured out how to pass two additional stations and conceal the vehicle in a relative's stable. They remained hid for seven days in the crude states of a predominately Jewish town. At the point when the time had come to leave that region, Joe said they left behind the greater part of their cash, all adornments and all pressed attire. Joe wore no shorts and socks when he left.

On getting back to Kyiv after 12 PM, they moved toward a remote watchman station with their headlights wound down. They zoomed past a getting up watch. At the following watched station, they were waved to stop. Joe, grinning, waved back and avoided around the outfitted gatekeeper, who didn't fire. At the entry to Kyiv, the gatekeepers were cautioned and sitting tight for Joe. A few hours delay followed, as Joe streaked Russian and Canadian reports. He clarified that they had become lost in the open country. Joe talked negligible Ukrainian. At last they were accompanied to the airport.

istening to Joe inform me concerning his experience was the point at which I previously discovered that his predecessors were from Ukraine. He was brought into the world in Vegreville, Canada, an unassuming community occupied for the most part by Ukrainians. I never heard Joe express a derisive word about Ukraine or Ukrainian individuals. Joe aroused my curiosity in Ukraine. At the point when Joe kicked the bucket, Doreen went to his burial service as I was out of Canada. Joe's girl Marilyn referenced my name in the tribute. Index 5 on page 250 has a "Background marked by the Jews in Bukovina".

Religion

Sterling Demchinsky is a Canadian Ukrainian who is the writer of the site "Ukrainian Churches In Canada." I replicated the accompanying areas from his site page, which can be seen here:

www.ukrainianchurchesofcanada.ca/history/highlights.html

Throughout this passage, I changed his spelling of "Kiev" to coordinate with my spelling in this book: "Kyiv".

egardless of whether Ukrainians are Greek, Roman or Ukrainian Catholic, Greek, Russian or Ukrainian Orthodox, they share a

strict inheritance that begins two centuries prior. As per legends, the Apostle St. Andrew voyaged [up the] Dnieper River in his central goal to the

Scythians (a group who involved huge spaces of what is presently current Ukraine.) On the slopes of what is today the city of Kyiv, St. Andrew anticipated that on those slopes would sometime emerge an impressive city with a large number temples. While the proof is deficient to demonstrate this legend, the 1621 Kyiv Synod passed a goal announcing it valid. Subsequently, for some Ukrainians, this legend involves confidence, paying little mind to any authoritative memorable proof.

While there is proof that to some extent little pockets of Christians resided in the Ukrainian countries all through the primary thousand years, Grand Princess Ohla (St. Ohla), who governed as official during her child's minority, was the principal Kievan ruler known with assurance to be a Christian. Writers discuss both her excellence and astuteness. Nonetheless, while she got political changes, she didn't endeavor strict changes for her people.

Arguably the main occasion throughout the entire existence of the religion of the [Eastern] Slav was the "Absolution of Rus". In around 988, Ohla's grandson, Grand Prince Volodymyr the Great (St. Volodymyr) changed over to Christianity, hitched the Byzantine sovereign's sister for dynastic reasons, and furthermore requested of his whole domain that all individuals convert to Christianity. Recorders express that Volodymyr guided Greek ministers to take tremendous quantities of Kievans into the stream and submerse them. Today in Canada, there are many temples named for Volodymyr and Olga [Ohla], including the metropolitan basilica for the Ukrainian Catholic Church in Canada and the house of God for the Western Diocese of the Ukrainian Orthodox Church of Canada.

When Volodymyr the Great passed on, his child Sviatopolk the Accursed killed his more youthful siblings, Boris and Hleb, for dynastic reasons and these two young fellows are perceived as the main Eastern Slavs that were celebrated as holy people. They are still extraordinarily revered by Eastern Slavs right up 'til the present time. Another sibling in the end thusly killed Sviatopolk. He is known as Grand Prince Yaroslav the Wise. He turned into the best leader of Kyiv and further fortified the foundation of the

Church all through the domain. Yaroslav was liable for building St. Sophia Cathedral in Kyiv, which right up 'til today is seemingly the best milestone in all of Ukraine. At the point when Yaroslav kicked the bucket in 1054,

Kievan Rus had arrived at its peak. In any case, fratricide again broke out among his children, and political strength was only occasionally enduring in Kievan Rus after Yaroslav's rule.

notwithstanding political issues, Kievan Rus fell into financial diminishment for different reasons. The last hit to Kievan Rus was the attack of Mongols in the thirteenth century. The Metropolitans of Kyiv deserted it and in the long run moved the see to Moscow. By the fourteenth century, the Lithuanians were pushing out the Mongols on one side, while the Muscovites battled them on the opposite side. The Lithuanians re-initiated the Metropolitan See of Kyiv and afterward there were metropolitans in both Moscow and Kyiv. As Moscow rose in power, it wiped out the last remnants of the Mongol burden by the fifteenth century. [...]

What had once been Kievan Rus was presently for the most part administered by the Russians in the east and by the Polish-Lithuanian Commonwealth in the west and there was additionally a crushed land in the south-focal region in which groups of Cossacks lived. After the Union of Lublin in 1569, all the Ukrainian countries vanquished by Lithuania went under the Crown of Poland. Accordingly, the vast majority of what is today Ukraine came to be in the political control of Roman Catholic Poland.

By the finish of the [sixteenth] century, the Ukrainian honorability had generally become ethnically Polanized and strictly Latinized, while Jesuits anxiously looked to change over the Orthodox public. The Ukrainian Orthodox Church [Kievan] became less fortunate and under consistent danger. With few aristocrats ready to secure them the Orthodox public started to shape fellowships at a grassroots level. Many individuals ran toward the south-focal [Ukraine] to join the Cossacks, as a method of liberating themselves from overwhelming overlords.

Eventually, a few Ukrainian diocesans made a bid to acquire equivalent status for their congregation by entering association with Rome. The Union of Brest (1596) was an arrangement between Ukrainian clerics, the Pope, and

the Polish Crown, wherein the Ukrainian Church would change devotion from Constantinople to Rome as a trade-off for ensures that the Eastern Rite would be secured by Rome and the Ukrainian diocesans would have equivalent status with Roman Catholic priests in Poland. […]

While the Ukrainian diocesans more likely than not been persuaded that the Union of Brest would be the solution to their concerns, they couldn't have envisioned that the Union would profoundly separate the Ukrainian public and dive them into hundreds of years of harsh battling. The Union had left loyal Orthodox individuals without priests, yet in 1620 Cossacks having a place with an Orthodox fellowship accompanied the Orthodox Patriarch of Jerusalem to Kyiv to sanctify another Orthodox pecking order. Severe battling broke out over the ownership of temples and religious communities. Hundreds kicked the bucket, including the exceptionally questionable Greek Catholic Archbishop, Josaphat Kuntsevych who was subsequently sanctified and is loved in Greek Catholic temples right up 'til the present time. The savagery turned out to be a lot for the Polish government and it interceded to perceive the Orthodox order and split the congregation property between the Greek Catholics and the Orthodox.

After the Partition of Poland in the eighteenth century, a large portion of what is today Ukraine went under control of the Russian Empire. Ukrainian Greek Catholics and Ukrainian Orthodox individuals were ultimately compelled to change over to the Russian Orthodox Church. A little piece of western Ukraine called Halychyna (Galicia) went under the control of the Austrian Empire and Ukrainians there stayed Greek Catholics generally, albeit some would have been affected to change over to the Roman Catholic Church. Also, the Austrians had taken a little area called Bukovyna from the Ottoman Empire and it contained a large number of Ukrainian individuals who had consistently been Orthodox on the grounds that that domain didn't go under the ward of the Union of Brest.

When the Soviets came to control, religion overall went under incredible abuse. At the point when eastern Poland was added by the Soviets, the Greek Catholic Church went under specific mistreatment as the

Soviets endeavored to snuff it out totally. This period, which finished with the fall of the Iron Curtain and the Soviet Union, was to be a severe time for Christians with an uncommon number of martyrs.

The ill will among Catholic and Orthodox Ukrainians erupted irregularly throughout the long term and it raised its head again in

Canada, especially during the interwar time of the 20th century. This ill will cooled during the post-war time frame and today, generally, Ukrainian wards have more significant things to stress over than the contrasts between being Ukrainian Catholic or Ukrainian Orthodox. For sure, the two places of worship currently get along well indeed in any case their proceeding differences.

Serhiy Chyrkov provided details regarding political parts of religion in contemporary Ukraine in an article distributed in the Euromaidan Press on April 28, 2016. The article is accessible here:

euromaidanpress.com/2016/04/28/how-the-moscow-patriarchate-is-making a-dissenter lavra-republic-in-kyiv/#arvlbdata

I replicated the stressed passages in the following segment from Chyrkov's piece:

On April 23, 2016, Petro Poroshenko welcomed delegates from the All-Ukrainian Council of Churches and Religious Organizations to his office […] not long before Easter.

"Under the states of cross breed war, when Ukraine is opposing the furnished hostility of the adjoining state, our foes are endeavoring to exploit the strict element for their own advantages," Poroshenko said. "The foe tries to part our nation and sabotage it from within."

[He] encouraged church pioneers to focus on the craving of Orthodox residents of Ukraine to have "a solitary public autocephalous church," as do most Orthodox nations. "A congregation joined through the Eucharist and supplication and authoritatively autonomous from different states," he added.

The official message was clearly focused on heads of the Ukrainian part of the Moscow Patriarchate. This Ukrainian Orthodox Church of the

Moscow Patriarchate has impeded the new Ukrainian government since Ukraine's Revolution of Dignity. At the point when Ukraine's congregation chiefs joined in a petition administration for harmony, the Ukraine Orthodox Church, Moscow branch, (UOCm) declined to join.

UOCm Bishop Pavlo (Petro Lebid) is the legislative head of the Kyiv

Pechersk Lavra (Monastery of the Caves). He lives in extravagance on a home close to Kyiv in a way of life like Ukraine's past president, Victor Yanukovych, who, as a manikin of Putin, escaped to Moscow during individuals' Revolution of Dignity, Maidan, in 2014.

The [UOCm] peril [to Ukraine] lies somewhere else. The Bishop Pavlo has made a virtual "republic" on the region of the blessed religious community, which now and then looks like the regional manifestations of the Muscovites in the Donbas. A "republic" heavily influenced by one individual, where Ukrainian laws are diminished to the base. Individuals can evaporate here, secret poisonings can occur, death endeavors on insubordinate pioneers, which the late Metropolitan Volodymyr became as of late. There, at the order of the Lavra head or even with his immediate interest, hands of columnists are broken [and their gear smashed].

[…] Pavlo communicates recently recorded video dangers to individual adversaries […] all through Ukraine." When approved government authorities highlight infringement of the nation's laws, he replies, "I violated the law? All things considered, brilliance be to God," and shuts the entryway of his own "republic" behind him.

In Moscow, the Ukraine Orthodox Church, Moscow Patriarchate (UOCm), Metropolitan Onufriy "openly announces his craving to see a free Ukraine 'in a casket in white shoes' [according to the Euromaidan Press proofreader, this is a "Russian curse"]. Cleric Pavlo is the most terrible of the workers of the Moscow Patriarchate […]. [H]is autonomous Lavra "republic" is the biggest […] that adheres to directions from Moscow. […] [T]hese regional areas [receive] fortifications from Moscow. On April 16 [2016], Gundayev's Synod chose to dispatch 1450 Russian clerics and 700 seminarians to the chapels and religious communities of Ukraine. […] [Now] Putin's armed

officers will be supported by Gundayev's troopers and new floods of [Putin's] mixture war will turn over [my progenitors' soil].

Separation of chapel and state are found in free, progressed nations. In post-battling Soviet Russia, the congregation is viably a branch of Putin's administration. Most Ukrainians do need detachment of chapel from the state.

Not excessively far away in my hereditary town is the huge, old Ukrainian Orthodox Church went to by the vast majority of my family members for over a century. This congregation isn't related with the Russian Orthodox Church (ROC) or the Ukraine Orthodox Church based from Moscow (UOCm). As of late, Frozena discovered that the Russian-based Orthodox church (ROC) that she goes to is a branch of the Russian government. She was stunned to become familiar with certain ministers were Russian supporters, giving data and cash to help Putin. The littlest of towns currently comprehend Putin's relationship to the ROC and the UOCm. These are enthusiastic occasions for chapel participants.

Tsars, tyrants and Putin today have confiscated or contaminated a great many non-ROC places of worship in Ukraine. UOCm are heavily influenced by Putin, by means of his manikin Bishop Pavlo in Kyiv. Most locals basically acknowledged the robbery of their congregation, avoiding the chance cause trouble. Townspeople since Perebudova have developed new holy places as indicated by their religion. One model is the new church in Ispas, twenty minutes south of Banyliv, where Doreen and I gave. The congregation seniors set our commitment in their affirmation book on page 100. A large number of my Ukrainian family members, particularly the Vatrich family drove and upheld the congregation construction.

In 1994, Ivan Vatrich drove us to the close by Anna Horade Shrine, where a supernatural occurrence is said to have happened in the fourteenth century. Legend says the Turks, endeavoring to catch Anna, were impeded when the bluff imploded and gulped Anna, leaving behind just a lock of her hair. This altar was kept up with on the site for travelers to visit for many years. At the point when we showed up at the congregation; nobody was there. Ivan, acquainted with the site, driven us to the sanctuary at the edge of the slope. Anna's hair and arranged archives were shown in a glass-shrouded case. A topped rooftop shielded the sanctuary. An edge of the glass was missing and I came to in contacting the coarse silver hair.

Fifteen years after the fact, Doreen and I returned to the site. An enormous multi-million-dollar ROC currently lingered before us. The design ruled the scene. A few inhabitant nuns in their teenagers with dark strict robes attempted to obstruct us from going behind the congregation to the site of Anna's holy place. We burst on. The place of worship rooftop was missing, and not very many of the relics we saw before remained. The place of worship was deliberately passed on to the components to before long be destroyed.

Today, lovers and sightseers from all over wonder about the congregation's lavishness. Church authorities guarantee assets to construct were from an unknown Russian benefactor. Frozena's grandson was as of late wedded at the congregation. I'm certain it was a glad second for her. She is a Moisey and like numerous Ukrainians has become mindful of rebellious activities by the Russian based temples. Pitiful Ukrainian gifts are supporting Putin, the viable top of the ROC and the UOCm.

aily, news fills the wireless transmissions, depicting exhaustively the passing of Ukrainian troopers on Ukrainian soil. A large number of those killed are neighbors, and passionate town memorial service parades regarding the dead are excessively normal. Roads are fixed with grievers on their knees, their heads twisted in despondency. Parishioners and all strict gatherings are beginning to scrutinize their help and resilience of the Russian based places of worship. They realize Putin's warriors and his Russian-supported dissidents are the killers.

Canada has a couple of ROC places of worship, all under a definitive control of Putin. The main Russian Orthodox Church (ROC) administration in Canada was at Wostok, Alberta, on July 18, 1897. It is found roughly twenty kilometers from my extraordinary granddad's estate ranch. That July, Theodore Nemirsky reached Bishop Nicholas of the ROC Mission in San Francisco, mentioning a cleric for strict administrations for the space. A reverend and minister voyaged in excess of 1,600 kilometers via train to Edmonton, and by cart to the Nemirsky ranch. There under an open sky, a help was held. Theodore Nemirsky's grandson and my dad John Moisey were awesome of companions. My dad, not long before his passing, gave me a five-centimeter-thick record of Nemirsky archives.

Galicia and Bukovina Ukrainians were quick to leave Ukraine, beginning in 1891. The reasonable larger part were Greek Orthodox Catholics, who preferred houses of worship of their own strict request. Extraordinary granddad Stefan Moisey and his children Nikolai and Olexsa joined neighbors and developed a congregation at Shandro, Alberta, in 1901. Their names are perceived with others on a plaque as the first developers. It is said that Stefan likewise helped develop the congregation in Banyliv.

The Shandro, Alberta church is a conventional wooden Bukovinian "three sided" of a three-segmented plan with rakish rooftops and peaks, topped by three little onion-molded vaults. It has a ringer tower. The burial ground is situated on a similar property, where Wasylena and Stefan Moisey's grave is handily situated as it has the biggest tombstone. Their little girl, Anna Rose Moisey and spouse Bill Caunt's remains are covered at the foot of the grave. It is set apart by plate-sized, red-rock stones, portraying a wild rose, the flower seal of Alberta. Stefan Rosichuk, who could neither read nor compose, from memory drove the plan and carpentry of the church.

The historical backdrop of the Shandro, Alberta Church is all around reported by Anna Navalkowsky (mother is Mary Moisey), in the magazine Alberta History, fall 1982. In 1903, these first region pilgrims begged Bukovina Metropolitan Repta of the Greek-Orthdox Church (situated in Chernivtsi) to send a minister for their nearly finished church. Repta reacted that he had a deficiency of clerics, suggesting they demand a minister from the Russian Orthodox Mission in San Francisco, guaranteeing them the Orthodox confidence was something very similar in all countries.

On August 28, 1979, the Shandro gathering commended their seventy-fifth commemoration of their congregation, which is presently an Alberta noteworthy site. In 2017, I am dubious who a definitive top of the Shandro Church is. In 1904, a couple of Moisey families are recorded as parishioners. This congregation is found fourteen kilometers N.E. of my incredible grandparents' Moisey ranch, the other way from the Wostock Church.

Today, the Russian Orthodox Church (ROC) in Canada is going by an Edmonton ecclesiastical overseer under the locale of the Moscow Patriarchate. I can't help thinking about what data and accounts the ROC in Canada adds to their definitive chief Putin. In Ukraine, this crucial exchange has been uncovered. Most Canadians of Ukrainian drop don't know about the Church-Putin association. In Ukraine, on April 2016, when the ROC would not join in ecumenical petitions for Peace in Ukraine, it was justifiable as Putin is the preeminent master of the ROC. He would rather not petition God for harmony. He needs Ukraine. Under Putin, the State is top of the Church. The ROC in Canada, settled in Edmonton, didn't and doesn't petition God for harmony in Ukraine all things considered. It is clear they take walking orders from Putin without question.

My mom, Nell Moisey, went to Edmonton's St. Barbara's ROC. Mother, subsequent to visiting Ukraine, was stunned to learn direct of Putin's killings in Ukraine. Mother deserted St. Barbara Church quickly before her demise. She was pleased to leave the ROC and spread the word of Putin's control.

anyliv Kolhosp and Farming

In 2017 by far most of ranchers have left the Kolhosp framework. Some lease enormous areas of the previous, useless aggregate homesteads and are creating great benefits. Most Kolhosp previous individuals lease more modest bundles and are inferring a preferred way of life over when in the Kolhosp. The land presently is all around focused on and useful. The Soviet horticultural framework was an outright disappointment, making pointless misery and demise millions.

In 2017, Putin keeps endeavoring dinosaur strategies in Eastern Ukraine that he utilized in Georgia and other close by nations. His hunger for reestablishing the previous Soviet framework is unquenchable. He advances his own depository by denying provincial Russians and adding portions of neighboring nations. It doesn't trouble him to shed honest blood. He is abhorrent, obliterating huge number of lives and making a great many refugees.

In Ukraine, Putin has experienced opposition that won't ever submit to his oppressive every day activities. He has experienced Wolves, while anticipating Dogs. Most Ukrainians today, and practically all young, realize it is "Smarter to Die a Wolf than to Live the Life of a Dog". Ukraine's new purposeful publicity machine is presently opened max speed. Combined with current computerized interchanges, they will crush down the repressor Putin. In excess of 1,000 years of beating intrusions has delivered a versatile populace. Like the boxing champion Klitschko siblings, Ukraine realizes how to deal with punches and convey the knockout. Ukraine has done this more frequently than the Klitschkos have won in the ring. Forceful Putin continues tormenting Ukraine, however he is fizzling. He will be taken out, to the cheering hordes of the worldwide local area, including the great people of Russia, who in 2017 should remain quiet or be prosecuted.

Son of a Kholhosp Member

On one of our first visits, Ivan Moisey, a Banyliv understudy, took me to his secondary school PC room. He gladly organized the PC's eight-inch measurement floppy-plate. This is only an underlying activity to begin the PC. Brilliant and hopeful, Ivan began giving PC examples in Banyliv with three resigned PCs gave from our Lingcomp Computer and English school in Vyzhnytsia. Ivan in the long run sold the PCs and inclined toward cultivating, where today he and his family are flourishing ranchers. In my September 2014 visit to his and his close by father's ranch, Ivan, sister Svetlana and their delightful youngsters, covered with field dust, immediately participated for lunch. The young men quickly devoured the scrumptious supper arranged by productive grandma Maria and girl Svetlana. This very useful family joined the most recent innovations and ranch hardware they can bear. I detected the positive thinking about their monetary future, rather than my first gathering in 1994 at this equivalent table, when the greatest wish was to procure a workhorse and expectation for old fashioned days.

Farming was a characteristic movement for the majority of the around 400 Banyliv Kolhosp families, who battled with old cultivating rehearses. Visiting this Kolhosp in 1994 with welder Wasyl Paraniuk, I was stunned to see weather beaten consolidates and other ranch gear. Wasyl was given a solitary welding bar every day to fix the gear. He told me, the common principle was for the Kolhosp to have 400 cows and 400 pigs, alongside other problematic rules. Today, the normal Canadian and American ranch family work 400 hectares of grain, or own 400 dairy cattle or 4,000 pigs. Ukrainians will ultimately be serious, and they are building it on a sound establishment to turn out to be again known as the bread container of Europe. I anticipate the Ivan Moisey family will build their abundance to contend with huge western side of the equator ranches. Their main potential deterrent is the danger from the Russian bear, dictator Putin.

The accompanying showed up in the "Emergency in Ukraine: Daily

Briefing – 14 October 2016, 3PM Kyiv Time" accessible on the site of the Ukrainian

Canadian Congress at the accompanying address:

www.ucc.ca/2016/10/14/crisis-in-ukraine-daily-briefing-14-october-2016-3-pm-kyiv-time/

The piece depends on an October 13, 2016 Bloomberg article called "That Boom You Hear Is Ukraine's Agriculture." Those with a membership to Bloomberg can see the full report at

www.bloomberg.com/news/articles/2016-10-14/that-boom-you-hear-is-ukraine-s-agriculture

Bloomberg revealed, "Ukraine sold $7.6 billion of mass ranch items worldwide in 2015, quintupling its income from 10 years sooner and fixing Russia, its nearest rival on world business sectors. By the mid-2020s, 'Ukraine will be no. 3 after the US and Brazil,' in food creation around the world, says Martin Schuldt, the top agent in Ukraine for Cargill, the world's biggest grain broker. [Cargill] is putting $100 million in another grain terminal in Ukraine. Bunge, the world's greatest soy processor, opened a port [in 2016] at a function with Ukrainian President Poroshenko.[…] [In 2017] [a]bout 1 in each 6 sections of land of horticultural land in Ukraine isn't being cultivated. Of land underway, John Shmorhun [CEO of AgroGeneration] says just a quarter is arriving at yields fair and square of those in the created world. in light of lower-quality seeds, manures, and gear. 'It's an enormous potential gain. It's amazing,' he says. [President] Poroshenko upholds making a business opportunity for farmland, yet the Parliament consistently expands the prohibition on selling agrarian property. Prior in October, officials upheld a bill delaying the ban through 2018, yet the president still can't seem to sign it. The dread is that huge Ukrainian organizations and unfamiliar financial backers will eat up the land and dislodge little ranchers. […] Despite the troubles, Ukraine's rise as a worldwide agro force to be reckoned with might be a sure thing for a basic explanation: the world necessities more food, and Ukraine can create it."

Holodomor

The accompanying segment is excerpted from the Ukrainian Canadian Congress

(UCC) President Paul Grod's Statement on the 82nd Anniversary of the Holodomor, conveyed November 2015 in Kyiv. The full assertion can be seen at: www.ucc.ca/2015/11/28/ucc-presidents-proclamation on-the-82nd-commemoration of-the-holodomor/The UCC can be visited online at www.ucc.ca; followed on Twitter at @ukrcancongress; or on Facebook at www.facebook.com/ukrcancongress.

his week we recall and recognize the awfulness of the Holodomor where incalculable great many men, ladies and youngsters were pointlessly killed through starvation by the socialist system of Joseph Stalin. Today the Holodomor stays a unimaginably significant and important basic freedoms story.

In attempting to get decimation, I have regularly wondered why did despots like Joseph Stalin or Adolph Hitler try to obliterate a whole group and for what reason would endless colleagues do their offering? And
– for what reason is this applicable to us today? It appears so long ago.

Unfortunately, over 80 years after the fact, the Holodomor has more importance to individuals of Ukraine and the world than it has at any point had. At a new Annual Toronto Ukrainian Famine Lecture, Pulitzer prize champ Anne Applebaum examined how Stalin found in Ukraine an existential danger, as Putin finds in Ukraine today. Stalin dispatched his attack on Ukraine since he realized that Ukraine was impervious to brought together standard, that Ukrainians were appended to their territory and their customs, and that Ukrainians could challenge Bolshevism and even reason it to fall. Today Russia's President Vladimir Putin fears the connection of Ukrainians to thoughts of opportunity, vote based system, and western qualities like basic freedoms. Indeed Putin's system as did Stalin's, pessimistically keeps the very presence from getting a different Ukrainian individuals. As Anne Applebaum said in her talk, "Assuming Stalin expected that Ukrainian patriotism could cut down the Soviet system, Putin fears that Ukraine's model could cut down his own system, an advanced despotic kleptocracy."

Ukraine today is under military, monetary and political assault by the Putin system, similar as it was under Stalin north of 80 years prior. There is no polite conflict nor was there ever any rebel development in eastern

Ukraine. This is struggle, which has brought about more than 8,000 daeths in the beyond two years [10,000 passings to 2017], is totally designed, coordinated and run by Putin's system and is driven by a malicious promulgation war.

The harmony and opportunity cherishing individuals of the world should strongly and effectively stand up together against this incredible danger to worldwide harmony and security.

Ukrainians have taken in their illustration from the Holodomor and won't turn over to the Putin's endeavor to destroy the Ukrainian country. All over the planet Ukrainian people group are working in their individual nations to acquire support for the situation of the Ukrainian individuals [who] want just to live in a country that is liberated from unfamiliar hostility and regards the human nobility of its people.

Now] we see the present predicament of the Ukrainian individuals through the verifiable focal point of the Holodomor. Numerous drives are in progress in Canada, including the new dispatch of the National Holodomor Awareness Tour, an inventive portable homeroom; the Memorial to Victims of Communism planned to be underlying Parliamentary Precinct of Ottawa; and numerous significant showing devices are accessible, for example, the exceptionally moving web-based video tributes of Holodomor survivors at www.holodomorsurvivors.com.

Teaching the basic liberties illustration from the Holodomor will assist with guaranteeing we stay watchful and able to stop cutting edge dictators like Vladimir Putin who today has released a conflict to annihilate the Ukrainian people.

May God rouse us to carry out altruistic things, and may the memory of the casualties of the Holodomor be everlasting — Вічная Їм Пам'ять".

n 2017, Canadian film chief George Mendeluk debuted the Holodomor film "Harsh Harvest." It is an unquestionable requirement film to encounter the mercilessness vouched for Doreen and me by Moisey overcomers of the Ukraine Holodomor. Video tributes from real Holodomor survivors can be seen at www.holodomorsurvivors.ca/Survivors.html

Canada 150 Years Old

hundred and fifty years prior, Canada had a populace of around 3,000,000, the vast majority of whom lived in a little space of Central Canada. A hundred and a quarter century prior, the initial not many Ukrainians came to Canada and got comfortable the uninhabited shrub grounds of Alberta. After fourteen years in 1905, Alberta turned into an area. Today in 2017, Alberta is by a long shot the biggest benefactor of cash to adjust the way of life in other Canadian provinces.

anada, a youthful nation, has perhaps the best quality of living. Ukraine is an old nation and, by the last long stretches of the Soviet Union, had an unfortunate way of life despite the fact that Ukraine is wealthy in assets, with dedicated and exceptionally taught people.

ow did quick thriving and harmony become conceivable in Canada? The vast majority of Canada's populace, involved "hungry" settlers, shown up from many nations before the 20th century and basically needed to work and raise their families. They wanted harmony and opportunity. What they procured had a place with them.

In the main third of Canada's 150 years as a country; workers in Western Canada were left to get by and flourish with their own. There were next to zero states and hardly any landowners in their lives. Western Canada, where most Ukrainians settled, needed police, prisons, schools, streets or fundamental framework. The people were left alone and set up a strong base to assist with making one of the most prosperous nations on planet earth.

In 2017, new workers' longings are similarly as prior migrants' fantasies, yet the present outsiders are not as fortunate. They have property managers, smothering guidelines and a self-serving government, pampering to all their longings. Canada's administration of today, with its substitutes and experts, erroneously accept they realize what is best for new immigrants.

There is no question Ukraine is currently shedding the burden of unfamiliar, severe tyrants, and is attempting to eliminate debasement. Ukraine is a fantastic model for its neighbors, including Russia, to show how it rose from a low expectation for everyday comforts by advancing toward independence from oppression.

Putin would be a worldwide legend of the twenty-first century in case he shed his pride and took cues from Ukraine. Does Putin have the gastrointestinal determination to change? It is conceivable, yet such a change would take a really incredible man. He has the capacity and power, and with hints from past-President Gorbachev, he would turn into a genuine saint. Putin can do it. I wish him karma.

Otpor

Steve York coordinated Orange Revolution, a 2007 full length narrative on the huge fights following the Ukrainian official decisions in 2004. It won a few honors from film celebrations, and has screened at numerous renowned celebrations since its delivery. The film's makers, the organization York Zimmerman organization, have even delivered a review guide, trusting that the film will be utilized in schools. The accompanying segment has been duplicated from the review guide, which can be seen in full at: www.orangerevolutionmovie.com/pdf/orange-transformation study-guide.pdf

The Orange Revolution was the third time in only four years that a peaceful common opposition development crushed bad or dictator systems in focal Europe. The previously was in 2000 when Slobodan Milosevic was overturned in Serbia. Next was Georgia's "Rose Revolution" in 2003 which eliminated Eduard Shevardnadze from power. In every one of the three nations, the sparkle was a fake political race [similar to that in ongoing Russian history] followed by monstrous common resistance.

Each of these accounts included a disliked pioneer, a huge and efficient resistance, and a framework to recognize and quickly announce vote extortion all through the country. Understudy and youth obstruction bunches likewise played a critical, albeit not indistinguishable, job. Each of the three resistance developments were affected and roused by effective peaceful battles of the 1980s – the Solidarity worker's organization development in Poland, the Velvet Revolution in Czechoslovakia, and "Individuals Power" development which crushed Philippine tyrant Ferdinand Marcos.

Many political specialists believe these scenes to be "majority rule forward leaps," whose shared objectives were free and reasonable elections,

responsive and straightforward popularity based establishments, and adherence to law and order, regard for common liberties, a free media, and legal independence.

In Serbia, resistance ideological groups quarreled and battled among themselves for no less than 10 years, at long last joining behind a solitary contender to run against Milosevic in 2000. En route, Serbian youth, driven by college understudies, gained authoritative and key abilities over a time of quite a while, which drove them to establish Otpor! (the Serbian word for opposition), a development which set up branches in north of 70 urban communities and towns. Known for their gripped clench hand image, splash painted on dividers, and imprinted on shirts, banners, and stickers, the gathering activated youngsters, yet the entire populace. Depending on humor, disparagement, and exciting music, Otpor individuals assisted individuals with conquering dread, the way to building investment. Numerous youngsters were captured, which assembled their beforehand unresponsive guardians. Otpor was additionally successful in sabotaging police and security power unwaveringness to the system. A large number of its methods were taken on by youth opposition bunches in Georgia, Ukraine, and different nations, where Otpor activists in some cases went about as counsels and trainers.

Otpor's techniques and strategies couldn't just be replicated by different developments, however the simple reality that Milosevic, a man broadly accepted to control all regular wellsprings of force, was taken out by a common obstruction development without turning to savagery, propelled and engaged others. In Georgia, the Kmara ("Enough") development was demonstrated on Otpor; in Ukraine, the development was called Pora! ("It's time!"). By late 2004, the expression "shading upheaval" had entered the famous jargon, and potential for an efficient peaceful development to prevail against a settled in tyrant had been broadly acknowledged. Lebanon encountered the Cedar Revolution; Kyrgyzstan, the Tulip Revolution; Iran, the Green Revolution. While none of these brought the indisputable or palatable advancement accomplished in Serbia, Georgia or Ukraine, peaceful developments are at the front line of acquiring change the present reality. [Are there comparative newborn child developments in Russia? Indeed there are.] [...]

In only months, the Orange Revolution appeared to have changed Ukraine irreversibly. Appointive change brought free and reasonable decisions; an exuberant and autonomous media arose, and established change brought a better harmony among leader and administrative power. These accomplishments were before long eclipsed by close to home power battles, and the proceeding with control of parliament by the oligarchs. By late 2005, the Orange alliance had fragmented. Yulia Tymoshenko, who had been a Yushchenko partner during the upset, turned into his opponent. He excused her as top state leader in September 2005; she was prevailed by Viktor Yanukovych for a considerable length of time. The Orange camp rejoined to win parliamentary decisions in 2007, which brought Tymoshenko back as prime minister.

Disappointed by Yushchenko's powerless administration, Ukrainians have become negative with regards to legislative issues. A staggering financial slump in 2008 added to the sadness. Toward the finish of his official term in late 2009, Yushchenko's notoriety slipped underneath 5%, leaving Tymoshenko and Yanukovych as the main suitable possibility to succeed him in 2010. One might say that ridiculous assumptions ensured the Orange Revolution would frustrate its supporters, yet powerless authority, a captivated country, determined defilement, and Russian endeavors to reassert provincial incomparability have played their parts.

kraine's vote based change stays deficient, however since the Orange Revolution, no races have been taken, and no writers have been killed by the state. While the objectives of the individuals who produced the upset and persevered through the cold and snow presently can't seem to be reflected in strategy, the political framework and the principles by which political choices are made have been changed - - to one that, notwithstanding its imperfections, is more equitable and conscious of law and order than it was under previous Kuchma's rule.

Pora

The accompanying comes from something very similar "Study Guide" accessible at the site of the Orange Revolution movie.

Pora! (Now is the right time!), showed up in late 2002, as a young association demonstrated freely on the understudy bunches which assumed noticeable parts in the loss of Milosevic in Serbia. […] Pora was truly two separate associations, referred to casually as Black Pora and Yellow Pora for the shades of their flags, stickers, and flyers. In spite of some contention, they cooperated, particularly in late 2004. Pora was less than [Serbia's] Otpor, not as firmly coordinated, and could just gauge its enrollment – at around 10,000. Many were understudies, and many had been dynamic in the Ukraine Without Kuchma development of 2001. Starting in 2003, Pora activists talked with, and got preparing from, veterans of the Otpor and Kmara gatherings. Pora activists were called psychological militants and lawbreakers by their administration, and they were now and again genuinely assaulted. They were quick to raise tents in Maidan, the evening of the deceitful spillover political race, and they assumed a vital part in getting sorted out and keeping control for the makeshift camps and groups on Maidan all through the revolution.

Electronic Media in Ukraine: Temnyky is the name given to secret email messages sent every day by Ukraine's official organization to TV channels, letting them know what to report, how to report it, and what to disregard. This arrangement of media oversight was initiated in 2002 by Russian political experts utilized by then-President Kuchma. During the 2004 political race, TV news programs were requested to depict the president, the supportive of official gatherings, and Viktor Yanukovych in a positive light, to give negligible inclusion to the Yushchenko lobby, and to dishonor him sooner rather than later. In covering Yushchenko's first mission rally, one temnyk requested: "... don't show wide shots of the assembly and shots of the group; show just gatherings of smashed individuals with socially improper, degenerate behavior."

Ukraine's TV stations: UT1 is the state-controlled telecaster. 1+1 and Inter are networks possessed by Viktor Medvedchuk, an oligarch who headed President Kuchma's official organization in 2002-2004. Three other TV channels are possessed by Kuchma's child in-law, Viktor Pinchuk: STB, ICTV, and Novy Kanal. During the 2004 official mission, this multitude of stations showed a solid predisposition towards Yanukovych. Just two stations created adjusted news. The first

was Channel 5, a little station with a more fragile sign, covering just around 15% of the country, with no inclusion at all in Eastern Ukraine. Channel 5 is claimed by Petro Poroshenko, an oligarch cordial to Yushchenko. Period TV gave comparative inclusion, yet was distinctly broadcasting live for parts of the day, and not in the evening. After the appointive extortion was uncovered, columnists and the news staff at UT1 and 1+1 undermined a strike to fight control. They pronounced to the executives, "Possibly you let us broadcast what's going on in the nation, or we as a whole leave." Management surrendered, and at 9pm they conveyed the primary uncensored news reports.

Russian pioneers [ie: Putin] considered the 2004 political race to be a defining moment: Would Ukraine take a favorable to Russian or a supportive of Western bearing after Kuchma? A year prior to the political decision, they [Putin] chose to help the applicant picked by Kuchma. Costly Russian political guides and twist specialists dealt with the Yanukovych lobby, which likewise got cash commitments from the Kremlin. The all out total isn't known. Fifty million is the least gauge; the sum most generally refered to is $300 million. Russian political experts utilized techniques normal in Russian races remembering putting huge strain to decide in favor of Yanukovych for state workers, beneficiaries, and others whose business relies upon the state. They fostered a supportive of Yanukovych promoting rush, which ran noticeably in Russia, focused on the million qualified Ukrainian citizens living there. Russian President Vladimir Putin by and by visited Ukraine to embrace Yanukovych. Afterward, Putin praised Yanukovych on his triumph multiple times before the votes had even been counted. Through and through, the Russian job put on a show of being ponderous, a straightforward endeavor to re-force Russian impact in Ukraine. A few investigators accept the Russian endeavors hurt Yanukovych. Russian pioneers were stunned and shocked by the enormous fights in Ukraine. Accordingly, they have given a high need to forestalling comparative "shading upheavals" in Russia or different nations. [...]

hen the Soviet Union broke down in 1991, Ukraine became autonomous. Inside a year, previous Soviet authorities and ex-directors of state-possessed endeavors arose as "oligarchs," buying former

state organizations like weighty industry, coal mineshafts, and news sources, at deal costs. These short-term moguls, who possessed colossal organizations and aggregates, delighted in close binds with the president and controlled huge groups in parliament. Their political associations permitted them to win such advantages as territorial syndications, charge exceptions, appropriations, and exchange preferences.

espite incidental enemy of debasement programs, the oligarchs stay key power communities in Ukraine. As head of the state (2000-01), Viktor Yushchenko pulled out large numbers of the duty exclusions and advantages appreciated by the oligarchs, while turning Ukraine's shortage to an excess and developing the economy interestingly since autonomy. In 2002, President Kuchma supplanted his bureau with clergymen attracted completely from the oligarchic groups parliament. In the situation of top state leader, Viktor Yushchenko was out, and Viktor Yanukovych was in.

As the official political race drew nearer in 2004, the oligarchs were predominant – yet not brought together. Among the in excess of twenty official applicants, just two were valid competitors: Yushchenko, the reformer, and Yanukovych, the up-and-comer of the oligarchs and the state of affairs. To be reasonable, Yushchenko partook in the help of certain oligarchs as well, however Yanukovych enjoyed a novel benefit. He was embraced by the officeholder president and upheld by the whole managerial part of government. He was likewise upheld by Russia.

Maidan and Wasyl Мойсей (Moisey) renew Nationalism

The Maidan uprising of February 2014 came about when Ukraine's President Yanukovych singularly, and without a second to spare, didn't sign a financial European Union arrangement. He all the while announced nearer attaches with Russia. Maidan was a famous public objection, confronting an all around settled in Yanukovych police framework to secure him, which thusly oversaw city and city police powers. Blood started to stream as Yanukovych's exceptional Russian-prepared marksmen started taking out demonstrators in the focal square of Kyiv.

The fifth dissident to be killed by a marksman was Wasyl Moisey, a far off relative of mine. The shooting was caught on film and included in the narrative "Winter on Fire". You can hear Wasyl's name got down on twice as he lay kicking the bucket. This youthful Moisey kid said before he passed on, "Preferable to Die a Wolf over to Live the Life of a Dog." His entombment and that of others of the "Glorious 100" attracted the biggest participation to memorial services to at any point happen in Ukraine.

Yanukovych was immediately presented to the world; his rich property and individual possessions in the billions of dollars were uncovered. He avoided for Donetsk and was immediately accompanied with regards to the country by Russians to Moscow. It was February 2014, and presently Putin provided the order to the military to assume responsibility for Crimea. Putin recognized this on the Russian government-possessed media during the second seven day stretch of March 2015. During this time, Russian troublemakers associated with mixing starting turmoil in Georgia and Northern Moldavia were additionally positioned in Donbas. Photographs of a portion of these Russian thugs recently showed up in media inclusion while creating problems in three different nations and showed up routinely in Donbas in 2014. In 2016, Putin actually asserted Russia didn't have anything to do with the issues in Eastern Ukraine, which had by then guaranteed in excess of 6,000 Ukrainian lives. In 2015 Yanukovych's abundance was assessed by Forbes to be in excess of a billion dollars, and Putin's at $40 billion. Putin's abundance in 2016 was supposed to be $200 billion. Where is his own abundance coming from?

2017 Ukraine Crisis Created by Putin

The accompanying timetable is taken from a BBC article about a narrative film made by Andrei Kondrashov, "a writer with state-run channel Rossiya-1", which offers the Russian view on how Crimea was attached. Kondrashov's film, called Crimea. The Way Home showed up on Russian TV and YouTube on 15 March 2015. The BBC article can be seen at: www.bbc.com/news/world-europe-31796226

- *22 February, [2014] former Ukrainian President Viktor Yanukovych flees [Kyiv] after violent protests*

- *23 February, Russian President Vladimir Putin plans to rescue Mr. Yanukovych and annex Crimea*

   24

   25

- *27 February, pro-Russian gunmen seize Crimea's Parliament and other key buildings*

- *28 February, unidentified soldiers in combat fatigues occupy two airports in Crimea*

- *1 March, Russian Parliament approves Mr. Putin's request to use force in Ukraine*

- *16 March, 97% of voters in [a Russian-sponsored referendum in] Crimea agree to join Russia*

- *18 March, Mr Putin signs a bill absorbing Crimea into the Russian Federation*

All this was cultivated in 26 days by the unbelievably careful Putin. A similar course of events showed up in other BBC articles, including one dated March 15, 2015 portraying a portion of the subtleties that arose out of Kondrashov's narrative. Coming up next is taken from that article, which can be seen at: www.bbc.com/news/world-europe-31899680

The Ukrainian government, Western pioneers and NATO say there is obvious proof that Russia is assisting the separatists with weighty weapons and troopers. Autonomous specialists reverberation that allegation. Moscow denies it, demanding that any Russians presenting with the revolutionaries are "volunteers" [… doing a…] "great deed".

Full subtleties of Mr. Yanukovych's break from Ukraine are indistinct in spite of the fact that Mr. Putin discussed Russian endeavors to empty him and dangers against [Yanukovych's] life.

For us it turned out to be clear and we got data that there were plans for his catch, at the same time, ideally for the individuals who did the upset, additionally for his actual end," Mr. Putin says in the film. He said arrangements to extricate Mr. Yanukovych were made via land, ocean and air, saying "substantial assault rifles" were put in Donetsk "so as not to sit around idly talking." Russia's Interfax news office cited Putin as saying that saving the existence of Ukraine's previous chief and his family was a "great deed".

Ukraine and Russia on Different Paths

coming up next is taken from a February 24, 2015 article called "Isolated At Birth: Ukraine's and Russia's Divergent Paths," composed by Brian Whitmore, and which showed up on his blog The Power Vertical on the site of Radio Free Europe/Radio Liberty. The full article can be seen here:

www.rferl.org/a/separated-at-birth/26867185.html

[…] Two days in two nations over twenty years prior. Two days, nine months separated, set Russia and Ukraine on the fundamentally various directions that finished in the contention we are seeing today. As the Russia-Ukraine struggle delays, as we watch with anxiety as the Minsk-2 truce disintegrates, as Mariupol and perhaps Kharkiv prepare for dissenter attacks, it merits reviewing how and why these two nations showed up at the spot they are today.

he prompt reason for the current emergency, obviously, is Russia's assurance to keep Ukraine from coordinating with the West. Be that as it may, the fundamental reason can be found in the unique ways they took after 1991.

And those various courses are typified in two pivotal days in the early stages after the Soviet breakup.

[…] The primary day is October 4, 1993, when Russian President Boris Yeltsin settled his longstanding clash with Parliament by sending tanks and shelling it into submission.

At the time, it resembled a triumph for Yeltsin's group of reformers over a retrograde and traditionalist lawmaking body. Allies of Yeltsin called it one of those occasions when it is important to utilize biased means to accomplish liberal finishes. Yet, in actuality, it was post-Soviet Russia's unique sin.

he shelling of the Russian Parliament set up the perilous point of reference that political questions could be settled forcibly. The Russian administration transformed into an untouchable behemoth – one that Vladimir Putin would at last use to the fullest.

The leader weighty power upward, the unapproachable super administration and the embellishing pocket parliament also called the State Duma were the immediate aftereffect of the manner in which the 1993 emergency was settled. So is the way that law and order in Russia is a deception, best case scenario, reliably bested by a lot more seasoned rule: Might makes right.

"Throughout the previous 20 years, we've kept on utilizing similar techniques," Sergei Filatov, Yeltsin's head of staff at the hour of the emergency, told RFE/RL's Russian Service in October 2013, on the twentieth commemoration of the shelling.

"We endure that time and we ought to have taken in something from it, yet tragically we got the hang of nothing. We as a whole had that Soviet, magnificent attitude, where strength will in every case better take care of the issue, instead of dealings and compromise. Assuming we're truly going to turn into a majority rule society, we want to change our techniques for dealing with the nation and the strategies for connection among the authorities."

The Ukraine Alternative

Fast-forward to the accompanying summer - - July 10, 1994 - - in Ukraine.

n that boiling summer day, in the second round of Ukraine's first post-Soviet political decision, citizens dismissed officeholder President Leonid Kravchuk and chose his challenger, Leonid Kuchma.

And Kravchuk accomplished something amazing for the previous Soviet Union. He ventured down without episode and permitted Kuchma to take power.

The appointment of 1994 came directly following a political emergency in Ukraine that was like the one Yeltsin had looked in Russia.

Ukraine] was in a monetary breakdown and an incapacitating series of coal-diggers' strikes. Kravchuk was secured a severe debate with the Ukrainian parliament, the Verkhovna Rada. However, as opposed to Russia, the emergency in Ukraine was settled calmly with a consent to hold early official and parliamentary elections.

Initially the customary way of thinking about the 1994 political race was that it was a triumph for Moscow in light of the fact that Kuchma, who hailed from eastern Ukraine, was more amiable to Russia than Kravchuk.

But the point of reference that was set by a tranquil exchange of force ended up being more significant and seriously persevering.

It's significant that in the five official decisions Ukraine has held since freedom, the occupant or the officeholder's handpicked replacement has lost multiple times. Just a single occupant, Kuchma in 1999, won re-election.

By contrast, in Russia, the officeholder or the officeholder's picked replacement has won every one of the five official decisions since the Soviet Union separated. Plots to undermine and control the popularity based cycle - - like Yeltsin giving the Kremlin to Putin with his New Year's Eve renunciation in 1999 or the "projecting" move Putin and Dmitry Medvedev pulled off in 2011-12 - - have been the norm.

Study in Contrasts

Not just have Ukraine's races consistently been more aggressive than Russia's; its political and financial world class has consistently been more pluralistic.

On [a] Power Vertical Podcast, Sean Guillory of the University of Pittsburgh's Center for Russian and Eastern European Studies, noticed that "the subduing of the tip top in Russia instead of Ukraine" was a critical element in deciding the various ways the two nations followed since independence.

In Russia, "the state stepped in and decimated the political force of the oligarchs in the mid 2000s and set Putin up as the focal point of the state framework. Every one of them consented to have a strongman in control", Guillory said. "We didn't have this in Ukraine. No one proved to be the best in Ukrainian first class legislative issues. It was consistently a challenge among different oligarchs situated in different pieces of the country".

t was the shelling of the Russian Parliament in 1993 and its political repercussions that set up for Putin's tyrant rule. "The

making of an extremely amazing administration is the thing that permitted this to occur", Guillory said.

And maybe above all, from the 1994 political decision and ahead, Ukraine's considerate society has consistently been more grounded and more autonomous than its Russian counterpart.

In Ukraine, free urban gatherings and NGOs flourished, prospered, and duplicated and eventually turned into an awe-inspiring phenomenon in the country's politics.

In Russia, they were on the other hand minimized, co-picked, and controlled by the specialists, or irritated out of presence. They have been known as a fifth segment and marked as unfamiliar agents.

ltimately, Ukraine's considerate society turned into the Third Force as Kyiv's and Moscow's political ways separated and the Kremlin plotted and struggled to keep its neighbor in its political orbit.

Irreconcilable Differences

So any reasonable person would agree that since the Soviet breakdown, Ukraine has logically become more equitable. Russia, less so.

But Ukraine's advancement starting around 1991 has been a long way from awesome. Debasement was uncontrolled and oligarchs dominated. Be that as it may, by the late spring of 2013, Ukraine's inexorably sure respectful society needed something better. Also the initial move toward something better was Ukraine consenting to an affiliation arrangement with the European Union.

"Assuming that you are an understudy or an entrepreneur in Ukraine, you comprehend Europe in the accompanying way: Europe is important for our set of experiences, and Europe today implies the European Union. What's more the European Union means regulatory consistency and law and order," Yale University history specialist Timothy Snyder said in a new lecture.

Snyder added that the Euromaidan uprising was "a working class unrest" to move the country "from oligarchic pluralism to genuine pluralism".

What made this definitive was that top oligarchs like Rinat Akhmetov

and Ihor Kolomoysky determined that they had a superior shot at securing their abundance in an European-style framework than in a Ukraine that was basically a province of Russia.

And when that occurred, the dissimilar ways that Ukraine and Russia had taken starting around 1991 became hostile differences.

Writing in […] Foreign Affairs, Princeton University antiquarian Stephen Kotkin takes note of that Ukraine is "a country that is too enormous and autonomous for Russia to gobble up", while "Russia is a harmed at this point still imposing incredible power whose rulers can't be threatened into permitting Ukraine to enter the Western circle. Consequently the standoff."

Spontaneous Revolution: Maidan

Nov. 22, 2013 a jam-packed makeshift camp involved Maidan Square makeshift camp where an evening execution was arranged. The accompanying area is likewise from the Orange Revolution film's "Study Guide":

way from Maidan, a less noticeable fight was being battled. Legal counselors for Yushchenko and his ideological group recorded north of 100 legal disputes refering to political decision inconsistencies. 300 legal counselors worked without pay to set up the legitimate cases. The key activity was at Ukraine's Supreme Court where the tension of mass activity and law and order joined. Eventually, reviews Mykola Katerynchuk, the legal advisor who administered the cases, "We demonstrated that the aftereffects of the political race second round were distorted, and uncovered the techniques and members in these misrepresentations. The adjudicators understood that individuals in the roads may attempt to hold onto power all of a sudden, and this might have incited them to settle on their choice rapidly – in seven days. Since the Supreme Court played out its notable job, a brutal situation was stayed away from. It changed the upheaval from an emergency of wrongness into one of lawfulness. It legitimized a change from misrepresentation to the foundation of vote based decisions. It was a decision that leaned toward government officials, leaned toward citizens, and leaned toward the popularity based eventual fate of Ukraine. Also this one case washed away all the filthy cash and the force of those oligarchs."

An individual from the mission staff who coordinated the occasions on Maidan clarified, "I envisioned this mission as a conflict. I was unable to consider it some other way, and we were unable to coordinate it some other way. We would need to work in a severe discipline, if not it would be difficult to win".

he [illegitimate] system expected to be that following a couple of days the bone chilling temperatures would constrain nonconformists to return home. In any case, as one of the coordinators noticed, "These individuals were truly ready to do anything, to give everything, to be freed of this criminal government." Night subsequent to freezing night, they stayed.

To deal with the mass of individuals in the makeshift camps, in Maidan, and around the Parliament and Presidential organization structures, severe guidelines were set up. Individuals from Pora!, the young opposition association, were the masters. Cocktails and medications were restricted in the tent camps. Junk was pulled away day by day. Pora volunteers controlled the designated spots, watched the settlements, and maintained control. […]

All of Ukraine's senior legislators were conceived, instructed, and started their vocations when Ukraine was a Soviet republic. Viktor Yushchenko [was conceived in] 1954, in northeastern Ukraine. By 1991, when Ukraine became autonomous, Yushchenko had acquired degrees in financial matters and finance, and set up a good foundation for himself as a regarded business analyst, utilized by neighborhood, provincial, and public banks. In 1994, he turned into the primary legislative leader of Ukraine's national bank, where he procured high acclaim for settling the cash and diminishing expansion. President Kuchma selected him state leader in 1999, however his forceful anti-corruption programs made him disagreeable, and he was pushed out of the state head's office in 2001. Inside a year, he became head of Our Ukraine, a reform-oriented political alliance. Our Ukraine won more parliamentary seats than any alliance in 2002. His run for president in 2004 stimulated the large numbers who considered it to be an opportunity to break, or if nothing else extricate, the oligarchs' hold on their country.

Leonid Kuchma [was conceived in] 1938, in north focal Ukraine. Instructed as a designer, Kuchma was fruitful in Soviet industry

and perceived for his plan and improvement of rocket and space innovation. He entered governmental issues in 1990, first as an individual from parliament, then, at that point, momentarily as top state leader. He was chosen president in 1994, promising to switch a genuine monetary decay through nearer participation with Russia. Designated by allegations of culpability and defilement all through his administration, he kept up with close connections to the affluent oligarchs who controlled quite a bit of Ukraine's economy. As his ubiquity plunged, he became suddenly angry at the media, particularly TV. Tape accounts purportedly made in his office were broadly acknowledged as proof of his inclusion in the homicide of writer Georgiy Gongadze and different wrongdoings. Following the fake appointment of 2004, he was forced to proclaim a highly sensitive situation and initiate Viktor Yanukovych, yet he would not do so.

Viktor Yanukovych [was conceived in] 1950, in the Donetsk area in Eastern Ukraine. Following eight years as an electrical technician at a nearby transport organization, he acquired a science certification by correspondence courses. Later he stood firm on administration footings in the vehicle area. He was vice-governor, lead representative, and top of the territory chamber of

Donetsk somewhere in the range of 1996 and 2001. His political vocation has been damaged by charges of guiltiness and defilement. He was indicted for burglary in 1967 and of assault in 1970, violations for which he served an aggregate of five years in jail. President Leonid Kuchma named him top state leader in 2002, and upheld his run for president in 2004. Coming from a Russian-talking locale, Yanukovych inclined toward close relations with Russia. During the mission, he upheld making Russian an authority language of Ukraine.

ulia Tymoshenko was brought into the world in 1960, in south-focal Ukraine. During an effective and questionable business profession, she joined the positions of Ukraine's oligarchs, working with a significant number of the country's generally well known (and scandalous) moguls. As leader of United Energy Systems of Ukraine, the principle shipper of Russian flammable gas around then, she was blamed for selling enormous volumes of taken gas and of avoiding charges; her moniker turned into "the gas princess". She was chosen for Parliament in 1996, and served two years as agent head of the state for fuel and energy. As a forerunner in the

2001 Ukraine Without Kuchma development, Tymoshenko was known for her enthusiastic, in some cases incendiary, manner of speaking. That very year, she framed the Yulia Tymoshenko alliance, a political alliance that joined the Orange powers working for Yushchenko's official mission in 2004. She turned into Ukraine's first female head of the state in mid 2005. Numerous Ukrainians acknowledge her as a reformer, disregarding or pardoning her hazardous history. She represents law and order, against debasement, and for an offset of relations with Russia and the EU. In 2009, she reported her expectation to run for leader of Ukraine.

Protesters stayed in the harsh virus makeshift camp the entire winter with irate groups and a couple of little lethal engagements until Feburary 20, 2014 when all hellfire broke out with Russian prepared expert marksmen from rooftop tops killing what is presently known as the "Glorious 100" (around hundred and thirty regular folks and eighteen police). The fifth regular citizen to pass on was a far off family member, 21 year-old Wasyl Moisey, shot in the chest. He was notable for saying it is "Smarter to Die a Wolf than to Live the Life of a Dog".

A year after the fact on February 20, 2015 President Poroshenko post mortem broadcasted these "Wonderful 100" be granted the "Saint of Ukraine" honor. Incredibly this decree is 100 years to the month when my third cousin eliminated, Olena (Yarema) Kuz in 1915 drove a gathering of eight men and threw explosives to eliminate the last Russian tsar's powers from popular Mount Makivka, for which she was regarded with two awards of bravery.

profoundly feel these two far off relative's feeling of obligation for our cherished Ukraine and would readily surrender my life to discard the current despot Putin for his deadly conflict presently seething in Ukraine as this book is being published.

After Maidan; my 12th Visit to Ukraine

In September 2014, I ready for the twelfth visit to Ukraine, a long time since the last visit. Contact with companions and family members during this time uncovered nobody was especially stressed over the progression of Ukraine. They were for the most part satisfied that the nation was moving to be more European and forsaking the Soviet framework. The Maidan dissents in early

2014 plainly uncovered the interfering and violence of Putin. They were hopeful Putin would ultimately be driven out of Ukraine. On the prior night leaving, as I arranged to head to sleep right on time to be new for the long excursion, Doreen called me to the TV to watch an Omni narrative on Canadian-Ukrainian craftsman Mykola Bidniak.

Mykola carried on with most his life under 200 kilometers from our Alberta home. He was brought into the world in Ontario, Canada in 1930, the child of foreigners from Bukovina. I wanted to watch the long narrative for a couple of moments. Promptly, we both were charmed with this gifted man's achievements and his affection for Ukraine. While visiting Ukraine with his folks during WWII, at age fifteen, Mykola lost the two arms and an eye in a hidden mortar blast. In the wake of residing in focal Canada, he had workmanship preparing in Calgary, Alberta, where close by he kept a little ranch with his actual inability. He was an autonomous soul, and his advanced symbol artworks are stupendous. The narrative recounted to different anecdotes about Mykola's life and showed him painting by holding a brush in his mouth.

Doreen and I examined the narrative for one more hour as we Googled more with regards to Mykola Bidniak. His affection for Ukraine was infectious. He experienced his most recent ten years in Ukraine and was covered in Lviv's Lychakiv Cemetery. I didn't rest soundly and was up before dawn, to travel to Lviv. In my fantasy, I was constrained to visit his grave. I imagined support through craftsmanship, and not shooting, to carry harmony to Ukraine. I needed to visit nationalist Mykola Bidniaks' grave. I just had to.

I messaged Valentyn to illuminate steadfast driver Tanasi (his mom was a Moisey) to find the graveyard so I could make a visit before dusk, as I was showing up in Lviv late in the day. In the wake of clearing customs, Tanasi and I set out for Lychakiv Cemetery. Tanasi stopped at the entry and was welcomed by the guardian, whom he got to know before in the day. The grinning guardian drove us through the lengthened shadows of the primary entry. The graveyard entryways were shut behind us, as visiting hours were finished. Driven by the guardian in agreeable discussion with Tanasi, we moved toward five close by raised caskets, inserted in a pile of new cut blossoms. Close to each final resting place was a metal and glass-outlined photograph of each man, some in uniform. Rapidly Tanasi clarified they were ongoing saints killed battling Putin's manikins close to Donetsk, Ukraine. Out of nowhere I detected what the vast majority of my companions dreaded about

the conflict currently seething on Ukraine's soil.

The sun had set as we strolled a couple dozen stages across the primary walkway towards the fundamental burial ground, and there, abruptly, lingered Mykola Bidniak's grave marker, a bronze radiant model. There he was in the principal line, in Ukraine's most regarded creative and respected local area individuals. Wow!

set a Canadian banner on the salt-and-pepper-shaded stone section. We three remained and talked for quite a while, long past the overseer's functioning hours. He strolled with us to Tanasi's vehicle, and we left for the five-hour drive to rest at Maria and Valentyn's Vyzhnytsia home. See Appendix 7, page 257 for additional on Bidniak, who, past his livelihood, exemplifies the energy Canadians of Ukrainian legacy hold for their homeland. I presently better know why I love Ukraine.The next morning with interpreter Oksana Chorney and Tatyana Krasniuk (her grandma Frozena was a Moisey) we visited the Banyliv house where metal stone carver, Roman Paraniuk lives. Roman showed significant interest when I enlightened him regarding craftsman Mykola Bidniak, who so profoundly cherished Ukraine. I referenced my fantasy about carrying harmony to Ukraine by utilizing craftsmanship and not weapons. Abruptly Roman broke into tears as a companion of his was as of late killed in the conflict. He asked his mom and family to leave the room, and we talked about Bidniak and the war.

Zen at Canadian Mykola Bidniak's grave in Lviv, 2014.

Roman needed to examine with his craftsman companions the idea of introducing a huge figure of fellowship among Eastern and Western Ukraine. After three days he had a plan for a two-meter high, 3,500-kilogram harmony mold, which I then, at that point, charged him to construct. It would be finished in under a year.

ight of us, generally youthful relatives (I was twofold to significantly increase the time of most individuals), shaped a casual gathering. We observed local area support in Banyliv to have younger students march the figure, hung with the Ukrainian blue and yellow banner, through towns from Ukraine's western boundary toward Donetsk. Kids from one town, with their banners, would lead the motorcade of the figure entering the following town. An exchange to new understudies would walk the model through their town.

Ivan Vatrich would buy a vehicle to pull a trailer with the mounted model. Tanasi, with his road and street smarts, would be the driver on the extended excursion. This lethargic walk would ultimately catch media consideration, and the harmony drive would bring attention to kinship from Western Ukraine to the Donetsk region.

Now, one of my family members in Kyiv reached a school in Eastern Ukraine to get the model. I conversed with and messaged this invigorated contact on many events. Following a while, the circumstance turned out to be so risky in the Donetsk area that the contacts dreaded for their lives. I consented to stop the task as not a solitary one of us needed blameless guilty conscience. The harmony project kicked the bucket. Presently in 2017, it is too risky to even think about referencing this harmony disapproved of contact's name. Ideally one day we will meet.

Survival rates in Ukraine and Canada

Survival was amazingly troublesome in Ukraine's nineteenth century. Notwithstanding killings from five word related powers, the rate of birth was merciless. Mary Ann (née Moisey) Tymchuk, my Canadian cousin, explored the Chernivtsi chronicles to uncover the accompanying measurements of a couple of our predecessors' endurance rates:

Stefan's dad, Tanasi Moysey (1821 – 1881) had seven kids; three kicked the bucket as infants, a 43 percent demise rate). Stefan (1846 – 1918) had eight kids; two young ladies kicked the bucket at ages three and five, a 25 percent demise rate). Stefan's more established sibling Ignati (1843 – 1893) had nine youngsters; five passed on before the age of five, a 56 percent demise rate). In Canada, Stefan's child, my granddad Gregory (1887 – 1974) had ten kids in Canada; first-conceived Helen kicked the bucket upon entering the world, a 10% demise rate. Of Gregory's 29 grandkids (counting me) just one bunch of twins passed on upon entering the world, a six or three percent demise rate in the event that the twins are considered one birth. My kids and grandkids have all survived.

In the time of Stefan's introduction to the world, when abusive unfamiliar property managers controlled individuals, the seeds of transformation were planted. This unrest gradually brought about the present post-Perebudova Ukraine. As mistreatment expanded in Ukraine and the populace developed on non-accessible grounds, pressures bubbled, and prompting movement in the late nineteenth and mid 20th hundreds of years. Relocation was principally to Canada, Brazil, Europe and the United States. During the 1930s and 40s, ruthless tyrant Stalin coercively eliminated a great many Ukrainians to the Siberian Gulag, what halfway clarifies the huge Ukrainian populace in the present Russia.

Chapter 7

My Last Visit

Three Apartments Purchased

In the 1990s, I bought three adjoining lofts of five in a palatial structure on 75 Ukraine Street, Vyzhnytsia, Chernivtsi Oblast to begin Lingcomp, a non-public school. The buy from Mila cost $8,500 US, from Klym $10,500 US, and from Orletsky $11,500 US. The lofts were bought for the sake of Valentyn and stayed in his name for a considerable length of time. They were in this manner moved to my name.

ash was given to Valentyn, as we didn't confide in a bank to deal with the cash. Banks couldn't be trusted following Perebudova, as they were known to become penniless frequently. Valentyn's pockets swell with money, and he stressed over being robbed.

The three lofts were revamped with delicate love and care by Maria's loved ones. They then, at that point, bought decorations and gear for the Lingcomp Computer and English schools. After over a time of working as a school, Valentyn's family keep on keeping up with the lofts, work their two stores and laser fabricating focus, just as Valentyn's law office.

On my thirteenth visit in 2016, Doreen and I chose to will the three condos to far off relatives. The Klym loft is willed to Tatyana Krasniuk, Mila's to Svetlana (née Moisey) and Orletski's to Valentyna Moisei (her visa says Мойсей). The three ladies marked a enrolled contract permitting Tatyana to work her organizations to a particular date. To will the condos was the practical technique to pass them on to keep away from quick restrictive gift charges. The ladies are relatives of my extraordinary granddad's sibling Ignati Moysey (spelling forced by the then involving Austrians). Doreen and I got much joy

from my tragically missing Ukrainian family and felt sharing our favorable luck was the least we could do to offer our thanks. See Appendix 3 for additional on history of the three condos, page 245.

Svetlana, Tatyana, Zen, Valentya and translator Ohla in Chernivtsi, 2016.

My Thirteenth 2016 Visit, Nikolai th e 3rd,

Luba and Mount Makivka

On the last day at the Lingcomp building, a lady grinned as I strolled around her to enter the store in the structure. On leaving to enter Valentyn's law office, she again grinned; I delayed, realizing I had met her previously. Grinning, she said "I'm Luba". A man ventured forward, saying "I'm Nikolai"

(Nikolai the third, the grandson of the main Moisey we met in Ukraine). What an unforeseen and charming encounter.

alentyn knew about the multiple occasions I enquired about the kid Nikolai's exercises, and he had organized this unexpected gathering. Valentyn, in his calm way consistently considered others and is very viable in accomplishing results for other people. We entered Valentyn's law office with interpreter Ohla. He left to give us privacy.

The kid, presently 32 years of age and wedded, let us know he had a seven-year-old little girl with a serious thyroid issue from birth. They all live in

Luba's home, where the girl was conceived. It is the house my dad and I visited 21 years sooner, when the kid Nikolai the third was residing at the Yabluniv Internat School for destitute children.

We talked for over 60 minutes, now and again genuinely clasping hands. Life for them, albeit better, was as yet troublesome. We were sitting under a duplicate of one of Ukraine's most well known canvases, in what was once Orletski's enormous living room.

We were examining the painting as Tatyana strolled in for certain reports. She eliminated the composition from the divider and later surrendered us the moved material for our Canadian Ukraine room. Tatyana, similar to her dad, consistently made a special effort to please us.

Luba reacted to my enquiry of how she lived in Ukraine's Perebedova times. During the 1970s, 1980s and mid 1990s, she ventured out to all the Soviet and a couple neighoboring nations, getting by selling organic product in season, apparel and woodcarvings she bought principally from Stari Kuty and Vyhznytsya. She went with a companion or two, and now and again with enormous gatherings via train on in excess of 100 events. These voyagers are among the most astute road individuals one can experience. Luba currently doesn't travel abroad, rather zeroing in on making fine arts available to be purchased. She gave me a cunningly embellished alcohol decanter made for basically no-cost from reused materials, which we use on each conceivable event. Nikolai the third works intimately with his Mom,

and he is once again working subsequent to falling while at the same time fixing their cracked rooftop and supporting two broken legs.

Nikolai related encountering a couple of other tragic minutes. Once more, he tried also his alcoholic dad and a couple of different family members who treated his family selfishly. Luba and Nikolai are agreeable and cheerful survivors, who are ordinary of many leftover in far off Ukrainian towns. The conveniences of the enormous urban communities will require a very long time to come to these folks.

Poet Stefan Kuz and writer Zen with books 2016.

and author Zen with books 2016.

Through the glass entryway, Tatyana and a man were pausing, as I embraced Luba and Nikolai. As they left, Tatyana entered the workplace with artist Степан Кузъ (Stefan Kuz), a relative of my extraordinary grandma Wasylena and Heroine Olena (Yarema) Kuz.

Tatyana got new herbata, as I pardoned myself for a washroom break, and after returning Stefan was hectically composing verse in a thick, all around worn scribbler with a short, yellow pencil. He had all the earmarks of being a habitual essayist, and I later scholarly he regularly conveyed a scribbler any place he went.

met Stefan's better half on September 22, 2014, while he was working in Kyiv. She gave me his just-distributed verse book, Не Ділітъ

Україну (Ukraine Do Not Believe). He is no fanatic of the past socialist framework and takes a few jabs at Putin's eyes. Stefan loved the title and first draft of my book cover. He concurred it was "Smarter to DIE a WOLF than to LIVE the LIFE of a DOG."

Conclusion

In the last a quarter century since the disappointment of the Soviet Union, I saw extraordinary expansions in Ukraine's way of life, a pride of language, a blast in artistic expression, and a flood in patriotism, positive energy and the certainty of the adolescent to try to achieve the impossible. Artistic expressions have bloomed. Artists win European rivalries, and Ukrainian apparel configuration is seen all through Europe and quickly spreading to the Americas. Conventional society moving, provincial ensembles and brightening have reappeared from close to blankness. The way of life in numerous towns went from trading and resource to money and advanced cells in pockets. Houses advanced from consuming wood to gas. Gas is not generally imported from Russia. Putin's cohorts in Ukraine's Rada have been uncovered for accepting his bribes.

Tsarist and past occupiers regularly attempted to change Ukraine's rich history, trying to keep local people as serfs. An influx of patriotism has and is clearing the country. Schools are current and clean. Most old commies have ceased to exist. The adolescent are really sure and battle to uncover the last remnants of socialism and defilement. They are ravenous for opportunity and have accepted the European Union. Nothing will prevent them from taking an interest in the ways of the West. The Soviets constrained the utilization of the Russian language. Today the nation has returned to Ukrainian being spoken in families and on roads. This has additionally happened in Eastern Oblasts, where the greater part communicated in Russian, and presently communicate in Ukrainian, with the exception of little areas.

Ukrainian youth have accepted their nearly lost culture, and no occupier will at any point get them to change. The memory of two six-year olds earnestly needing to kill Putin in my 2014 visit is still new. The present Ukrainians have betrayed the smothering Soviet Union and the burden of Russian mastery and corruption.

kraine's Ministry of Economic Development and Trade announced Ukraine's 2017 commodities developed by 24.2% (or $4.3 billion) when contrasted with the principal half of 2016. Horticultural commodities developed by 28.9%; metallurgy exports

by 23.4%; mineral products by 61.4%; machine building items by 14.2%; different modern items by 23.1% and light industry items by 9.7%. Ukraine is on a positive move and will turn into a vital contributing gear-tooth in the European Union.

Most houses we previously remained at had open air latrines; not really in 2017. Most provincial people strolled previously, however presently own vehicles. We were stunned on our first visit that transport administration didn't exist. Today, the streets are utilized by transports. Power in provincial Ukraine was accessible just hours of the day, if fortunate. Ukraine in 1991 resembled rustic Canada of the 1930s, best case scenario. Soviet Ukraine had an amazingly low expectation for everyday life, in spite of the pride of the lying Kremlin and its tyrants. Today, a portion of my family members own corner stores, eateries, lodgings and partake in claiming paintbrush, plastic and block processing plants. They are artists, clothing originators and fabricators. The normal Ukrainian depends less on government than we do in Canada. They are significantly more independent than Canadians.

A p p e n d i x

Appendix 1

Ukraine a Part of Europe for a Millenium

Ukraine has been important for Europe for almost 1,000 years. It is indeed at the focal point of European conversation, and in 2017, an arrangement was endorsed to join the EU (European Union). This is the very arrangement that started fights and disturbance all through Ukraine in November 2013, when then, at that point, President Viktor Yanukovych (Putin's manikin) wouldn't sign it. In June 2014, recently chose President Petro Poroshenko consented to the arrangement, venturing out towards full EU membership.

To comprehend present-day Europe, we want to comprehend European history. A gander at archaic guides and genealogical records uncovers that Ukraine has consistently been important for Europe.

Early Kievan Rus lands were essential for Bukovina associations of ancestral territories identified with the focal government obligation to take an interest in military missions of the Kievan rulers and to honor them. From the tenth century, current Bukovina domain was essential for the Kievan state, and in the twelfth century of the Galicia-Volyn Principality. In 1241, it was subject to the authority of the Tatar khans. In 1514, Bukovina was under Turkish domination.

Because of the Russo-Turkish War of 1768-1774, Russia involved Bukovina and after a year in 1775 Austria attached it. Bukovina was under military control, and in 1786, it was associated with Galicia, and in 1849, Bukovina turned into a different area; three years after the introduction of my incredible granddad Stefan Moisey. As of now, the greater part of Bukovina had minimal composed law. After the breakdown of the Austro-Hungarian Empire, Bukovina turned out to be important for Romania, and in 1940 turned out to be essential for the USSR.

Appendix 2

WWII Finally Ukraine's Version

The Ukrainian Institute of National Remembrance has distributed a booklet introducing Ukraine's form of World War II. The booklet can be seen in English at: issuu.com/memory.ua/docs/ukraina_u_2_pdf_eng_inter/2 The accompanying a few pages of stressed segments have been replicated from that booklet.

The Ukrainians in the Transcarpathia were the first during the interwar period, who in March 1939 didn't sit tight for the extension of their area by unfamiliar powers however remained strong with arms for their opportunity against the animosity of outside countries.

From September 1, 1939 onwards, the Luftwaffe besieged Galicia and

Volynia.

During the Second World War, the front passed the entire of the Ukrainian region twice. Through Kharkiv, the second biggest city in the country, the front passed by four times.

Ukrainians became gun grain for two tyrants – Hitler and Stalin. Each third man in the Red Army was lost (contrasted with each twentieth in the British armed force). The justification for this horrendous circumstance was basic – Stalin didn't count misfortunes on the grounds that, as he said: "Ladies can bring forth more children!"

The survivors of this conflict of two tyrannies were both the military and regular citizen Ukrainians, the region between the Carpathians and the Don River became known as the "Blood Lands." That was the value Ukrainians paid for their very own absence autonomous state.

The Ukrainians battled against Hitler and his partners in the Polish, Soviet, Canadian and French armed forces, alongside those of the American and Czechoslovakian and in the European, African and Asian battlefields and on the Pacific and Atlantic oceans.

Ukrainian Alexei Berest was one of the individuals who put the Soviet banner on

the Reichstag in Berlin, the Ukrainian Michael Strank – was one of the American Marines who raised the American banner at Iwo Jima. In any case, just a single armed force arrangement battled under the Ukrainian banner during the conflict – the Ukrainian Insurgent Army (UPA).

[World War II's] inexact misfortunes as indicated by the United Nations [were:] China 15 millions, Russia 14 millions, Ukraine 8-10 millions, Poland 6 millions, Yugoslavia 1.1 millions, France 550,000, Great Britain 450,000 [and] USA 420,000.
Ukrainians – the Heroes of Second World War:

Olena Viter: Mother Superior of a cloister in the Lviv region. During the German occupation, she concealed individuals against extreme restraint. By saving the Jews during the Holocaust, she was granted the title of a "Honorable Among the Nations."

Kateryna Zarycka: Organizer of the Women's secret exercises organization,

Head of the Ukrainian Red Cross for the UPA. Granted the Silver Cross of Merit.

Stefan Vaida: Lieutenant of the first Czechoslovak Army Corps. Member in the Battle of the Dnieper and the fights in the Carpathian Mountains. Killed in Poland. He was granted the Czechoslovak War Cross 1939-1945 and the Hero of the Soviet Union.

Michael Oparenko: Polish plane pilot. He took part in the fights against the Nazi aggressors in Poland and later in France and the UK. Was granted the Polish Cross of Valor twice.

Alex Diatchenko: Sailor U.S. Naval force. By the cost of his own life attempted to save caught german boat from obliteration. For his accomplishment of arms he was compensated by the Silver Star. American military vehicle ship was named after him (USS Diachenko (APD-123)

Nicholas Oresko: Master Sergeant U.S. Armed force. For a trying assault on the foe's braced position in Germany, he was granted the most elevated American distinctions: the Medal of Honor, the Bronze Star and the Purple Heart.

Peter Dmytruk: Canadian military pilot. He was killed and joined the French Resistance. Saved regular citizens from German constraint. Granted the Cross of War.

Ivan Kozhedub: Soviet military pilot. The best Allied expert. Had 64 air triumphs. Granted the Hero of the Soviet Union three times.

My Father's sibling, my Canadian uncle Steve Moisey from Andrew, Alberta, additionally battled in World War II, shed blood, and was fortunate to survive.

During the Second World War, most of Ukrainians battled on the Allies.

The conflict started on 1 September 1939 and 120 thousand Ukrainians battled against the Wehrmacht as a feature of the Polish Army. Most were Polish residents who came from Galicia and Volynia, which was a piece of interwar Poland.

what's more, there were a couple dozen veterans of the Ukrainian

Army from 1917-1920 serving in the Polish military. These officials additionally protected Poland in 1939.

After the loss of Poland in 1939, Ukrainians likewise battled as a feature of the Polish military under Soviet and British order. Entering the Polish developments under the USSR, Ukrainians saved themselves from capital punishment that came in the GULAG camps. Thus, Ukrainians brought into the world in Transcarpathia, additionally joined the first Czechoslovak Army Corps under the order of Ludvík Svoboda

My father's brother Steve Moisey, WWII Canadian Army

On 17 September 1939, the Red Army crossed Poland's eastern line. This was the means by which Soviet Ukrainians entered the Second World War.

any Ukrainians battled on the Soviet side against Finland in 1939-1940.

ore than 6 million Ukrainians battled in the Red Army during the 1941-1945 German-Soviet War.

In the late spring of 1945, Ukrainians as a component of the Soviet armed force participated in the loss of Japan.

At the front from the Atlantic to the Pacific and Norway to Egypt, Ukrainians battled in the Armed Forces of the United States of America (80 thousand), the British Empire (45 thousand), France (6 thousand) and different nations. These were overwhelmingly individuals from the Ukrainian Diaspora.

During 1942–1950 the Ukrainian Insurgent Army battled in Ukraine, with roughly 100 thousand individuals traveling through its ranks.

Some Ukrainians battled close by Germany's partners. A large portion of them had to make this stride by attempting to endure the German occupation. Some related with Germany, anticipating autonomy from Soviet Ukraine. Playing on these public sentiments, the German trespassers made Ukrainian military units during the last phases of the war.

n June 1940, a Soviet Union final offer requested that Romania move all of Bessarabia and northern Bukovyna. Without the help of Berlin and not needing a conflict, Bucharest gave their regions to the Soviet Union without a solitary shot fired.

n these recently involved regions, the Soviet system carried out a huge scope constraint. In Western Ukraine in 1940 and the principal half of 1941, more than 10% of the populace was expelled. In the recently settled Ukraine, there were 25 jails made where a huge number of nearby inhabitants were imprisoned.

Even before the finish of battle with Poland, on 28 September 1939 the German-Soviet Treaty of Friendship, Cooperation and Demarcation was endorsed, in which a mysterious convention was incorporated that predetermined the ranges of prominence in Europe. Thereafter, economic deals were finished up because of which Germany got basic unrefined components and provided the Soviet Union with current strategies and innovation. Because of this collaboration, the Third Reich had the option to take up arms in the West and couldn't announce battle against their Soviet partners in 1940.

Hot Summer of 1941

Blitzkrieg. At day break on 22 June 1941, German soldiers crossed the USSR line. During the battling along the boundary locale of Dubno,

Lutsk and Brody, Soviet soldiers were crushed. The Red Army really lost their order and started the retreat to the Dnieper River.

simultaneously, in Lviv, Lutsk, Stanislav, Dubno and in many different urban areas in Western Ukraine there started a mass execution of political detainees. During the initial fourteen days of the conflict, in excess of 21 thousand individuals were shot by the NKVD in the penitentiaries of Western Ukraine. With the toward the east takeoff of the Red Army, mass executions occurred in Vinnytsia, Uman, Kyiv and other cities.

"Seared Earth" The retreat of the Red Army was joined by the utilization of the "burned earth" strategies. Its need was proclaimed by Stalin in a discourse on 3 July 1941. Various goals of the Council of People's Commissars of the USSR and the Central Committee of the Communist Party of the Soviet Union arranged the obliteration of all that couldn't be cleared toward the eastern locales of the USSR including plant hardware, apparatus, grain and so on One of the awful violations of the Stalin system was the annihilation of the Dnieper Dam by NKVD troops in August 1941. This brought about the passing of a huge number of Red Army fighters and regular folks who were nearby.

Military Disaster. The Red Army's battle in Ukraine in 1941 transformed into a calamity. In August-October 1941, the Red Army in Ukraine was really annihilated. The quantity of dead Soviet officers is at this point unclear. In circles ("pockets") close to Uman, Kyiv and Melitopol around 1 million Red Army warriors were lost.

Only toward the start of 1942 did Soviet order attempt to start hostile tasks, yet they all finished in a devastating loss for the Red Army. In May-July 1942, Soviet soldiers were crushed in Kerch, Sevastopol and Kharkiv. The Red Army lost 500 thousand warriors as detainees of war. By 22 July 1942, the whole domain of Ukraine was involved by German soldiers and their allies.

[…]

Battle for Kyiv

The Battle for Kyiv endured from early July to 26 September 1941. In August, Hitler dismissed the proposition of his General Staff to think their entire existence toward Moscow. A mandate was immediately marked which moved the hostile south. Toward the beginning of September, Kyiv was "in a bad habit."

The Soviet post in the invigorated Kyiv region proceeded with their battle. The Kyiv opposition went on for a considerable length of time – longer than the obstruction for the entire of Poland in September 1939. Just on 19 September, when the Nazis shut their circle toward the east of Kyiv, did the Red Army leave the capital of Ukraine.

In the pocket at Kyiv, as indicated by German information around 665 thousand Red Army warriors were captured.

Adolf Hitler expressed on the Battle for Kyiv: "The best fight in the historical backdrop of the world!"

According to David Stahel, creator of "Kyiv 1941, Hitler's Battle for Supremacy in the East," this hostile was a victory for Hitler, yet it was here and not in Moscow or Stalingrad, that he lost the Second World War. Hitler lost time for his Blitzkrieg, erred the degree of opposition from the foe, neglected to anticipate the climate and experienced issues providing ammo, fuel and rewards to the involved domains. These variables were lethal to the war.

Crimes of the Communists in Kyiv

Before their takeoff from the Ukrainian capital, the Soviet government had mass executions of political detainees in Kyiv penitentiaries. Many houses were mined by the NKVD and afterward annihilated. Eighteen months after the fall of the city, there was a wrongdoing against culture: Soviet commando units exploded the eleventh century Cathedral of the Assumption, the primary church of the Kyiv Pechersk Lavra.

On 24 September 1941, NKVD exploded radio-controlled mines that they laid ahead of time in houses along the focal roads of the Ukrainian capital.

KVD saboteurs obliterated the focal point of Kyiv, alongside its kin. Blasts and flames annihilated 324 old houses. Large number of individuals in Kyiv were killed and 50,000 were left homeless.

The word related specialists blamed the obliteration of focal Kyiv for their allegations against the Jews and before long started their mass killings at

Babi Yar.
[...]
Prisoners of War

During the 1941-1942 retreat, the Red Army lost practically 70% of its faculty in Ukraine. A large number of Red Army officers were taken to German bondage, a huge part of which went willfully. During the conflict, there were 180 inhumane imprisonments in Ukraine where almost 1.8 million POWs were killed.

Holocaust

During the occupation, Ukraine lost in excess of 5 million regular folks, of which 1.5 million were Jews. Mass executions started from the principal days of the German-Soviet conflict. Nazi Einsatzkommando bunches totally obliterated the Jewish people group in Lviv, Drohobych, Lutsk, Rivne, Zhytomyr, Kharkiv and many different urban communities in Ukraine.

Babi Yar

During the 1941-1943 Kyiv occupation, Babi Yar turned into the spot of mass executions of regular folks, detainees of war and opposition development individuals. In simply two days – 29 to 30 September 1941 – the Nazis shot just about 34 thousand Jews at Babi Yar. The mass shootings at Babi Yar and the adjoining Syrets Concentration Camp were constantly held until the freedom of Kyiv. During the long stretches of the occupation, there were roughly 70-200 thousands individuals took shots at Babi Yar.

Koriukivka

On 1-2 March 1943, in light of the activities of the Soviet sectarians, the German and Hungarian units held pu-nitive activities against the regular folks of Koriukivka in the Chernihiv area. They shot a few thousand neighborhood occupants and consumed practically every one of the houses. On 9 March 1943, the invad-ers again came to Koriukivka. On this day, they collected every one of the enduring townspeople and consumed them alive. In three sad days, the intruders killed 6700 individuals and consumed 1290 houses. It was the biggest settlement in Europe that was totally annihilated by the Nazis as a component of their correctional tasks during the Second World War.

During the German control of Ukraine, there were in excess of 1370 settlements obliterated. The quantity of survivors of these reformatory tasks were something like 50 thousand people.

Righteous

According to Yad Vashem, the country al Holocaust remembrance, 2472 Ukraini-ans are perceived as saving the existences of the Jews during the Holocaust and given the title "Upright among the Nations."

During the Nazi control of Kyiv, Father Alexander Glagolev and his family saved the Jews of Kyiv from annihilation. He concealed them in his condo and in the structures that had a place with his ward. He likewise provided them with an authentication of submersion on old endorsements that stayed from the hour of his dad. In the harvest time of 1943, he was captured by German police and shipped off Germany. En route, he figured out how to get away and gotten back to Kyiv. The "YadVashem" Institute granted him and his wife

and kids the title of "Noble among the Nations."

Trying to save the Jews from killing, Father OmelyanKovch gave them baptismal authentications. Generally speaking, he delivered in excess of 600 endorsements. He composed a letter to Hitler, which denounced the mass killings of Jews and looked for consent to visit them in the ghetto. For this, in the spring of 1943 he was captured by the Gestapo and detained in the Majdanek Concentration Camp, where he subtly proceeded with his consecrated exercises until his demise in 1944. In 1999, the Jewish Council of Ukraine provided him with the title of "Equitable of Ukraine."

Guerillas

The absence of political privileges, the financial double-dealing and the fear against the regular folks and detainees of war made individuals disdain the trespassers. A huge number of Ukrainians participated in the opposition against the Nazi occupation regime.

Soviet Partisans

The underground organization was coordinated by the insight offices of the USSR and the Communist Party. Prepared commandos were tossed across the forefronts. The Red hardliners were framed from messengers of the Soviet order, neighborhood inhabitants and officers of the Red Army who got away from bondage. Administration and arms for the Red sectarians was accommodated by Moscow. Enormous guerrilla bunches were framed in military units, which did assaults in the German back. The Red hardliners battled against the occupation's powers and organization, serious harm tasks of correspondence lines and led insight activities.

Polish Partisans

In western Ukraine, notwithstanding the Red sectarians, there was likewise the Polish underground. The Polish government someplace far off, banished for good tried to reestablish their pre-1939 eastern line. To do this, they set up the premise of the Home Army (AK). They depended on Polish settlements that were dispersed among the Ukrainian population.

Apart from Soviet and Polish hardliners, the battle against the German occupiers was likewise completed by the Ukrainian Insurgent Army (UPA).

Ukrainian Liberation Movement

The Ukrainian freedom development existed in western Ukraine before the Second World War. The Organization of Ukrainian Nationalists (OUN) battled for Ukrainian autonomy against Poland until 1939, from 1939-1941 against the Soviet Union, and after that against Germany.

The mid year 1941 endeavor of the freedom development to attempt to reestablish Ukrainian freedom was stifled by the German occupiers. The OUN pioneers were detained in focus camps.

uring the German occupation, the OUN underground worked across Ukraine from the Carpathians to the Donbas. In eastern Ukraine, attacks were coordinated by individuals from the OUN who advanced from Galicia and Volynia. Individuals from these gatherings tracked down partners among the neighborhood populace in Kyiv, Dnipropetrovsk, Donetsk, Simferopol and other cities.

Halyna Kuzmenko: brought into the world in Chernihiv, experienced childhood in the Donbas, battled with the UPA in the Carpathian Mountains.

In the lush spaces of western Ukraine, Ukrainian patriots made the Ukrainian Insurgent Army in 1942. The UPA was comprised of neighborhood individuals went against to the German designs for the monetary existence of their nation and the commodity of the populace to the Reich for constrained work. The UPA disordered the German occupation's organization in Volynia: a few regions were briefly freed from the Nazis. In the freed domains, the Ukrainian self-government acted under the security of the UPA. An illustration of this domain the region around the Kolky settlement – the guerilla's "Kolky Republic".

In their fights against the German occupiers, the UPA annihilated almost 13 thousand adversaries. The targets of the UPA, AK and the Red sectarians were unique, which is the reason in 1943-1944 there were ridiculous fights between them. An especially merciless type of contention happened during the Polish-Ukrainian struggle, the survivors of which became

regular folks from both sides.

The Expulsion of the Nazis from Ukraine and Central Europe

In 1943, the militaries of the counter Hitler alliance, after their triumphs in Stalingrad and Al Alamein, started to a let area out of Nazi occupation. In the second 50% of 1943 to the furthest limit of 1944, Ukraine turned into the primary venue of tasks in the Eastern Front. In 1944, of the Red Army most were concentrated infantry, shielded and motorized formations.

Ukrainian Fronts

On 20 October 1943, four Ukrainian fronts were shaped based on military units which battled in Ukraine. Hereafter, they particularly selected Ukrainians who were activated into the Red Army. From just February 1943 to October 1944, almost 3.7 million individuals were activated in Ukraine.

Black Infantry ("Chornosvytnyky")

During the hostile, Soviet order began the complete assembly of the non military personnel male populace in Ukraine. An exceptional field armed force was made which even activated long term olds. Ukrainians, without appropriate preparing, were utilized as "gun grain". The socialist system respected everybody in the Nazi-involved domains as double crossers. In fight, they frequently went unarmed and in regular citizen garments thus they were designated "Chornosvytnyky" or the "Dark Infantry"

Battle of the Dnieper

In the fall of 1943, Soviet soldiers arrived at the Dnieper River and Stalin requested them to take Kyiv at any expenses by 7 November, an emblematic date for the socialist system – the commemoration of the October Revolution. The

Battle of the Dnieper was the bloodiest fight activity in Europe.

In request to take the capital of Ukraine before the predetermined date, Soviet

order tossed all their accessible powers into the fight, paying little mind to their misfortunes. Kyiv was won on 6 November 1943 at the expense of no less than 380 thousand warrior's lives. Among them – around 250-270 thousand coercively activated "Chornosvytnyky".

The Rescue of Krakow

In 1944, the withdrawing Nazis arranged their arrangements to begin mining Krakow. To begin with, transportation and modern offices were mined. Then, the authentic downtown area. Soviet insight, which was driven by Ukrainian Yevhen Berezniak from Dnipropetrovsk and Oleksiy Shapovalov from Kirovohrad, got data about this arrangement. With this data, designs immediately obliterated the explosives and the city was saved.

Yevhen Berezniak – scout, Hero of Ukraine, granted the Polish War Order of Virtuti Militari. In 1944, he drove a gathering of scouts, code-named "Voice", which worked in Poland. Chief Yevhen Berezniak worked in suburbia of Krakow in August 1944. Was captured by the Gestop however figured out how to get away. Worked 156 days behind adversary lines. His most noteworthy accomplishment – saving Krakow from obliteration. Subsequent to getting back, security officials blamed him for needing to remain in bondage. He was taken to a NKVD filtration camp. After his delivery, he filled in as a Ukrainian language educator. By the 1960's, he was under reconnaissance by the mysterious knowledge administrations. He passed on in his 99th year.

Auschwitz Liberators

On 27 January 1945 came the finish of the most over the top horrible misfortune for the detainees of the biggest Nazi "demise manufacturing plants" – Auschwitz. On 24 January, the 60th Army of the first Ukrainian Front dispatched a hostile against the city of Oswiecim. Close to half of the officers of the Army came from Ukraine. During the assault, on 27-28 January, the accompanying death camps were liberated: Auschwitz-I, Auschwitz II Birkenau and Auschwitz-III Monowitz. The principal entryway of the principle camp was opened by the troopers of the legion headed by Poltava-Jew, Anatoly Shapiro of the 100thLviv Division.

Anataoly Shapiro – member of the Auschwitz focus camp

freedom, Hero of Ukraine. Brought into the world in 1913 in the city of Krasnohrad, in the Poltava region to a Jewish family. Was a prepared designer. During the Second World War, directed a different infantry brigade of the 100th Infantry Division. Granted 20 orders and medals.

Victory, But Not Liberation

After the removal of the Nazis in October 1944, the Soviet extremist system got back to Ukraine. Albeit, given the significant commitments and huge penances, Ukraine was one of the establishing individuals from the UN, there was no space for a free Ukraine in the new world order.

The Punished People

The removal of the Nazis from Crimea finished on 12 May 1944 and after seven days the Soviet government started the extradition of Crimean Tatars. They were blamed for mass abandonment toward the start of the conflict and with wild cooperation with the occupiers. There were additionally comparative charges made against others living in Crimea.

The Crimean Tatars added to the triumph over Nazism. By 1941, the Red Army assembled in excess of 12 thousand Crimean Tatars out of which multiple thousand passed on. The title "Saint of the Soviet Union" was granted to 5 Crimean Tatars, 2 were with distinction and one – Amet-khan Sultan – was given the "Legend" title twice.

On 18 May 1944 started the constrained removal of every one of the Crimean Tatars to Central Asia. By early July, 225 thousand individuals were expelled: 183 thousand Crimean Tatars, 12 thousand Bulgarians, 9.5 thousand Armenians, 15 thousand Greeks and 4 thousand different identities.

One more 9 thousand Crimeans were banished from the Red Army in 1945. Because of the extradition conditions, in excess of 30 thousand deportees were killed before the finish of the war.

The World, Divided in Half

just before the last loss of the Third Reich, the heads of the "Enormous Three" – Roosevelt, Stalin and Churchill, met on 4-11 February 1945 at

the Yalta Conference. As indicated by the USSR, its choices confirmed their right to western Ukraine and Belarus, handles that were segregated from Poland in 1939.

because of these Yalta arrangements, and later at Potsdam, Europe was partitioned into two sections: the freedom popularity based West and the socialist extremist East.

Quote: "From Stettin in the Baltic to Trieste in the Adriatic an "Iron Curtain" has slipped across the landmass." W. Churchill

Ukrainians kept on enduring misfortunes and after the conflict, mass restraint proceeded until Stalin's demise. A coordinated protection from Soviet principle in western Ukraine existed until 1954 and a few conflicts happened until 1960. During the concealment of the public development, around 500 thousand individuals were stifled (killed, detained or deported).

Another 200 thousand Ukrainians who were in Western European Displaced Person's Camps were not ready to get back to the Soviet Union.

Ukraine's Contribution to Victory

Ukrainians made a significant commitment to the triumph over Nazism, becoming one of the successful nations.

illions of Ukrainians, with weapons in their grasp, battled against Nazism during the conflict. Ukraine gave the Red Army: 7 Front and Army Commanders, 200 Generals, in excess of 6 million warriors, NCO's and officers.

About 120 thousand Ukrainians met the Nazis in September 1939 as a component of the Polish Army. In resulting years, in excess of 130 thousand Ukrainians battled in the militaries of other enemy of Hitler Allies (USA,

British Empire, France). Countless Ukrainians battled Nazism in the obstruction movement.

because of the battling, in excess of 700 urban communities and towns were annihilated in Ukraine alongside a huge number of towns. Kyiv was 85% obliterated, Kharkiv – 70%, Dnipropetrovsk, Zaporizhzhia and Poltava experienced incredible pulverization and Ternopilwas totally destroyed.

Nearly 2 million homes were annihilated which brought about in excess of 10 million vagrants. Generally speaking, Ukraine's material misfortunes in the conflict were 285 billion rubles or $100 billion.

During the Soviet retreat of 1941, 550 modern organizations, property and animals from great many ranches was taken from Ukraine alongside homesteads and many scholarly and instructive offices, social focuses and verifiable assets. Almost 3.5 million occupants left the republic – gifted specialists and experts, researchers, scholarly people who gave their work and scholarly power in the advancement of the military and financial capability of the USSR.

In request to acquire support in Ukraine, in 1943 Stalin had to make specific concessions to Ukrainians. The Ukrainian Fronts were made, the public authority of the Ukrainian Soviet Socialist Republic was framed based on the People's Commissars (Ministries) of Defense and Foreign Affairs.

In acknowledgment of this Ukrainian commitment to the triumph over Germany, Ukraine was remembered for one of the establishing conditions of the United Nations.

[…] Proclamation of the Third Universal [occurred] on Sofia Square in Kyiv, 20 November 1917 [led by] Ukrainian political pioneers Symon Petliura, Mykhailo Hrushevksyi, and Volodymyr Vynnychenko.

[…] Declaration of Independence of Carpathian-Ukraine [occurred on] 15 March 1939.

…] On 23 August 1939, the Non-Aggression Pact was closed between the Third Reich and the Soviet Union (the Molotov-Ribbentrop Pact) […]

Russian extension by Tsars neglected to vanquish all of Ukraine up to WWI. Despot Lenin, and even to Putin today have attempted to eradicate Ukrainian culture. This was not to be; and never will be, due to the permanent Ukrainian soul. The soul is reflected in tune, verse, ensemble, dance and numerous family exercises. It is a culture created on the hard working attitude. The hard working attitude of many past ages was needed to just make due. Generally nineteenth and twentieth century Canadian Ukrainians acquired this

work ethic.

he globally perceived Ukrainian People's Republic just arose out of its own common conflict removing the last Tsar in 1915. Very quickly a tumultuous time of fighting followed after the Russian Revolution of 1917. The Ukrainian Soviet-Socialist Republic (SSR) on December 30, 1922 became one of the establishing republics of the Soviet Union. Beginning Soviet arrangement assaulted the Ukrainian language and culture. Russian had to be the authority language of organizations and schools. A strategy during the 1930s attempted to force everything Russian. In 1932 and 1933, under Stalin, a huge number of individuals, generally laborers, in Ukraine starved to death in a politically initiated starvation (Holodomor) to a great extent due to the "liquidation of the Kulak class." Six to 8,000,000 individuals passed on from hunger in the Soviet Union during this period, of whom four to 5,000,000 were Ukrainians. Despot Nikita Khrushchev was top of the Communist Party in 1953.

Appendix 3

History of the Author's three lofts in Vyzhnytsia

Mila Koshovetz (had one girl) was given the condo free of charge. Assessed cost in 1994 recorded as 75,400 rubles. Orletski (spouse Stefa, husband and little girl), March 29, 1991 paid 3,741 rubles for their loft. Klym clearly paid more than the others for his loft. All the above unique proprietors have passed on, with the exception of the girls of Koshovetz and Orletski.

Zen bought the three lofts from Mila, Klym and Orletski for
$8,000 US, $11,000 US and $11,500 US separately during the 1990s. The
condos were for the sake of our far off relative Valentyn Krasniuk for a long
time and afterward moved to the creator's name. The condos were utilized by
Lingcomp, a lawful Ukraine/Canada Joint Venture for a Computer and
English school for over 10 years. Therefore the Krasniuks utilized the lofts
for a PC store.

In September 2016, Zen willed the three apartments to three Ukraine
female family members. The will is registered in the central registry at
Vyzhnytsia. Each recipient has a copy of the willed units. In addition, each
inheritor has a hand-written copy, signed by all of us and witnessed by Ohla
Sokivka, my translator from Kosiv while we lunched at a Chernivtsi
restaurant on Sept 20, 2016. This hand-written document provided Tatyana
twelve years of triple net, free rent, including her providing annual proof of
fire insurance and use of the units for her various businesses. When I die,
they will have their specified apartment in their name.

Stefa Orletski, the previous owner of one of the apartments, stated there
was a main street door entrance with a carving. As a young girl living here,
she heard horrible things below in the now-filled basement (beatings,
shootings, bodies removed – and she told me where they were buried). Stefa
asked me not to reveal more of our discussion as some Russian supporters
still live nearby. I promised I would wait for many years before telling.

ur faithful lawyer Valentyn was told by Mr. Kordiak how he was beaten

and woke up on a dead body in this basement. This occurred between 1945
and the 1950s. Apparently, the building was a former driving school.

Appendix 4

Scholarships

You can learn more about the Moisey Scholarships by visiting
www.moiseyscholarship.org. Here is a list of the Banyliv winners of the
Wasylena and Stefan Moisey Scholarship:

- 2005: Maya Andryuk, Mykolaivna Doutchak Mykola Mykolayovych, Lesya Andryuk, Mytskan Petro Petrovych and Choboryak Alina Viktorivna.

- 2006: Havrysh Nadiya, Serhiivna Marchouk, Oleksandr Tanasiyovych,

- 2007: Zahul Iryna Ivanivna, Kuz Oleksandr Ivanovych,

- 2008: Dasevych Kateryna Dmytrivna, Strynadko Galyna Tanasiivna

- 2009: Terteryan Larysa Levonivna, Oleksandryuk Kateryna Ivanivna, Pylypyk Nazariy Tarasovych

- 2010: Magalyas Maryana Vasylivna, Zvarych Oleksiy Ivanovych

- 2011: Kolotylo Mariya Mykhailio, Andryuk Ivan Mykolayovych

- 2012: Chronoguz Tetyana Ivanaivna, Mandryk Ivan Gregorovich

- 2013: Godovanets Tetyana Stepanivna, Stafiychuk Ivan Olekisyovych

- 2014: Kolotylo Yulia and Ivanchuk Grygoriy

- 2015: Romanyuk Alina and Ostashek Petro

- 2016: Anna Andryuk, Mykhailo Kovtunovych

- 2017: Zinovilia and Antonolii Myronov

CUF (Canada Ukraine Foundation)

Here is a list of additional student award winners of the "Doreen & Zenith Moisey Fund" distributed by the Canada Ukraine Foundation in the Lviv office area. First, we have the winners in the Ivano-Frankivsk region:

- Bunziak Oksana, Secondary School of Obertyn, Tlumach region

- Vozniak Taras, Kolomya Secondary School #6

- Grynechko Mariana, Secondary School of Stary Lysets, Tysmenytsa district

- Grynkiv Anastasia, Ivano-Frankivsk Secondary School #21

- Drohomeretsky Yuriy, Secondary School of Pechenizhyn, Kolomya district

- Kozak Mychailo Nadvirna, Secondary School #3

- Konopka Ihor Rogatyn, Grammar School named after Volodymyr Velyky

- Melnichek Ivanna Rogatyn, Secondary School #1 specialized in foreign languages

- Semkiv Yaroslav, Ivano-Frankivsk oblast Boarding Lyceum for talented children from rural regions.

- Stasiuk Nazar, Secondary School of Dovgy Voinyliv, Kalush District, Scholarship Awards Event, Chernivtsi Region.

Here is the winners list for the Chernivtsi region:

- Marko Olesya Volodymyrivna, Secondary School #3 of Novoselytsya

- Poturnak Kseniya Bohdanivna, Liceum #3 of Chernivtsi

- Oleksyuk Olga Serhiivna, Gymnazium of Kitsman

- Muzyka Dmytro Stanislavovych, Gymnazium of Klishkivtsi

Dovhan Viktoriya Mykolayivna, Secondary School of Kelmyntsi

Moldavan Volodymyr Ivanovych, Gymnazium of Zastavna

Cherednychenko Viktor Ihorovych, Liceum of Hlyboka

Kuzyk Oleksiy Dmytrovych, Secondary School of Zamostya

Shvets Bohdana Vyacheslavivna, Secondary School of Sokyryany

Yakivyuk Dmytro Yuriyovych, NVK "Perlyna Hutsulschyny" of Pidzakharychi

Appendix 5

History of Jews in Bukovina

he following section is an excerpt of the chapter "Rus-Banila" from the book Geschichte der Juden in der Bukowina (History of Jews in Bukovina) edited by Hugo Gold, and translated to English by Jerome Silverbush. The original can be found at:

www.jewishgen.org/yizkor/Bukowinabook/buk2_097a.html#f3

As told by Jakob Enzenberg, Kfar Ata, Israel, Published in Tel Aviv, 1962

Rus-Banila which had many Jews lay between Waschkoutz and Wiznitz. In 1888, of the 4222 residents, 818 were Jewish (19.39%) of whom 358 had citizen's voting rights. The Jews of the town farmed and raised cattle. Among these were landowners and those that leased their land. Mendl Thau, Jankel Leder, and Leiser Nagel should be mentioned. The lessee in Slob. Banila, Eisik Lipmann Eifermann was the father of the lawyer Dr. Nathan Eifermann who lives in Argentina. In the forests of Rus-Banila, engineer Schlomo Geller (died 1961 in Tel-Aviv) had a model enterprise. In 1918, a Zionist organization came into existence in Rus-Banila. Its founders were Israel Sattinger (died in Israel), Hermann Neumeier (both were mentioned in the Golden Book of the K.K.L. for their services), also Hermann Bildner the estate owner in the nearby village of Millie who together with his brother-in-law Benno Herer was deported to Siberia by the Russians. Both perished there. The Zionist organization of Rus-Banila participated in an outstanding way in all collections for the K.K.L. and the K.H. and was always at the forefront in all collection efforts. The leadership of the successful and hard working organization was in the hands of Herman Neumeier who later served many years as secretary of the regional Zionist organization in Chernivtsi, the lawyer Dr. Elias Burg (died in Transnistrien) who was in the Bukovina section of the Jewish political federal party and Moses Bildner (presently active in the Defense Ministry in Tel-Aviv). The above named were

responsible for the opening of a well attended Hebrew school in Rus- Banila in 1918. Rus-Banila took active part in every Zionist campaign. The first national battle took place with the regional parliment election (1910) as Prof. Kellner and Dr. Straucher ran for office. 705 of the Jewish voters of Rus-Banila voted for Prof. Kellner. David Bildner, a good Talmud scholar and an expert on Maymonides stated at that time that it was in the interest of the national Jews to vote for Prof. Kellner's list. His example was decisive in the outcome of the election. There were 1200 Jews in Rus-Banila.

he rabbi of Rus-Banila, Rabbi Berisch Reimann and his son Elieser and family died on the way to Transnistrien. After, the occupation of Rus-Banila by the German-Romanian armies, 263 Jews were murdered by the Soldateska and the Ukrainian village residents. They were buried in two mass graves in the Jewish cemetery. About 70 families lost their lives in Transnistrien, 15 were transported over the Bug and then murdered by the SS. It is certain that we will remember their fate with great sadness.

As told by Zwi Hermann Neumeier, Tel –Aviv

Appendix 6A

Moisey Family Tree, Canada

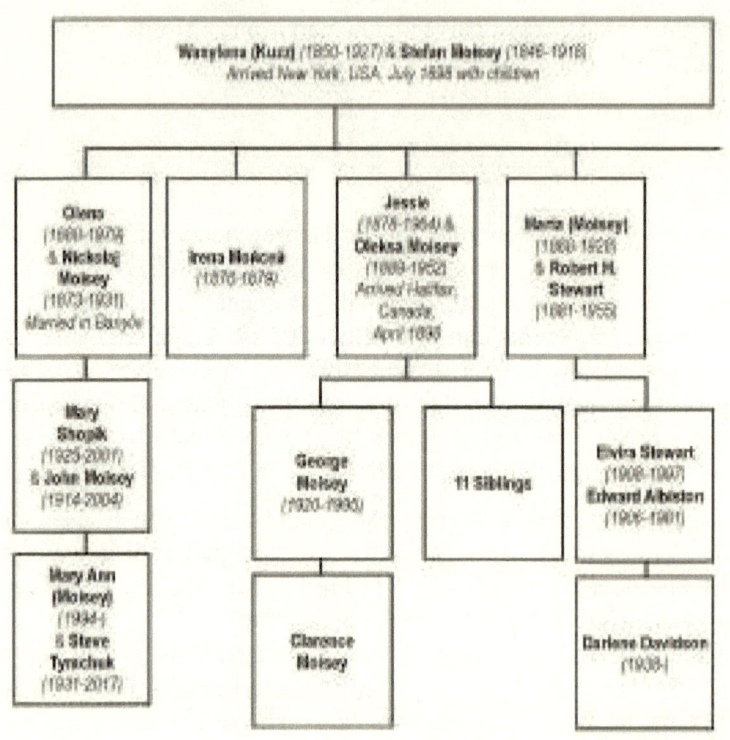

Wasylena (Kuzi) (1850-1927) & Stefan Moisey (1846-1918)
Arrived New York, USA, July 1898 with children

Olena (1880-1978) & Nickolaj Moisey (1873-1931) Married in Baujów

Irena Moisea (1876-1879)

Jessie (1878-1964) & Oleksa Moisey (1889-1952) Arrived Halifax, Canada, April 1898

Nana (Moisey) (1880-1928) & Robert M. Stewart (1881-1955)

Mary Shopik (1925-2001) & John Moisey (1914-2004)

George Moisey (1920-1995)

11 Siblings

Elvira Stewart (1906-1997) Edward Albiston (1905-1981)

Mary Ann (Moisey) (1944-) & Steve Tymchuk (1931-2017)

Clarence Moisey

Darlene Davidson (1938-)

Myriah (1991-)

Taro (1994-)

Laszlo (1997-)

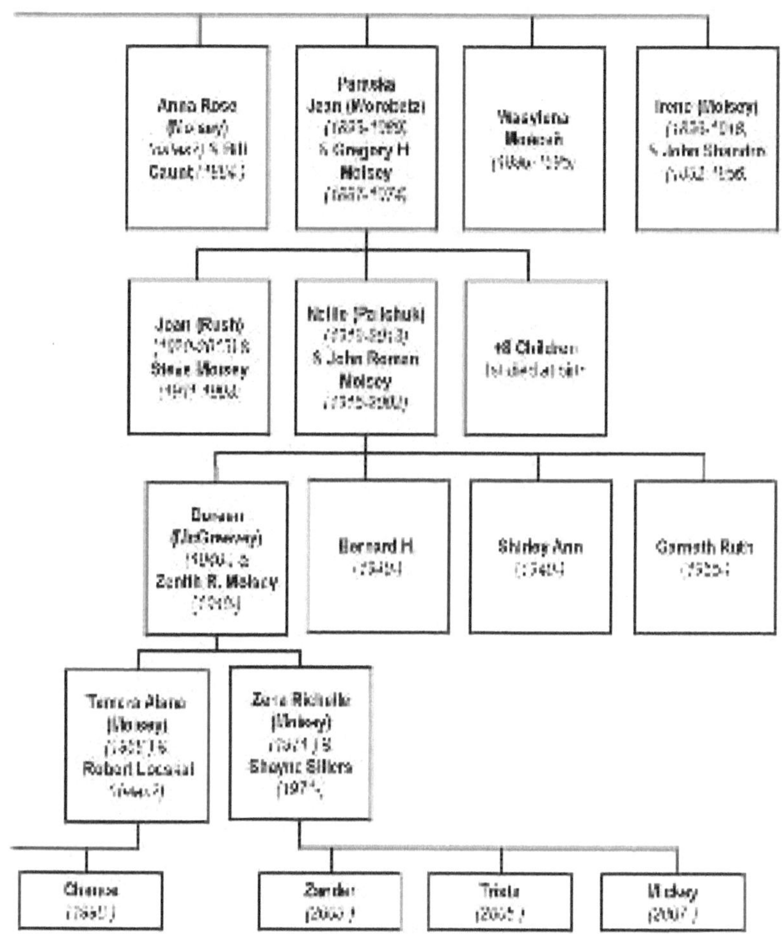

Appendix 6B

oisey Family Tree, Ukraine

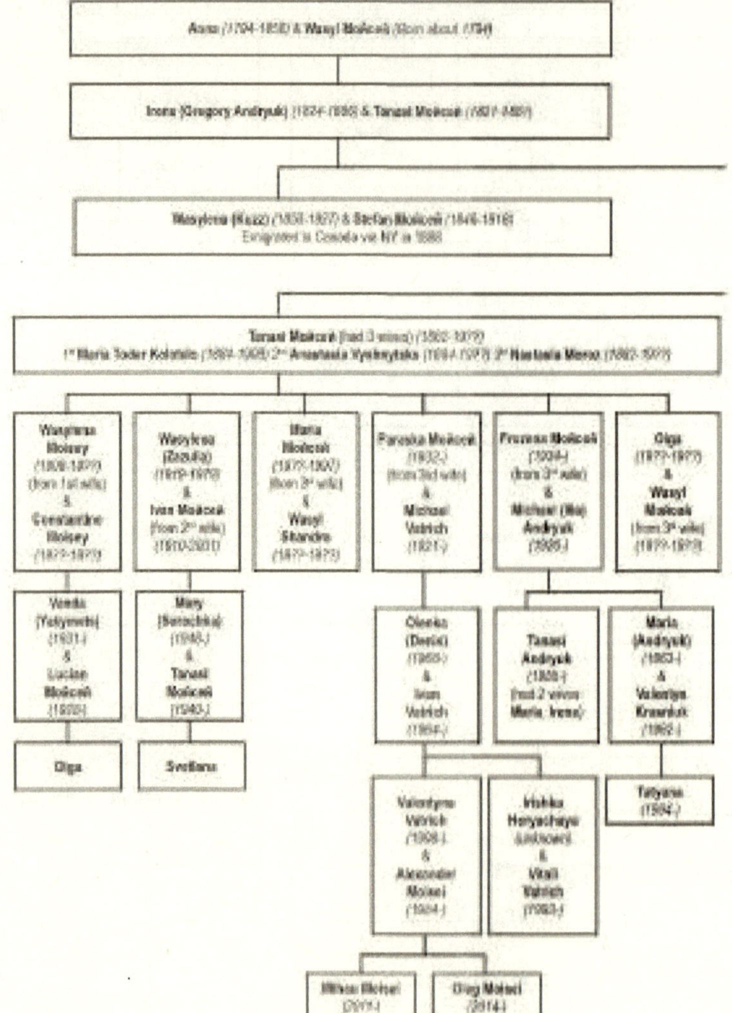

Anna (1794-1850) & Wasyl Moscei (Born about 1794)
Irena (Gregory Andryuk) (1824-1895) & Tanasi Moscei (1827-1887)
Wasylena (Kuzz) (1858-1877) & Stefan Moscei (1846-1918)
Emigrated to Canada via NY in 1888
Tanasi Moscei (had 3 wives) (1863-1979)
1st Maria Soder Kolohole (1864-1908) 2nd Anastasia Wyshnytska (1894-1979) 3rd Nastasia Mesoz (1882-1979)
Wasylena Moisey (1908-1979) (from 1st wife) & Constantine Moisey (1879-1979)
Wasylena (Zazula) (1919-1979) & Ivan Moscei (from 2nd wife) (1910-2001)
Maria Moscei (1977-1997) (from 3rd wife) & Wasyl Skandra (1977-1997)
Pareska Moscei (1932-) (from 3rd wife) & Michael Vetrich (1921-)
Prunea Moscei (1934-) (from 3rd wife) & Michael (Ma) Andryuk (1935-)
Olga (1977-1977) & Wasyl Moscei (from 3rd wife) (1977-1979)
Venda (Yelymeta) (1931-) & Lucian Moscei (1925-)
Mary (Senschka) (1946-) & Tanasi Moscei (1943-)
Olenka (Desia) (1955-) & Ivan Vetrich (1954-)
Tanasi Andryuk (1958-) (had 2 wives Maria, Irena)
Maria (Andryuk) (1953-) & Valentyn Krawczuk (1962-)
Olga
Svetlana
Valentyna Vetrich (1988-) & Alexander Moisei (1984-)
Vishka Horyachaya (unknown) & Vitali Vetrich (1983-)
Tetyana (1994-)
Mihau Moisei (2011-)
Oleg Moisei (2014-)

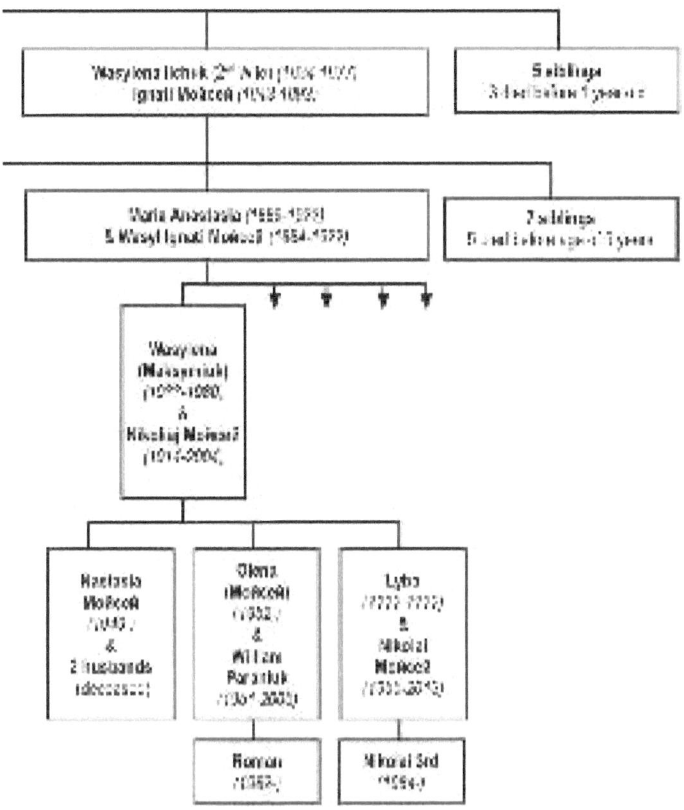

Appendix 7

krainian Sculptor Roman Paranuik

& Canadian Artist Mykola Bidniak

The following has been copied from the article "Angel In Flight" by Iryna Yehorova published on December 12, 2006 in Dyen' (The Day). The original can be read here: day.kyiv.ua/en/article/culture/angel-flight

Only those who loved Mykola Bidniak and appreciated his talent were present at the unveiling of his gravestone in Lychakiv Cemetery. Perhaps this is the way it was meant to be? Maybe outsiders shouldn't go there. From now on, a bronze "Angel in Flight" will always greet those who walk down one of the central alleys of Lviv's Lychakiv Cemetery and remind them of this remarkable man and artist (see Den, March 11, 2006).

In his last will Bidniak said that he wanted to be buried in the city of lions, where he spent the last 10 years of his life. He lived most of his adult life in Canada, where he was educated, created his works by painting with his mouth, and dreamed of Ukraine, which he had left as a small boy and where he would be able to return only after it became independent. The artist's wife, the noted singer from Lviv, Mariika Maichyk, introduced Mykola Bidniak to Ukraine, while the international community learned about him thanks to the Association of Mouth and Foot Painting Artists of the World, based in Liechtenstein. Bidniak, who lost his arms at age 15, when a mine exploded, headed this organization for many years.

Remarkably, all those who learn about Bidniak's creative legacy and life since his death agree that he is the most dramatic personality of the second half of the 20 th century. His friends, who remember his infectious laughter and optimism, say that Mykola was a happy man. They valued his company so much when he was alive that they do not want to let go of him even now.

Perhaps some people would think this unimportant, but Bidniak is in excellent company in Lychakiv Cemetery. Lying next to him is Dmytro Krvavych, the sculptor and veteran lecturer from the art academy, who said of Bidniak: "He is a giant of 20th-century Ukrainian icon painting. We do not have a more spectacular personality in the sacred art of our time. I think that only a man who has access to another, higher, world can create such masterpieces. The creativity of this genius spans many genres and is unique in terms of complex techniques and rich palette. It is extremely important to study every aspect of his creativity. We still do not know who Mykola Bidniak is for us; we do not realize in whose company we are."

On the other side of Bidniak's grave is Emanuil Mysko, probably one of his closest friends with whom he shared his joys and sorrows. Prof. Mysko, rector of Lviv's Academy of Arts, marveled at the Mykola Bidniak phenomenon. He wrote: "Does not Mykola represent an enigma? He was raised and educated in a foreign modern environment but nevertheless remained Ukrainian by profession, vocation, and creative orientation. Does he not set an example worthy of being emulated by some of our homegrown aesthetes, who are trying to outstrip cosmopolitans and amaze the formalistic world?

"This world has not conquered Mykola Bidniak with his inherently creative way of thinking and national mentality. From a great distance, he clearly saw, sensed, and appreciated the native Ukrainian creative heritage that dates back centuries and has undergone natural selection, in which the finest humanistic ideas have continued to evolve."

To say that it is a shame that Ukraine knows so little about this artist is to say very little. Only art specialists and a handful of aesthetes know which of his creations are stored in which museums. Chornobyl Madonna is at the National Art Museum of Ukraine; Man Engulfed by Fire is in Kaniv. Some works are at the Culture Foundation and the Shevchenko Committee, but most of his creations -about 40 in all — are in the storerooms of the National Museum in Lviv. All these works are gifts.

Meanwhile, Ukraine failed to bestow citizenship on him and did not even contribute any funds to his gravestone. All the expenses — the sculpture by Mykola Posikira, the bronze cast, and installation — were paid for by Moscow businessman Valerii Levin.

"We met in the Crimea," he recalls. "I watched him work on his plein-air paintings for three years. I heard him speak English and tried to communicate in the same language, but I wasn't much good at it. And then I heard him speak Ukrainian. I was so happy! I was raised in an orphanage in Sambir and then lived in Kyiv for quite some time, so I can say that Ukraine is not a foreign land for me.

"After Mykola and I became friends, my life acquired a somewhat different meaning. For those who met him even once, Mykola Bidniak served as an example of vital strength and courage. To healthy people he gave strength and sincerity, something we so often lack in this world today. So my wife Ludmila and I wanted to do something for him."

Mykola Bidniak's widow is looking forward to publishing a monograph written by the art historian, Dr. Volodymyr Ovsiichuk. The manuscript has been collecting dust for three years. "Three times I have tried to contact the president of Ukraine, Kateryna Yushchenko, and the Ministry of Culture, let alone lower-ranking bureaucrats, asking them to help publish it, but to no avail," says Mrs. Bidniak. "There is still no money to publish it, despite the fact that Mykola donated his best works to various prestigious Ukrainian museums. The impression is that Ukraine does not need him even after his death, although his destiny and creative work may be regarded as the best example of patriotism, civic, and purely human courage."

Those who watched him decorate churches, perched high on top of

scaffolding, those who heard his excellent lectures at the Chair of Sacred Art at the Art Academy of Lviv, and those who saw his works dedicated to Ukraine's liberation efforts, painted long before the 1990s or in independent Ukraine, will forever cherish their memories of Mykola Bidniak. After he was awarded the Taras Shevchenko Prize and the Order of Yaroslav the Wise, and after becoming a member of the National Artists' Union of Ukraine, the artist said, "I have been and remain simply Mykola Bidniak." Such a statement is possible only from one who has untold riches in his soul.

Appendix 8

IMF Publishes a Ukraine Report

he International Monetary Fund published its Ukraine country report on October 3, 2016. The following is an excerpt from the report. The full report can be viewed here: www.imf.org/en/Publications/CR/Issues/2016/12/31/Ukraine-Second-Review-Under-the-Extended-Fund-Facility-and-Requests-for-Waivers-of-Non-44318

> The authorities have continued to make progress in implementing the program. Notwithstanding the delay in completing this review, mainly related to a difficult approval process of the 2016 budget and political tensions culminating in a change in government in April 2016, important policy measures have been taken since the last review. This includes a sizable fiscal adjustment; a successful completion of the debt operation with private bondholders; the increase in gas and heating tariffs to full cost recovery; and decisive steps to rehabilitate the banking system. However, progress in tackling corruption,

privatizing state-owned enterprises (SOEs), and advancing pension reform has been slower than envisaged against significant political resistance.

he economy has stabilized and is showing signs of a gradual recovery. Following a severe economic crisis, activity is picking up, inflation has receded quickly, and confidence is improving. International reserves have doubled to over US$14 billion.

ontinued determined policy implementation is needed to achieve program objectives, given the still significant challenges lying ahead. The new government has affirmed its commitment to the program's reform agenda. Policies in the period ahead aim to: (i) further strengthen public finances via expenditure consolidation— including pension reform—and improvements in tax administration; (ii) continue to improve banks' financial health; (iii) maintain prudent monetary policy and exchange rate flexibility; and (iv) speed up

structural reforms to overhaul the SOE sector, improve the business climate, and, importantly, tackle corruption, without which the program cannot be successful. The policy agenda is ambitious, and its timely implementation remains critical.

Staff supports the completion of the second review, and the authorities' requests for waivers of the missed performance criteria, rephasing of access, and financing assurances review. All prior actions have been met, demonstrating the authorities' commitment to the program and offering assurances of their ability to achieve program objectives. The purchase available upon completion of this review would be equivalent to SDR 716.110 million, bringing total purchases under the EFF to SDR 5,444.21 million.

The same day as the IMF report, October 3, 2016, the BBC reported slave labor is being used in prisons in Russian-occupied territories of Donetsk, Luhansk. The following is borrowed from the BBC article, which can be read here: www.bbc.com/news/magazine-37512356

uman rights activists in eastern Ukraine say they have evidence that slave labour camps reminiscent of Soviet gulags are operating in rebel-controlled areas. A newly published report alleges that 5,000 people in the self-declared Luhansk People's Republic are held in solitary confinement, beaten, starved or tortured if they refuse to carry out unpaid work. [...]

"About 5,000 people work without payment every day in order to preserve their life and health, to receive visits from relatives and not to die of hunger," [the report] goes on. "All this takes place for the purpose of enriching a certain group of people in the so-called LPR." [...]

The director of the Eastern Human Rights Group, Pavel Lisyansky, says he has evidence that a similar forced labour system is employed in prisons in the neighbouring Donetsk People's Republic (DPR), another rebel-held region, affecting a further 5,000 prisoners. A report on conditions in the DPR will be published next month.

It's hard to believe that we are witnessing slave labour in the middle

of Europe in the 21st Century. But this is happening, and something needs to be done," Lisyansky says.

The following is taken from an October 3, 2016 blog post by Alexei Sobchenko on the website of the Atlantic Council called "Kremlin Panics after Dutch Report, and it Should" The full article can be viewed here:

www.atlanticcouncil.org/blogs/ukrainealert/kremlin-panics-after-dutch-report-and-it-should

The report of the Dutch-led investigation team on the shoot down of Malaysian Airlines Flight 17 over eastern Ukraine offered a momentary glimpse into the true nature of the proverbial riddle wrapped in a mystery inside an enigma. Instead of denying any Russian involvement in the death of 298 people in July 2014, a number of official spokespersons, journalists, and bloggers known for their close ties to the Kremlin reacted nervously and with contradictory responses. [...]

This unusual variety of perspectives on such a crucial issue betrays fear in Moscow's official circles. Before the report, Kremlin propaganda denied not only Russian or separatist involvement in the tragedy, but even refused to admit that the Boeing was shot down by a

Russian-made missile. [...]

Putin and his cohorts have been caught red-handed in willful mendacity on many previous occasions and the Russian regime has invariably maintained its collective poker face. [...]

The international investigative team indicated that about a hundred individuals were "linked to the crash or to the transport of the Buk" missile, though the investigators have yet to determine who could be held criminally responsible. There is a chance that some of them belong to Russia's top leadership, perhaps all the way up to Putin himself. We know what happened to the Libyan leader Muammar Gaddafi after he was implicated in the 1988 bombing of Pan Am Flight 103, which blew up over Lockerbie, Scotland. Gaddafi became an international pariah, banned from visiting all Western capitals other than New York during UN General Assembly sessions.

A similar ban might be considered for the perpetrators of the MH17 shootdown. A quick detour through recent Soviet history can help clarify what such a ban would mean for contemporary Russian elites. [...]

Being cut off from enjoying their wealth in the West would render Russian elites' existence drab and even senseless. Nothing would scare them more than an extension of the 2012 Magnitsky Act, which banned a handful of Russian nationals from entering the US due to their complicity in the death of a Russian lawyer investigating corruption.

The people responsible for downing MH17 could be subject to a similar travel ban. [...]

Russian history has several examples of Russian elites turning against their national leader. Putin has every reason to fear the fate of Tsars Peter III and Pavel I, or even General Secretary Joseph Stalin, who died under mysterious circumstances.

Appendix 9

Olena (Yarema) Kuz, 1915 Heroine, Ukrainian Sich Riflemen.

Following are several accounts of Olena (Yarema) Kuz. She volunteered with the Sich Riflemen, about which Wikipedia has this to say:

> The unit was formed in August 1914 on the initiative of the Supreme Ukrainian Council. It was composed of members of different Ukrainian paramilitary organizations in Galicia, led by Frank Schott, and participated in hostilities on the Russian front.

In 1915, the Russian Tsar's forces pressed further west and battled for strategic Mount Makivka in Galicia, northwest of Banyliv. The control of the hill oscillated between the Tsar and Austrian forces.

Account #1: A Woman Who Fought Better than Men

The accounts below are from European and American newspapers:

Twenty-year-old Olena (Yarema) Kuz was a graduate of Chernivtsi teachers' seminary higher trade school and volunteered with the Sich Riflemen. She underwent training on par with men, and later fought in the cavalry, demonstrating unprecedented courage. Olena was twice wounded, the second time very seriously. Her treatment took her to Vienna. The Emperor's personal physician treated her. Olena Kuz, at the beginning of war, was with the Red Cross, then in the cavalry YCC. She was one of thirty women in the Austro-Hungarian army's independent Ukraine cavalry.

n documents in the United States, Austria and Germany, one can find a great deal of data about the wild Bukovina of the past and presently. Her story is an illustration of valor. A work of Ukrainian students of history recognizes the name as "A. Kuz" in the depictions of the battle of Sich Riflemen. Olena (Yarema) Kuz, 1885 — obscure date of death), cadet at the equestrian foundation in USS. She was granted silver and bronze decorations of valiance. Brought into the world in the town Banyliv, she graduated as an educator, turned into a champion and presently her activities are uncovered to us, in the wake of being disguised by the Soviet Union.

Chairman of the relationship of the "Ukrainian National Home" in Chernivtsi, Vladimir Starik, deciphered and distributed an article about her from the 1915 Viennese paper Neue Post Freie Press. Afterward, a mosaic of data about her from different sources (papers of that time, European and

American momentum distributions, research papers) arose. A few realities have as of late become known. For instance, Yarema Kuz (Кузъ) experienced genuine individual show, which drove her to enlisting with the Sich Shooters).

he Austrian specialists sent her dad Tanase Kuz (Кузъ) (my distant grandma's sibling) to the Talerhof death camp in Austria toward the start of the conflict on a bogus allegation of him double-crossing the Emperor by favoring the Tsar. He was tracked down guiltless, delivered and passed on of typhus prior to getting back. She carried on with an existence of practically Shakespearean dramatization: little girl and father were blamed for selling out the Emperor, a story recorded by the Legion Sich Riflemen (Ukrainian military unit in the Austrian armed force, which worked on the Russian front in 1914-1918).

Olena's dad, Tanase Kuz, was a local of the town of Ruska Banyliv, a reality recorded in the town evaluation book. George Menzak, an all around regarded man, states Tanase was an informed, keen man. At the point when hitched, he moved to Chernivtsi, where he purchased a house on Berezhansky Street. He was a rail line official with six youngsters, Olena (Yarema) being the fourth. The appearance of Russian soldiers had disastrous ramifications for Tanase. After the Austrian soldiers got back to Bukovina, somebody made an allegation against him that he worked together with the Russians. The Austrians captured and ousted him to the camp in Talerhof, an internment camp made by the Austro-Hungarian specialists during World War I, in a valley in the lower regions of the Alps, close to Graz, the primary city of the area of Styria. Styria is a state or Bundesland, in southeast Austria. An appointed authority viewed him not entirelyliable and delivered him. He didn't get back and passed on of typhoid in 1915.

ccount #2:

I needed to study in Vienna. A correspondent for the Regional news week after week, "Association of Liberation of Ukraine" wrote in 1915, about a seriously injured Olena (Yarema) Kuz at the Queen Elizabeth Hospital in Vienna, Austria.

Olena, an alum of educating from the University of Chernivtsi went to

Vienna to get a more significant level in instructing from the shipper IT Academy, yet rather tried out rifle sharpshooting classes in Vienna. She then, at that point, joined with the Sich Riflemen, cavalry division, driven by Hoffmann (Ukrainian Sich Riflemen [USS Riflemen]): the main free Ukrainian public military power, as a feature of the Austro-Hungarian armed force framed of volunteers, who reacted to the sets of the Ukrainian Supreme Council of 6 August 1914, and were driven by the Ukrainian Battle Board (UBU) in the primary legion division, Korsika, at the town of Upper Vyhnanka, presently Chortkivsk locale of Ternopil region.

The journalist expresses that Tanase Kuz, Olena's dad, was wrongly blamed, and that Tanase kicked the bucket. One sibling passed on at the front; the different was caught. Olena, a petit 20-year-old, with slim manly elements was alluring to guys. She was a decent warrior and wore standard male armed force boots and field regalia. Her chest is embellished with two decorations, silver and bronze, for courage.

The journalist expresses that Olena (Yarema) partook in many clashes of the early conflict. She was first injured in the leg in the Carpathians, and afterward got back to become well known in the fight at Mount Makivka, Ukraine, for which she got the title of senior official and awards of bravery.

At the highest point of Mount Makivka, monitoring an essential pass, the Russian Tsar's powers had a few sorts of weapons (rifled and smoothbore firearms, flintlock black powder guns, gun and the turning chamber automatic rifles, call "Chris" (a name utilized all the more habitually in Western Ukraine, particularly in the Carpathians). The Muscovites were very much dug in at the peak, with many soldiers, found straight over the essential pass. On a watch with eight officers drove by Olena Kuz, around evening time, the gathering tossed hand explosives, annihilating the automatic rifles of the detested enemy.

On my last visit to Ukraine I strolled the 4.5-kilometer new Makivka trail to a recently raised dedication at the essential top. I gauge Olena's rising by the briefest course in obscurity, without making commotion to caution guards, would have required no less than two evenings to climb.

The "Association of Liberation of Ukraine" columnist proceeds with that on another event Olena drove thirty Bukovina Hutzul Sharpshooters, who carried on their backs (dribbling with sweat and blood) ammo for the contenders in the Mountain Division. She progressed under the shots, stowing away in the pits made from bombs. With the ammo, her comrades scattered the enemy.

After Mount Makivka they went, to the Russian front moving east with the Allied powers, which were driven by the shooters. The Muscovites were dissipated. Olena gained from three occupants the concealing area of certain Muscovites. Riding a horse, she arrived at Hrebeniv (a town in Ukraine's Skole area, Lviv locale) and a worker lady informed Olena that the adjoining house had Cossacks. Olena, with a pistol, came up to the house, caught three Cossacks and took significant reports. From the hostages, she discovered that close by were senior Russian officials. She then, at that point, continued to catch one Russian lieutenant, who said, "I'm heartbroken and embarrassed that I am caught by a youthful girl."

coming up next is the engraving on a plaque on the Angel mold at the highest point of Mount Makivka. It is written in Ukrainian and English:

Пам'яті Олени (Яреми) Кузь уродженки с. Банилів стрільця з лав Українських Січових Стрільців, гора Маківка

29 квітня 1915 року разом з 8-ма іншими героями Олена гранатами знищила російське кулеметне гніздо, що посприяло припиненню царської влади в Україні.

Скульптура "Ангел"

Автор: Роман Паранюк, с.банилів

Встановлено: Іван Ватрич, с.іспас, 2017

На спільні пожертвування: мешканців с.банилів, с.іспас та канадців Doreen and Zen Moisey

BANYLIV HEROINE OLENA (YAREMA) KUZ,

olunteer "Ukraine Legion Sich Riflemen" at Mount Makivka with 8 men, at morning dawn, on April 29, 1915 explosive the Russian automatic weapon homes prompting the expulsion of the last from Ukraine.

ANGEL SCULPTURE by BANYLIV ROMAN PARANIUK, ERECTED by ISPAS, IVAN VATRICH, 2017.

DONATED by the RESIDENTS of BANYLIV, ISPAS and CANADIANS DOREEN and ZEN MOISEY

Account #3

About Olena Kuz, on January 24, 1916 more is written in a few American papers, says Vladimir Staruk, who acquired a photograph of Olena Kuz, which was circulated to the American Press Association.

The photograph subtitled: Countess Olena Kuz, Austrian lady official, twice granted for Honor. Bukovinka, came from a straightforward family to be called Countess; a particularly amazing privilege. What was the courageous woman's destiny after she left hospital?

Did she get back to battle? The report remembers just a short sentence for this inquiry: "Olena grounded in 1917 and resided with her sister Wasylena in Vienna, where she passed on." When, isn't known.

Account #4

Maria Tanasiyivna (née Kuz) Luchka who resides in Banyliv expressed "The most daring lady from Bukovina, who is popular everywhere" about Olena (Yarema) Kuz. Luchka states that Olena, while recovering in Vienna, functioned as a French language instructor. Maria and family consistently realized that her cousin was a champion, yet in Soviet occasions, to say this was inconceivable. The family knew the little girl of Tanase Kuz was a bold lady, who went to the Sich Riflemen for her dad. Maria's grandma Wasylena Kuz said that during the conflict, Olena Kuz went to her home. Maria's grandma said Olena came riding from across the Cheremosh River, joined by her officers. She was injured in the arm. Maria accepts this was the main injury from battling in the Carpathians. Maria said, "She lived with my grandma for a month, until the injury recuperated. My grandma prepared her food. Olena was conveying a guide, which she regularly checked out. This is all I am aware of her."

I met Maria Luchka, who composed the above article in September 2016. There was a slight sprinkle as we sat and talked in Tanasi's vehicle. Maria was toward the back and had her document with guides and news sections. It was right now I took in my incredible grandma was the more established sister of the champion's dad, Tanase. This was subsequently affirmed from the Chernivtsi archives.

Our vehicle was before Maria's home at the north edge of Banyliv, close to the Cheremosh River. She pointed toward the waterway to an enormous, two-story, uninhabited structure. This structure is on the specific area of an old house where champion Olena (Yarema) Kuz, injured interestingly, was breast fed by her grandmother.

After the charming gathering Maria got back with umbrella to her home. Tanasi, interpreter Ohla and I headed to the emptied fabricating, where we were quickly charged by two German shephelhards from a close by fish ranch. We immediately bounced back in the vehicle, throwing in the towel and withdrew for Valentyn's home.

Olena was on a rush of patriotism that saw Ukraine take on the present Flag, National Anthem and Tryzub symbol.

Account #5

Olena (Yarema) Kuz (Кузъ), injured interestingly recovered at her grandma's home in Banyliv. She returned and took on a few additional conflicts, acquiring the Silver and Bronze Metals for grit. In April of 1915, Olena with eight fearless volunteers in the night heaved explosives, taking out the key found automatic weapons on Mount Makivka and setting up the defining moment against the Tsar, for Austria and Western Ukraine.

Olena, injured again at Golden River, Ivano-Frankivsk Province with broke ribs of projectile shrapnel and tumbling from her pony lay in a state of unconsciousness for eight hours. She got clinical consideration in Budapest and afterward move to the Queen Elizabeth medical clinic in Vienna where she was taken care of by the individual doctor of the Emperor. The Emperor took an individual interest in Yarema (Olena) Кузъ, a dainty pretty lady, with remarkable fortitude. She turned into a legend in a somewhat free Ukraine. She stirred up independence.

Olena's sister was next to her during recovery. The sisters lived respectively in Vienna, where Olena earned enough to pay the rent educating French. She passed on youthful; the date and spot of her entombment in Vienna are as yet unclear. A few of us are sleuthing this far off family member. She was courageous and adored her darling family and Ukraine. Olena sincerely blended great many Ukrainians to dream of an autonomous Ukraine. Her activities were imprinted in the significant press of the day; in any event, arriving at America.

Wikipedia additionally has this to say about the Ukrainian Sich Riflemen:

After World War I, with Austria's crumbling, the unit turned into the customary military unit of the West Ukrainian People's Republic. During German and Austrian control of Ukraine in 1918 the unit was positioned in southern Ukraine. Previous unit troopers took an interest in the development of Sich Riflemen, a tactical unit of the Ukrainian People's Republic. In 1919 the Ukrainian Sich Riflemen ventured into the Ukrainian Galician Army […] They partook in the Polish–Ukrainian War around Lviv and experienced weighty misfortunes. On May 2, 1920, the unit was disbanded.

Account # 6: Wikipedia Entry on the Ukrainian Sich Riflemen

The Wikipedia passage on the Ukrainian Sich Riflemen clarifies the "Beginnings and Formation" of the Sich Riflemen. The page can be seen here:

en.wikipedia.org/wiki/Ukrainian_Sich_Riflemen

various Ukrainian youth associations shaped in Galicia as ahead of schedule as 1894, the aftereffect of the developing public awareness among Ukrainians in Galicia. In 1900, a games/firefighting association Sich was established by an attorney and social dissident Kyrylo Tryliovs'kyi in Sniatyn (the present Ivano-Frankivsk Oblast), which revived the thoughts of Cossack Zaporozhian Sich to cultivate the public positive energy among the youthful age. Close by these associations, shaping the whole way across Galicia, equal games/firefighting associations (Sokil) (Falcon) were likewise jumping up. By 1912, numerous more modest Sich organizations showed up in various Ukrainian people group. Alongside these young associations, a Women's Organizational Committee was set up to prepare attendants. The Ukrainian Sich Union composed the exercises of all nearby Sich organizations and printed its own paper, "The Sich News". By the beginning of the First World War there were no less than 2000 such associations in Galicia and Bukovyna.

In 1911, a truth seeker from Lviv, Ivan Chmola, coordinated a mysterious paramilitary gathering, made out of youngsters and ladies from Lviv University, Academic Gymnasium, and other nearby schools. These devotees figured out how to utilize guns, arranged military manuals, interpreted military phrasing and campaigned the Austrian specialists to legitimize the Ukrainian paramilitary associations. They were incredibly affected by the comparative Polish paramilitary associations, like Związek Strzelecki, that were very various, efficient and — in contrast to the Ukrainian associations — lawful. This gathering later distributed its own paper, "Vidhuk", and kept on getting sorted out Lviv's Ukrainian youth. Be that as it may, a few endeavors to sanction it were hindered by the nearby specialists, who were

generally Poles.

lthough at first Chmola picked the name "Plast" for this arrangement, this gathering addressed just one confined endeavor to coordinate the Ukrainian youth into a genuine exploring development under this name. In June 1912, Dr. Oleksandr Tysovs'kyi, an educator at the Academic Gymnasium in Lviv, managed a service, at which a gathering of youthful understudies under his tutelage made a scout's vow. Accordingly the authority Ukrainian exploring association Plast was conceived. Unequivocally paramilitary components were explicitly prohibited by the association's constitution, composed by Dr. Tysovs'kyi, on the grounds that he wanted to zero in the its endeavors principally on encouraging the philosophical part of public nationalism, just as, obviously, on propelling the standard exploring educational program. Having more noteworthy power and deserving admiration in the Lviv common society, Dr. Tysovs'kyi won the advantage, and Ivan Chmola in the end got endeavors together with him. By and by, Chmola proceeded with his endeavors to prepare the young, begun sorting out exploring camps and showing teenagers different basic instincts, orienteering in various landscapes and comparative helpful abilities dependent on independence, discipline and, in particular, cooperation. This drive pulled in a few noticeable people, who might later additionally assume significant parts in the making of the Sich Riflemen — for instance, Petro Franko, Ivan Franko's child. What's more numerous people proceeded to covertly prepare militarily, of their own accord.

Finally, Kyrylo Tryliovs'kyi deciphered a comparable resolution of a Polish paramilitary sharpshooter association and submitted it to the Austrian experts for endorsement. This time, the authorities had no real option except to give endorsement, and a general public of "Sich Sharpshooters" (Sichovi Stril'tsi) was at last authorized in the Kingdom of Galicia and Lodomeria on 18 March 1913. The primary such organization was set up in Lviv, destined to be increased by Ivan Chmola and his gathering. Sanctioning of Sich Sharpshooters gave catalyst to other Ukrainian youth associations, and the positions of Sich, Sokil and Plast therefore ballooned all over Western Ukraine.

n the spring of 1913, the Ukrainian Sich League was framed in Lviv,

and a rule of Ukrainian Sich Sharpshooters (USS) was drafted. On
25 January 1914 the subsequent society "Sich Sharpshooters II" was coordinated in Lviv, numbering more than 300 individuals. Sich Sharpshooters I included generally understudies and Sich Sharpshooters II - for the most part laborers and workers. By World War I, there were 96 Sich Sharpshooter social orders in Galicia alone. Plast was by then changed into an undeniable exploring association with branches in numerous towns and towns. A considerable lot of these youthful scouts would proceed to willfully join Ukrainian Sich Sharpshooter development even well after the conflict was finished, and people in the future would likewise take part in the freedom battles between the conflicts and in World War II. After numerous hardships, having made due in the Ukrainian Diaspora, Plast was rearranged in Ukraine in no time before Ukraine's freedom in 1991 and keeps on being the biggest exploring association in Ukraine, encouraging

the upsides of public positive energy among Ukrainian youth.

nitially there was no unanimity among the authors of the Ukrainian Sich League regarding its objectives: some needed total autonomy of the Ukrainian individuals from the Austro-Hungarian realm, and some needed restricted independence inside the domain. The supportive of Austrian group won, and just units faithful to the Habsburg government were permitted to exist. From its origin, Ukrainian Sich Sharpshooters considered Russia to be their fundamental foe and were planning to free Ukrainian terrains from under the burden of Russian Empire. In Galicia and Bukovyna, Sich Sharpshooters were likewise circling a magazine called "Vidhuk" ("Response"). In 1914, a rule of USS was distributed, which set up the request for administration and the garbs, given military wording and orders in the Ukrainian language. That very year ammo and rifles were acquired for a 10,000-in number Legion of Ukrainian Sich Sharpshooters, which took part in Lviv march on 28 June 1914, alongside all of the adolescent associations - Sich, Sokil and Plast. That very day, Archduke Franz Ferdinand was killed in Sarajevo by a Serbian patriot, hastening the chain of occasions that prompted World War I.

ne month after the fact, World War I broke out and the recently established

General Ukrainian Council distributed in a Lviv paper "Dilo" the call for Galician Ukrainians to shape volunteer units to battle the Russian Empire. The Ukrainian forerunners in Austria-Hungary trusted that the arrangement of these units would propel the reason for public freedom. They likewise looked to disperse the doubts of some Galician Russophiles that the Ukrainians in that space were thoughtful to Russia. The Austrian conflict service was not ready for this drive of the General Ukrainian Council and permitted making of a unit with just 2,500 men. The primary volunteers were primarily individuals from Ukrainian patriot associations like Sich, Sokil and Plast.

Account #7

The Internet Encyclopedia of Ukraine has a passage on the Ukrainian Sich Riflemen composed by Petro Sodol that the accompanying has been replicated from. The first can be seen at:

Ukrainian Sich Riflemen (Ukrainski sichovi striltsi [USS], Legion USS). The main Ukrainian unit in the Austrian armed force. Coordinated in Galicia in August 1914 at the drive of the Supreme Ukrainian Council, it was administered by the Ukrainian Combat Board. The principal volunteers were individuals from Ukrainian paramilitary associations, like the Sich social orders, Sokil, and the Plast Ukrainian Youth Association. In September 1914 just 2,500 of them were acknowledged into the military and shipped off Transcarpathia for brief preparing. Following fourteen days, individual USS organizations were moved to the Russian front in the Carpathian Mountains. [Of the 2500, 30 were women.]

The USS were separated into ten organizations, gathered at first into two and one-half regiments and afterward into three autonomous gatherings (told by Captain Mykhailo Voloshyn, Captain Hryhorii Kossak, and Maj Stefan Shukhevych). Put under the functional control of the Austrian 55th Infantry Division, they were utilized strategically as forces or organizations of the 129th and 130th Austrian

detachments. The army's commandant was Teodor Rozhankovsky, then, at that point, Mykhailo Halushchynsky. In March 1915 the post of army commandant was annulled, and the USS were partitioned into two autonomous units (instructed by Kossak and Semen Goruk and, later, V. Didushok), a save organization, and a preparation unit. The army separated itself fighting at Makivka (29 April–3 May 1915), Bolekhiv, Halych, Zavadiv, and Semykivtsi. In spite of setbacks, the power stayed at eight infantry organizations (in two units). In 1916 the units were converged into the First Regiment of the USS, under the order of Maj Kossak and afterward Lt Col Antin Varyvoda. In August–September 1916 the regiment lost north of 1,000 men at Lysonia and was diminished to a unit (instructed by Col F. Kikal). The USS experienced one more extreme misfortune at Koniukhy in July 1917. The overcomers of the USS Hutsul Company and the USS Kish were re-shaped into another unit (instructed by D. Krenzhalovsky). In February 1918, under Maj Myron

Tarnavsky, it walked with the Austrian armed force to the Kherson district. In October it was moved to Bukovyna. On 3 November, the USS showed up in Lviv, past the point where it is possible to hold the city against the Poles. […]

The Legion USS was the first and generally tough (5.5 years) Ukrainian military development during and after the First World War. Its previous officials turned into the coordinators and heads of the Sich Riflemen in Kyiv. Its officials likewise assumed a significant part in the November Uprising in Lviv, 1918. It had the best-prepared soldiers of the UHA, and its officials were the military's top commanders.

BIBLIOGRAPHY: Ukraïns'ki sichovi stril'tsi, 1914–1920 (Lviv 1935; third edn, Montreal 1955) Ripets'kyi, S. Ukraïns'ke sichove striletstvo (New York 1956)

Account # 8

Fighting for mountain Makivka — warmed positional fights on Mount Makivka in the Carpathians that there were from April 29 to May 4, 1915, during the First World War on the Eastern Front between units of the Austro-Hungarian 55th Infantry Division background

Flyayshnera (comprising of 700 first and second hut Ukrainian Sich Riflemen) and Russian Imperial soldiers of the 78th Infantry Division of General Alftana for securing of the predominant stature of Mount Makivka to command over the town Kozyova.

Because of the gallant guard of vaults totally separated vital plans of the Russian order. Acquiring the top, which was moved toward April 29, worked out as expected utilizing every accessible save. Because of enormous misfortunes, Russian soldiers couldn't proceed with the hostile, and after seven days needed to quickly withdraw before the Austrian divisions that came. There was an uncommon fortitude during the fight for the recognized top of the Ukrainian Sich Riflemen, which further reflected in individuals' memory.

Mount Makivka in February 1915 laid the forefront, comprising of three pinnacles — the north-western, focal and eastern. The most elevated pinnacle, was set apart on guides of the time as the "stature 958." In mid 1915, withdrawing in the German-Austrian winter Carpathian hostile Russian Imperial powers kept the eastern highest point arch; the other two were involved by Austro-German soldiers. The mountain is situated between the expressway (in the valley Oriava) and rail lines (in the valley of the opposition), interfacing Mukachevo from Lviv and Stry drew in Russian Imperial soldiers, and it was predominant over them, similar to the vital importance.

Account # 9:

On January 6, 2010, President of Ukraine Viktor Yushchenko marked a decree
№ 5 "On Measures for festivity, a far reaching study and objective inclusion of the Ukrainian Sich Riflemen." It denoted a critical job in restoring the Legion USS public military practices and the dynamic cooperation of these gatherings in the Ukrainian upheaval. A statute was proposed to put together, especially in pieces of the military of Ukraine in April 2010 the 95th year commemoration of the triumph of the Riflemen on Makivka. Research and instructive exercises at the highest point of Mount Makivka brought about a TV series and radio projects about the occasion. A postage stamp envelope was given just as a narrative to celebrate about the Ukrainian Sich Riflemen army. Government and neighborhood specialists Ukraine were asked to

consider renaming units and schools, roads and squares to pay tribute to USS.

According to the goal of the Verkhovna Rada of Ukraine № 184-VIII on 11 February 2015, one hundred years after the fight celebrated at the state level on April 21, the President of Ukraine Petro Poroshenko gave an announcement "On Measures to commend the Ukrainian Sich Riflemen on the 100th commemoration of triumph on Mount Makivka".

In 1998 – 1999, a graveyard was remade with 50 crosses at the mountain ridge and a landmark was raised to respect the fallen Sich.

n the Pantheon are covered:

1.Onufry Fedorchak.
.Dmitry Formusyak - 22 years.
3.Julian Shevchuk - 19 years.
4.Nicholas Yuzvyak - 18 years.

5.Dmitry Tsvilyniuk - 19 years.
6.Fed Tkachuk - 21 years.
7.Boris Tkachuk - 23 years.
8.Philip Tymchyshyn - 26 years.
9.Sumaruk.
0.John Tymchyshyn - 21 years.
11.Omelian Stratiychuk - 17 years.
12.Michael Stratiychuk.
13.Michael Stefano.
14.Grits Stefurak.
15.Dmitry Snitovych - 18 years.
16.Dmitry Savchuk - 19 years.
17.George Pitylyak - 20 years.
18.Bone Popenyuk - 26 years.
19.John Rebenchuk - 20 years.
20.Theodore   pinnacle   -   20
years.
21.Dmitry Petrov - 20 years.
22.Basil Paliychuk - 20 years
(My mom's Kosiv relative)
23.Nicholas Mytskanyuk - long
term. 24.Michael Mytskanyuk - 23
years.

25.Dmitry Mytskanyuk - 22 years.
26.Nicholas Mikhailyuk.
27.Osip Matkovskyi - 22 years.
28.Ilko Matiychuk.
32.Fed Matiychuk.icholas Maximyuk -
18 years. 31.John Lavruk - 19 years.Ivan
Cat - 19 years.
33.Osip Konyushevskyy - 25 years.
34.Alexa Kurendash - 19 years.35.Karpyn
says Fyodor - 22 years. 36.Basil Ilychuk - 18
years.
37.Michael Dyachuk. 38.Basil
Vitenyuk - 20 years.
39.Tanase Dupreychuk - 21 years.
40.Peter Danyschuk.
41.Ilko Hrytsiuk - 20 years. 42.Basil

Henyk - 21 years. 43.Ilko
Hanushchak - 19 years. 44.John
Hiltaychuk.
45.Alexa   Grigorchuk   -   18   years.
46.Yurko   Grigorchuk   -   20   years.
47.Stephen   Havryliuk   -   20   years.
48.Michael   Bilyachuk   -   18   years.
49.Ilko Behmetyuk - 22 years.
50.Theodore Belmeha - 17 years.

There on Mount Makivka a recognized lady bowman, Olena (Yarema) Kuz, who with explosives annihilated automatic weapon homes became known. Ukrainian every day paper in America "Opportunity" on August 19, 1915 recorded news from the front: "During Trebenovom range Bolekhiv was Kuzivna (Kuz) driving the establishing of the Tsar powers from the mountain ridge. Quickly followed by our soldiers. In a town, she caught two Cossacks, a Moscow general, just as significant conflict documents.

The Austrian diary Neue Freie Presse on July 10, 1915 portrayed in

detail the caught Russians, "Miss Kuz on this event caught archives and a few important things just as some Muscovite chiefs. One said; "most bites me that a young fellow (Olena Kuz) got me". At that an Austrian official answered: "Do you know what his identity is? - Ukrainian lyerionistka". The Muscovite pale and was quiet, ponuryvsya.

The Ukrainian Sich Riflemen deified Mount Makivka in a society song;

"There on the mountain at Makivka". There

on the mountain on top,

There sichoviyi be beat toxophilite.

Chorus:

uys, how about we go, battle for glory

or Ukraine, the vilniyi law and state. Folks,

go battle well

For Ukraine, the vilniyi law. Our

folks are battling well,

They come to battle, actually chuckling.

We have hundreds ready,

Set out to stem.

In Kyiv PLN gate,

At the door - blue and yellow banner.

There Lviv usususy –

Ukraine ought to be.

And we have folks like the Pearl, Sing

"we actually are alive … "

Appendix #10

Internally Displaced Persons

Women IDPs in Ukraine

The accompanying has been replicated from a July 29, 2016 article on the site of
the Organization for Security and Co-activity in Europe, which can be seen here: www.osce.org/ukraine-smm/251946

- *The number of IDPs in Ukraine is 1.8 million, according to Ukraine's Ministry for Social Policy as of July 2016;*

- *Of this figure, 1.1 million are women (61 per cent);*

- *Women make up 73 per cent of IDPs residing in collective centres, according to Global Shelter Cluster figures as of May 2016. Collective habitats are previous structures and constructions planned for the drawn out stay of IDPs. They incorporate residences and sanatoriums, particular sort habitats and leased houses.*

Appendix #11

Recent Momentous Events to January 2005 Shaping Ukraine

The accompanying has been duplicated from the Study Guide for the film Orange Revolution, which can be read here: www.orangerevolutionmovie.com/pdf/orange-upset review guide.pdf

- *1921 Ukraine joins the Soviet Union*

- *1941-45 Ukraine occupied by Nazi Germany*

- *1960s Covert opposition to Soviet rule grows*

- *1986 Nuclear reactor at Chernobyl explodes*

- *1991 Ukraine declares independence*

- *1994 Leonid Kuchma becomes second president of Ukraine*

- *1996 Democratic constitution adopted*

- *1997 Ukraine signs Friendship Treaty with Russia*

- *1999 Leonid Kuchma re-elected president*

- *September 2000 Journalist Georgiy Gongadze murdered*

- *December 2000 Ukraine Without Kuchma movement demands resignation of President Kuchma and investigation of Gongadze murder*

- *March 2001 Violence erupts at protests organized by Ukraine Without Kuchma; the movement dissolves*

- *2002 Viktor Yushchenko becomes leader of the political coalition, Our Ukraine*

- *2004 July 1 Presidential election campaign begins*

September 5 Following dinner with director of Ukrainian Security Service, presidential candidate Viktor Yushchenko becomes ill

September 10 Yushchenko seeks medical treatment in Austria. Rumors of poisoning begin to circulate

October 15-16 PORA youth movement offices raided by special police

October 20 Government freezes assets of pro-opposition TV Channel 5. Representatives of Channel 5 go on hunger strike

October 31 Presidential election — first round. Telephone records indicate fraud by Yanukovych

November 1 Central Election Commission [CEC] announces no candidate exceeded 50% and a runoff election will be necessary

November 21 Runoff election, marked by fraud and irregularities

November 22 Massive protests begin in Kyiv and other major cities International election observers (OSCE) declare election unfair. Russian President Putin praises Yanukovych on victory

November 24 Election results announced: Yanukovych 49%, Yushchenko 46%. Ukrainian opposition calls for general strike

November 25 Supreme Court prohibits publication of election results until Yushchenko's appeal of CEC vote count can be heard

November 26 Negotiations begin, mediated by EU, Russia and Poland

November 27 Parliament expresses "no-confidence" in CEC, orders Kuchma to disband CEC

November 28 (11 pm) Ukraine's Interior Minister orders 10,000 armed troops to disperse protesters in Kyiv. They begin driving toward Maidan, but Ukraine's Security Service successfully intervenes to stop them

November 29 Kuchma proposes a new election. Yushchenko demands that Kuchma dismiss Yanukovych as prime minister.

The Supreme Court begins hearing Yushchenko's case against the CEC

December 2 Kuchma flies to Moscow to consult Russian President Putin. They reject a re-run of Nov. 21 election, favoring entirely new elections instead

December 3 Supreme Court hears final arguments, begins private deliberations. At 6 pm, the Court invalidates the Nov. 21 election results and orders a repeat election not later than Dec. 26

December 5 Opposition demands electoral law reforms, appointment of new CEC members

December 6 Kuchma announces he will accept electoral reforms in exchange for constitutional amendments to limit the power of the president

December 8 Parliament passes constitutional changes and electoral reform

December 26 Second round of presidential election is repeated. Yushchenko receives 52% of votes; Yanukovych, 44%

January 23, 2005 Viktor Yushchenko is sworn in as president Ukraine.

Appendix #12

Orange Revolution

The accompanying has been replicated from the Study Guide for the film Orange Revolution. The first can be seen here: www.orangerevolutionmovie.com/pdf/orange-upset review guide.pdf

An Election Provides the Spark.

Before a solitary vote was projected, Ukraine's 2004 official political race had snatched an overall crowd. TV and print media announced each sensational contort starting in September, when Viktor Yushchenko, a reform-minded official competitor, was
afflingly harmed and traveled to Austria for crisis treatment. Yushchenko made due, however before-and-after pictures of the
competitor's once-attractive face, presently seriously scarred, drove the news all over the planet. The show proceeded in November when the second round of casting a ballot was defaced by explicit political decision misrepresentation. A great many offended residents flooded into the roads of Kyiv, Ukraine's capital, and other Ukrainian urban communities, in a monstrous dissent that incapacitated the country for quite a long time. It was the best commotion in Eastern European legislative issues in almost twenty years - - the most fantastic of the post-socialist uprisings for majority rules system, which had effectively spread through Slovakia, Serbia and Georgia.

Named for Viktor Yushchenko's mission tone, the Orange Revolution of 2004 was the perfection of an emergency started three years sooner. In 2001, gigantic fights had momentarily shook the nation when the Ukraine Without Kuchma (UWK) development requested the acquiescence of the profoundly disliked president, Leonid Kuchma. Kuchma's lethargic and degenerate initiative had as of now determined his fame into the single digits by December 2000 when accounts made by Kuchma's protector were pitched by an individual from parliament. Kuchma's voice is heard suggesting the snatching of Georgiy Gongadze, an analytical columnist who had accused

Kuchma of defilement. The so-called "tape embarrassment" started the formation of UWK. The development was phenomenal in current Ukraine, upheld by bunches across the political spectrum.

Gongadze had been absent since September 2000. His headless body was found close to Kyiv two months after the fact. Hearing the tape accounts, which attached Kuchma to Gongadze's homicide, however uncovered Kuchma to be at the focal point of a criminal system, the populace rioted. UWK proclaimed itself to be a rigorously peaceful development, however couldn't handle its extreme individuals, who assaulted revolt police in March

2001 at a meeting in Kyiv. At the point when police reacted, many dissenters were harmed. Working class allies of UWK abandoned the development short-term, unfortunate of further brutal incidents.

Ukrainians remained profoundly disappointed with the system, and the UWK development had given insight to another age of activists who might assume key parts in 2004. Yuriy Lutsenko oversaw road activities in both 2001 and 2004. He reviewed that the carnage of March 2001 had "rebuffed all of Ukraine I was the finish of the development." In 2004, he realized that peaceful discipline would be fundamental for any effective well known uprising.

Ineligible to serve a third term, Kuchma blessed the sitting state leader, Viktor Yanukovych, to succeed him. Despite the fact that Yanukovych needed moxy, he'd been a steadfast worker of the country's rich financial matters, and was relied upon to keep up with or even reinforce Ukraine's connections to Russia. With the whole hardware of the public authority supporting the Yanukovych application (at citizen cost), Kuchma was sure his man could win. In any case, the Kuchma/Yanukovych powers belittled the resistance. For a really long time, each stump discourse helped electors to remember Kuchma's disappointments. Viktor Yushchenko stood up over and over against defilement, considering Kuchma's administration a "criminal system." Even when assessments of public sentiment highlighted an unequivocal Yushchenko triumph, the Orange alliance maintained the tension. They accepted that Kuchma's party would do anything - - including vote misrepresentation - - to keep up with power, so they worked with metro gatherings to sort out voter

instruction crusades and a huge political decision checking framework. The Orange powers wanted to forestall elector misrepresentation, yet as a reinforcement, they arranged to record, uncover, promote and fight the extortion in the event that it occurred.

In the underlying round of deciding on October 31, Yushchenko completed first of the 25 up-and-comers, yet since no competitor prevailed upon half, a second round of casting a ballot was set for November 21. In this round, the extortion was obtrusive and inescapable. Yushchenko's Orange alliance was prepared; famous shock gave them the activating apparatus they required. At 2 a.m. on November 22, Orange pioneers broadcast an enticement for all residents to accumulate in the core of Kyiv at Independence Square (Maidan Nezalezhnosti), referred to just as Maidan.

A Planned Spontaneous Revolution

By early afternoon on November 22, 2004, almost 100,000 furious demonstrators had merged on Maidan and in different urban communities to fight the earlier day's political race misrepresentation. As the groups mushroomed, even the coordinators were astounded. Unexpectedly, Maidan turned into an image of the insurgency, obstruction, and resistance. "Maidan" itself took on a few implications; it was a spot, however a development, and a mode of interchanges. This was actually what the Yushchenko lobby and Orange alliance had planned. They had effectively expected a taken political decision - - and ready for it - - with Maidan as the point of convergence of their mass action.

Knowing they may need to possess the city for a long time or weeks, coordinators circulated food, tents, and covers. They impeded terrifically significant government structures and successfully shut down day-to-day government capacities. Every one of their activities were arranged to
forestall carnage. Realizing their allies would come face-to-face with police and security powers, Yushchenko and his
ranking staff had set up back channel contacts with leaders of safety powers to keep them educated regarding resistance arranging and to console them the dissent would remain nonviolent.

During the main days, as nonconformists and security powers looked at each

other without flinching, something amazing occurred. As one dissent pioneer noticed, "They got familiar and they became accustomed to one another. Inside a couple of days, they started offering food and tea to one another." Meanwhile, around evening time, Maidan pioneers met with officials from the equipped administrations to share information.

Members of Parliament developed the stage at Maidan with their own hands. Since they delighted in parliamentary invulnerability, the police were not permitted to capture them. The stage was the stage from which Yushchenko and the Orange chiefs could address individuals, clarify their arrangements, and give directions. 24 hour TV inclusion of the stage kept all Ukrainians informed with regards to occasions of the revolution.

[…]

Additional Resources

Ukraine and the Orange Revolution

slund, Anders and Michael McFaul, eds. Transformation in Orange: Origins of Ukraine's Democratic Breakthrough. Washington: Carnegie Endowment for International Peace, 2006.

Karatnycky, Adrian. "Ukraine's Orange Revolution." Foreign Affairs, vol 84, no. 2, March/April 2005.

Koshiw, J. V. Decapitated: The Killing of a Journalist. Perusing (UK): Artemia Press, 2003.

Subtelny, Orest. Ukraine: A History. Toronto: University of Toronto Press, 2000.

Wilson, Andrew. Ukraine's Orange Revolution. New Haven: Yale University Press, 2005.

Nonviolent Revolution in Serbia and Georgia

Collin, Matthew. The Time of the Rebels: Youth Resistance Movements and 21st century Revolutions. London: Serpent's Tail/Profile Books, 2007.

Doder, Dusko and Louise Branson. Milosevic: Portrait of a Tyrant. New York: The Free Press, 1999.

Glenny, Misha. The Balkans: Nationalism, War, and the Great Powers, 1804-1999. New York: Viking Penguin, 2000.

Gordy, Eric D. The Culture of Power in Serbia: Nationalism and the Destruction of Alternatives. College Park: The Pennsylvania State University Press, 1999.

Judah, Tim. The Serbs: History, Myth and the Destruction of Yugoslavia. ew Haven: Yale University Press, 1997.

arumidze, Zurab and James Wetsch, eds. Enough! The Rose Revolution in the Republic of Georgia 2003. Hauppauge, NY: Nova Science

Publishers, 2005.

General — Civil Resistance and Social Movements

Ackerman, Peter and Christopher Kruegler. Key Nonviolent Conflict: The Dynamics of People Power in the Twentieth Century. Westport, CT: Praeger, 1994.

ckerman, Peter and Jack DuVall. A Force More Powerful: A hundred years of Nonviolent Conflict. New York: Palgrave Macmillan, 2000.

rendt, Hannah. Emergencies of the Republic. New York: Harcourt Brace Jovanovich, 1972.

elvey, Robert. On Strategic Nonviolent Conflict: Thinking About the Fundamentals. Boston: Albert Einstein Institution, 2004. This book might be downloaded at www.aeinstein.org.

ing, Mary. Mahatma Gandhi and Martin Luther King, Jr. The Power of Nonviolent Action. Paris: UNESCO Publishing, 1999.

Meyer, David S. what's more Sidney Tarrow, Eds. The Social Movement Society: Contentious Politics for a New Century. Lanham, MD: Rowman and Littlefield, 1998.

agler, Michael N. Is There No Other Way? The Search for a Nonviolent Future. Berkeley: Berkeley Hills Books, 2001.

oberts, Adam and Timothy Garton Ash, eds. Common Resistance and Power Politics. Oxford (UK): Oxford University Press, 2009.

Schock, Kurt. Unarmed Insurrections: People Power Movements in Nondemocracies. Minneapolis: University of Minnesota Press, 2004.

Sharp, Gene. From Dictatorship to Democracy: A Conceptual Framework for Liberation. Boston: Albert Einstein Institution, 2002. Downloadable in a few dialects at www.aeinstein.org.

Sharp, Gene. Pursuing Nonviolent Struggle: twentieth century Practice and 21st century Potential. Boston: Porter Sargent Publishers, 2005.

Tarrow, Sidney. Power in Movement: Social Movements, Collective

Action and Politics. New York: Cambridge University Press, 1994.

Zunes, Stephen, Lester R. Kurtz and Sarah Beth Asher, eds. Peaceful Social Movements: A Geographical Perspective Malden, MA: Blackwell Publishers, 1999.

esources on the Internet Articles,

Papers & Study Guides

Beehner, Lionel. "One Year Afer Ukraine's Orange Revolution." Council on Foreign Relations, 22 Nov 2005. www.cfr.org http://www.cfr.org/distribution/9259/

Corwin, Julie A. "Fledgling Youth Groups Worry Post-Soviet Authorities." Eurasia.net 11 Apr 2005. http://www.eurasianet.org/departments/civilsociety/articles/pp041105.shtml

Corwin, Julie A. "Rock's Revolutionary Influence," Radio Free Europe Radio Liberty 12 Jun 2005. http://www.rferl.org/content/Article/1059220.html

Meier, Patrick. "Computerized Resistance and the Orange Revolution," blog passage at www.irevolution.wordpress.com 18 Feb 2009.

"Digital Resistance and the Orange Revolution," blog entry at www.irevolution.wordpress.com 18 Feb 2009.

http://irevolution.wordpress.com/2009/02/18/digital-resistance-and-the-orange-revolution

Simpson, John and Marcus Tanner. "Serb Activists Helped Inspire Ukraine Protests," Institute for War and Peace Reporting.

http://www.iwpr.net/index.php?
apc_state=hen&s=o&o=p=bcr&l=EN&s=f&o=155269

United States Institute of Peace. "Concentrate on Guide Series on Peace and Conflict." Washington, D.C. 2009.

Forty-page study guide, which can be downloaded at http://www.usip.org/documents/sg10.pdf.

Weir, Fred. "The Students Who Shook Ukraine -- Peacefully." Christian Science Monitor 9 Dec 2004.

Websites

The A Force More Powerful.org site contains broad data on every one of the movies and games on peaceful developments created by York Zimmerman Inc, including depictions, concentrate on guides, illustration designs, and proposed further readings. It likewise includes selections from the book, A Force More Powerful: A hundred years of Nonviolent Conflict. www.aForceMorePowerful.org

The Albert Einstein Institution is a non-benefit association propelling the review and utilization of vital peaceful activity in clashes all through the world. The site remembers downloadable material for forty languages.

www.aeinstein.org

The Center for Applied Nonviolent Action and Strategies (CANVAS) site contains articles about peaceful developments and methodologies of the previous decade. www.canvasopedia.org

The International Center on Nonviolent Conflict is a free, non-profit, instructive establishment that creates and energizes the review and utilization of civilian-based, non-military techniques to build up and guard common liberties, vote based system and equity around the world. Their site contains news about peaceful contentions all over the planet, just as connections to articles, webcasts and different assets of pertinence. www.nonviolent-conflict.org

Kyiv Post is an English-language day by day distributed in Kyiv. Documents tracing all the way back to 2004 are accessible for search at www.kyivpost.com.

aidan.org portrays itself as "a web center for Citizens Action Network in Ukraine." It was established in December 2000 to go around government concealment of data on resistance exercises, and to fight deception on the vanishing of the killed columnist, Georgy Gongadze. The English language variant can be found at http://eng.maidanua.org.

Mirror Weekly (Zerkalo Nedeli) is among Ukraine's most powerful print weeklies, having some expertise in political investigation, meetings,

and assessment, in Russian and Ukrainian. Established in 1996, the autonomous, non-partisan distribution is subsidized by Western (nongovernmental)

sources. The English language files can be gotten to at www.mw.ua.

Appendix #13

Daughter Olena's record of her dad

Nikolaij Moisey

On four of our visits to Ukraine, Nikolaij's little girl Olena (née Moisey) Paraniuk would get back from Italy to meet us. She was one of approximatley 700 ladies along the Cheremosh River who headed out abroad to give monetarily to their families. I requested that Olena pen what she recalled of a portion of her dad's accounts concerning his childhood and Canada.

She uncovered her dad Nikolaij Moisey, as a kid, apprenticed as a smithy under the direction of a Polish Jew. In his mid 20s, he proceeded with the exchange and had his own business. She composed that her granddad Wasyl Moisey (additionally spelled Moysey and Mojsej under Austrian and Polish occupations) wanted to go to work in Canada with one more Moisey about the hour of her dad Nikolaij's introduction to the world in 1914. Evidently Wasyl didn't go, yet the other Moisey proceeded to work in a coal mineshaft for a railroad organization in the Canadian Rocky Mountains. Coincidently, my granddad Gregory Moisey and his more seasoned sibling Oleksa worked in a similar region in various coal mineshafts. Their ways never crossed.

This Ukrainian Moisey got back to Ukraine following a year with huge amount of cash and bought a track of land on the old stream level toward the north of Forzena's home, where my Canadian extraordinary granddad Stefan Moisey had been conceived. I accept this might have been a Michaelo Moisey. No documentation has been found to validate this belief.

Olena Paraniuk with history of her Father Nikolaij Мойсей, 2014

Olena depicted how her dad was popular. "He acquired cash from the congregation to purchase the fourth parcel north of the congregation, where he worked his business and raised the family. Today it is the seventh house north of the congregation. Nikolaij was a diligent employee and consistently in his shop. Spouse Wasylena died in 1980. After two years, I (Olena) had my lone kid, Roman Paraniuk. We lived about a kilometer away from Dad, and Roman would invest energy with his granddad Nikolaij."

Acknowledgments

Sincere appreciation to loved ones from Ukraine and Canada for making this book conceivable. Mary Ann (nee Moisey) Tymchuk, Darlene Davidson, my dad John Roman and my significant other Doreen, an incredible accomplice for assisting with composing this book. Much thanks to you Sonia and John Shalewa for the principal draft survey and ideas. Because of Jan, proprietor of Bossonova Communications for the book's plan and illustrations and neice Kelly Picard of divantidesigns@shaw.ca for the intro page plan. Uncommon notice to Eddie Southern (perished) and Yaroslav (not his genuine name). On account of many Ukrainians from Canada and Ukraine; old buddies and partners, beyond any reasonable amount to specify, who motivated this book.

Thank you Rotarians from the Clubs of Kyiv, Lviv, Ivano-Frankivsk (particularly Natalie Ifonska), just as Rotary Clubs from Canadian RD5370. Because of town and territorial government authorities, church pioneers, Caritas and numerous Vyzhnytsia Region School instructors and chiefs. On account of the numerous craftsmans, stone worker Roman and family, carvers, artists, essayists, vocalists, artists, understudies and translators (Oxsana Chorney and Ohla Slokivka) that opened warm hearts and homes to Doreen and me.

In 13 visits to Ukraine, I rested in a lodging just three days. Inconceivable cordiality. Exceptional because of confiding in Lawyer Valentyn Krasniuk, loyal driver Tanasi Andryuk, Ivan Vatrich and family for taking us, my folks and numerous companions into your homes. Your accounts and love of Ukraine inticed Doreen and me to record 25 years of encounters and perceptions of excellent Ukraine. With you we facilitated tough spots to help many, including us and together we crossed over the family hole since Wasylena and Stefan Moisey, with youngsters left for Canada in 1898, never to see or speak with Ukraine again. How miserable this was. Ideally our grandkids will proceed with the relationship we developed.

verwhelming are the many natural last names from Banyliv that I recollect from my Canadian youth in Andrew, Alberta, Canada. Much obliged to every one of you for opening your hearts and assisting me with observing my family roots. In the vast majority of you I saw my caring Baba and in view of you I love

This book… about contemporary, Post-Soviet Ukraine is a must read to better understand Putin and how ordinary Ukrainian folks overcame oppression to achieve freedom. It is a page-turner, with interesting facts and stories.

Highly suggested perusing suggested by Bill Rankin, with fractional Ukrainian roots. I have worked thirty years for some Canadian papers including the Edmonton Journal, the National Post, the Globe and Mail and Opera Canada and am likewise an essayist, manager and talk at the University of Alberta and keep on showing rookie at MacEwan University. My mom experienced childhood with a ranch close to Mundare, somewhat southwest of the creator's unique Moisey estate. A passionate read.